iPhone 7 (

The iPhone Manual for Beginners, Seniors & for All iPhone Users

(The Simplified Manual for Kids and Adults)

Dale Brave

ISBN: 978-1-63750-238-9

Table of Contents

5

Introduction

The iPhone 7 and iPhone 7 Plus are faster than ever and have more powerful cameras. With the latest edition of this bestselling guide, you get a funny, simplified guide to the tips, shortcuts, and workarounds that will turn you into an iPhone master.

For those who want the most sophisticated technology available in a mobile phone, but without a sky-high price, the iPhone 7 and iPhone 7 Plus is perfect for you.

Millions of people all over the world are excited about this iPhone 7 and iPhone 7 Plus, simply because the iPhone offers many advance and exciting features, including a *camera like no other*, *Siri*, turn-by-turn driving directions, a calendar, and a lot more. But if you're acquiring the iPhone 7 and iPhone 7 Plus, for the first time, or you probably need more information on how to use your device optimally, that is why this book is your best choice of guide.

In this book you'll discover:

• How to set up your brand new iPhone 7

- iPhone 7 Series Security Features
- 27 essential iPhone 7 in-depth tips and tutorials
- Apple Face ID Hidden Features
- All iPhone 8 Gestures you should know
- How to Hide SMS notification content display on iPhone screen
- Software & hardware features of iPhone 7
- Surprising things you don't know your iPhone 7 can do
- The secrets of mastering mobile photography
- Troubleshooting tips
- How to use the virtual Home button
- How to enable limited USB settings
- Best Shortcuts you are never aware of
- Disabling Location-Based iAds
- How to Use Look Around feature in Apple Maps
- How to Customize Your Memoji and Animoji
- How to Use the New Gestures for Copy, Cut, Paste, Redo and Undo

...and a lot more.

It is the perfect guide for all iPhone users, as you would get simplified follow-through in-depth tips and tutorials on every possible thing you should know about iPhone 7 and iPhone 7 Plus.

Chapter 1

How to Set up Your brand-new iPhone 7

For many individuals, the iPhone 7 Series would radically not be the same as the previous iPhone model. Not surprisingly, the iPhone set up process hasn't transformed much. However, you might end up on the familiar ground; you may still find a lot of little things you honestly must do before you switch ON your new phone for the very first time (or soon after that).

Let's check out how to set up your brand-new iPhone 7 the proper way.

Setup iPhone 7 the Correct Way

With iPhone 7, you'll have the ability to take benefit of Apple's Automatic Setup. If you're on an updated iPhone without Face Identification, you would see that Touch ID is entirely gone. (Which means you'll save one face, rather than several.)

If you're a serial upgrader, and you're from the year-old

iPhone 6, less has changed. But you'll still need to update just as usual.

iPhone 7 Set up: The Fundamentals

Re-download only the applications you would need; that one is crucial. Most of us have so many applications on our iPhones that people do not use; this is the big reason we execute a clean set up, in all honesty. Utilize the App Store application and make sure you're authorized into the Apple accounts. (Touch the tiny icon of the Updates - panel to see which accounts you're logged on to.) Only download applications you've found in the past half a year. Or, be daring: download stuff you Utilize regularly. We're prepared to wager it'll be considered a very few.

Set up **DO NOT Disturb** - If you're like ordinary people, you're constantly getting notifications, iMessages, and other types of distractions through to your iPhone. Create **DO NOT Disturb** in the Configurations application (it's in the next section listed below, slightly below *Notifications* and *Control Centre*). You'll want to routine it for occasions when you need never to be bothered.

Toggle Alarm to On and then Messages when you want to keep Notifications away from that person. Try 9 p.m. to 8 a.m. when you can.

Pro suggestion: *Let some things through if there's an Emergency: Enable Allow Phone calls From your Favourites and toggle Repeated Phone calls to On. iOS 13 also enables you to switch on DO NOT Disturb at Bedtime, which mutes all notifications and even hides them from the lock screen, and that means you don't get distracted when you take the phone to check the time.*

Auto Setup for iPhone 7

Secondly; Auto Setup enables you to duplicate your Apple ID and home Wi-Fi configurations from another device, simply by getting them close collectively.

In case your old iPhone (or iPad) has already been operating iOS 12 or iOS 13, to put it simply the devices next to one another. Then follow the prompts to avoid needing to enter your Apple ID and Wi-Fi passwords;

this makes the original iPhone set up much smoother.

Set up a fresh iPhone 7 from Scratch

The guide below assumes you're establishing your brand-new iPhone from scratch. If you don't wish to accomplish that, you'll need to read further.

Restoring from a back-up of Your old iPhone

You'll probably be restoring your brand-new iPhone from a back-up of your present iPhone. If that's so, then you merely want to do a couple of things:

- Be sure you come with an up-to-date backup.

- Use Apple's new Auto Setup feature to get you started.

The first thing is as simple as going to the iCloud configurations on your iPhone, and looking at that, they're surely a recent automated back-up. If not, do one by hand. Head to *Configurations > Your Name > iCloud > iCloud Back-up and tap BACKUP Now*. Wait around until it is done.

Set up Face ID

Face ID is much simpler to use than Touch ID, and it's

also simpler to create.

Instead of needing to touch your iPhone with your fingerprints, one at a time, you simply check out the camera, and that's almost it. To create Face ID on your iPhone, do the next when prompted through the preliminary iPhone setup. (If you'd like to begin over with a phone you set up previously, check out *Settings > Face ID & Passcode, and type in your password, to begin*.)

Establishing Face ID is similar to the compass calibration your iPhone enables you to do from time to time when you use the Maps app. Only rather than rolling the iPhone around, you turn your head. You'll need to do two scans, and then the iPhone 7 would have your 3D head stored in its Secure Enclave, inaccessible to anything, even to iOS itself (despite some clickbait "news" stories).

Now, still, in Settings/*Configurations* > *Face ID & Passcode*, you can pick which features to use with Face ID, as everyone else did with *Touch ID*.

If you regularly sport another appearance - you're a clown, a doctor, an impersonator, or something similar - then additionally, you should create another impression. Just tap the button in the facial ID settings to set this up.

Create iPhone Email

- *Add your email accounts* - Whether you utilize Mail, Perspective, or something similar to Sparrow, you'll want to include your email accounts immediately. For Apple's Email app, touch *Configurations > Accounts & Passwords, then tap*

Add Accounts. Choose your email supplier and follow the steps to enter all the knowledge required.

- *See more email preview* - Email lets you start to see the content of a note without starting it. May as well see as a lot of it as you possibly can, right? Utilize Settings > Email and tap on the Preview button. Change your configurations to five lines and get more information from your email messages and never have to get them open up.

- *Established your default accounts* - For reasons unknown, our iOS Email settings always appear to default to a merchant account we never use, like *iCloud*. Tap *Configurations* > *Accounts & Passwords* > *Your email accounts name, and then touch Accounts* > *Email*. Once you reach the depths of the settings, you can touch your preferred email; this would be your address in new mails. (When there is only one address in here, you're all set.) That is also the spot to add some other email addresses associated with your email account.

Advanced iPhone Email tweaks

- *Swipe to control email* - It's much more helpful to have the ability to swipe your email messages away rather than clicking through and tapping on several control keys. Swipe to Archive, so that whenever you swipe that path, you'll have the ability to either quickly save a contact to your Archive. Or, if your email accounts support swiping left as a default Delete action, it'll offer a Garbage icon. Swipe left to Tag as Read, which is a smart way to slam through your electronic mails as you have them. This only impacts your built-in Email application from Apple. Each third-party email customer can do things differently.

- *Add an HTML signature* - A sound email signature really can cause you to look professional, so make sure to include an HTML signature to your email. If you've already got one on the desktop, duplicate and paste the code into contact and ahead to yourself.

You'll be able to copy and paste it into an Email application (or whichever email supplier you like, if it facilitates it). It could be as easy as textual content formatting tags or as complicated as adding a logo design from a webserver. You should use an iOS application to make one, too; however, they tend to look fairly basic.

Manage Calendars, iCloud, Communications and more

- ***Set default Calendar alert times*** - Calendar is ideal for alerting you to important occasions, but it's not necessarily at a convenient or useful time. Established the default timing on three types of occasions: Birthdays, Occasions, and All-Day Occasions, and that means you get reminders when they're helpful. Utilize *Configurations > Calendars*. Tap on Default Alert Times and set your Birthday reminders to 1 day before, your Occasions to quarter-hour before (or a period which makes more sense to your mind), and All-

Day Occasions on the day of the function (10 a.m.). You'll never miss a meeting again.

- ***Background application refresh*** - You'll desire to be selective about which applications you desire to be in a position to run in the background, so have a look at the list in *Settings > General > Background App Refresh*. Toggle Background App Refresh to ON, then toggle OFF all the applications you don't need being able to access anything in the background. When in question, toggle it to OFF and find out if you are slowed up by any applications that require to refresh when you release them. You'll want to allow Background Refresh for Cult of Macintosh Magazine!

Secure Your Web Experience

- ***Browser set up*** - Surfing the net is filled with forms to complete. Adding your name, address, email, and bank cards may take up a great deal of your power. Make sure to head into

Configurations > Browser > AutoFill to create your mobile internet browser the proper way. First, toggle Use Contact Info to On. Then tap on My Info and select the contact you want to use when you encounter form areas in Browser. Toggle Titles and Passwords on as well, and that means you can save that across appointments to the same website. (This pulls from *iCloud Keychain*, so make sure to have that allowed, too.)

Toggle *CREDIT CARDS* to ON as well, which means you can shop swiftly. (*be sure only to use SSL-encrypted websites.*)

Pro suggestion: Manage which bank cards your iPhone helps you to save with a tap on BANK CARDS. You can include new cards within, or delete ones that no more work or that you don't want to use via mobile Browser.

The browser in iOS 13 and later version also blocks cross-site monitoring, which are those cookies that follow you around and let online stores place the same advertisements on every subsequent web page you visit. That is On by default, and that means you should not do anything. Just relax and revel in your newfound personal privacy.

iCloud Everywhere

- *iCloud is everything* - There's without a doubt in our thoughts that iCloud is the easiest, optimum solution for keeping all of your stuff supported and safe. Utilize the Configurations > iCloud and be sure to register with your **Apple ID**. You can manage your storage space in here, but make sure to enable all you need immediately. Enable iCloud Drive, Photos, Connections, Reminders, Browser, Records, News, Wallet, Back-up, Keychain and others once you get the iPhone unpacked. You can enable Email and Calendars if you merely use Apple's applications and services; usually, you would keep those toggled OFF.

Services subscription during iPhone setup

- ***Enable iCloud Photo Library*** - We love the iCloud Photo Library. It maintains your photos and videos securely stored in the cloud and enable you to get full-quality copies of your documents in the event you misplace your originals. iCloud Picture Library depends on your iCloud storage space, if you have a lot of photos, you'll want to bump that up. Utilize Configurations > iCloud > Photos, then toggle iCloud Image Library to On. (Remember that this will switch off My Picture Stream. If you'd like both, you'll need to re-toggle Image Stream back again to On.)

- ***Use iTunes Match*** - Sure, Apple Music monitors all the music data files on your devices, but if you delete them from your iPhone and don't have a back-up elsewhere, you're heading to have to stay for whatever quality Apple Music will provide you with when you listen. If you wish to maintain your full-resolution music documents supported to the cloud, use iTunes Match.

You get all of your music files matched up or published to iCloud in the best bitrate possible. After that, you can stream or download the music to any device provided your iTunes Match membership is intact. Never be without your music (or have an over-filled iPhone) again. Go to *Configurations > Music*. Then touch on Sign up to iTunes Match to understand this valuable service allowed on your brand-new iPhone.

More iPhone set up Tweaks

- *Extend your Auto-Lock* - Let's face it. The default two minutes you get for the Volume of time your iPhone would remain on without turning off its screen may keep the battery higher much longer, but it's insufficient for anybody during regular use. Utilize Configurations, General, Auto-Lock to create this to the whole five minutes, which means you can stop tapping your screen at all times to keep it awake.

- ***Get texts everywhere*** - You can enable your Mac PC or iPad to get texts from your iPhone, provided you've set up iMessage to them (Settings, Text messages, toggle iMessage to ON on any iOS device, Messages Preferences on your Mac). Ensure that your other device is close by when you Utilize Settings on your iPhone, then touch Messages > TEXT Forwarding. Any devices available will arrive on the list. Toggle your Mac or iPad to On, and then check the prospective device for a code. Enter that code into your iPhone. Now all of your devices are certain to get not only iMessages but also texts from those not using iMessage.

- ***Equalise your tunes*** - Start the EQ in your Music application to be able to hear your preferred jams and never have trouble with a Bluetooth speaker. Go to Configurations > Music. Once there, touch on EQ and established your iPhone to NIGHT TIME; this will provide you with a great quantity rise for those times where you want to blast *The Clash* while you make a quick supper in the kitchen.

C h a p t e r   2

iPhone 7 Gestures You Should Know

Just like the iPhone 7 launched in 2017, the iPhone 7 doesn't include a physical home button, instead deciding on gestures to regulate the new user interface. It would require a couple of days to get used to the change but stay with it. By day three, you'll question how you ever coped without it, and using an "old" iPhone would appear old and antiquated.

1. **<u>Unlock your iPhone 7</u>:** Go through the phone and swipe up from underneath the screen. It truly is that easy, and also you don't need to hold back for the padlock icon at the very top to improve to the unlock visual before swiping up.

2. **<u>Touch to wake</u>:** Tap on your iPhone 7 screen when it's off to wake it up and find out what notifications you have. To unlock it with FaceID, you'll still have to set it up.

3. **<u>Back to the Homescreen</u>:** Whatever application

you are in, if you would like to return to the Home screen, swipe up from underneath of the screen. If you're within an application that is operating scenery, you'll need to keep in mind slipping up from underneath the screen (i.e., the medial side) rather than where the Home button used to be.

4. **<u>Have a screenshot</u>**: Press the power button and the volume up button together quickly, and it would snap a screenshot of whatever is on the screen.

5. **<u>Addressing Control Centre</u>**: It used to be always a swipe up, now it's a swipe down from the very best right of the screen. Even if your iPhone doesn't have 3D Touch, you can still long-press on the symbols to gain usage of further configurations within each icon.

6. **<u>Accessing open up apps</u>**: Previously, you raise tapped on the home button to uncover what apps you'd open. You now swipe up and then pause with your finger on the screen. After that, you can

see the applications you have opened up in the order you opened them.

7. **<u>Launch Siri</u>:** When you may use the "Hey Siri" hot term to awaken Apple's digital associate, there are still ways to release the function utilizing a button press. Press and contain the wake/rest button on the right aspect of the phone before Siri interface pops-up on screen.

8. **<u>Switch your phone off</u>:** Because long-pressing the wake/rest button launches Siri now, there's a fresh way for switching the phone off. To take action, you would need to press and contain the wake/rest button and the volume down button at the same time. Now glide to power off.

9. **<u>Release Apple Pay</u>:** Again, the wake/rest button is the main element here. Double touch it, and it would talk about your Apple Budget, then scan that person, and it'll request you to keep your phone near to the payment machine.

10. **<u>Gain access to widgets on the lock screen</u>:** Swipe

from still left to directly on your lock screen, ideal for checking your activity bands.

Using Memoji

- **<u>Create your Memoji</u>:** Open up Messages and begin a new meaning. Touch the tiny monkey icon above the keypad, and then strike the "+" button to generate your personality. You would customize face form, skin tone, curly hair color, eye, jewelry, plus much more.

- **<u>Use your Memoji/Animoji in a FaceTime call</u>:** Take up a FaceTime call, then press the tiny star icon underneath the corner. Now, tap the Memoji you want to use.

- **<u>Memoji your selfies</u>:** So, if you select your Memoji face, preferably to your real to life face, you can send selfies with the Memoji changing your head in Messages. Take up a new message and touch the camera icon, and then press that top button. Now choose the Animoji option by tapping that monkey's mind again. Choose your Memoji and tap the '*X*,' not the "done" button, and then take your picture.

- **Record a Memoji video:** Sadly, Memoji isn't available as a choice in the camera app, but that doesn't mean you can't record one. Much like the picture selfie, go to communications, touch on the camera icon and then slip to video and then tap on the superstar. Weight the Animoji or your Memoji, and off you decide to go.

iOS 13 iPhone 7 Notification Tips

- *Notifications collection to provide quietly*: If you're worried that you would be getting way too many notifications, you can place the way they deliver with an app by application basis. Swipe left when you've got a notification on the Lock screen and touch on Manage. Touch Deliver Quietly. Calm notifications come in Notification Centre, but do not show up on the Lock screen, play audio, present a banner or badge the application icon.

You've just surely got to be sure you check every once in a while.

- **Switch off notifications from an app**: Same method as the "Deliver Quietly" feature, other than you tap the "Switch off..." option.

- **Open up Notification Centre on Lock screen**: From your lock screen, swipe up from the center of the screen, and you would visit a long set of earlier notifications if you have any.

- **Check Notifications anytime**: To check on your Notifications anytime, swipe down from the very best left part of the screen to reveal them.

Using Screen Time

- **Checking your Screen Time**: You can examine how you've been making use of your phone with the new Screen Time feature in iOS 13. You'll find the reviews in *Configurations > Screen Time*.

- **Scheduled Downtime:** If you want just a little help

making use of your mobile phone less, you can restrict what applications you utilize when. Check out Settings > Screen Time and choose the Downtime option. Toggle the change to the "on" position and choose to routine a period when only specific applications and calls are allowed. It's ideal for preventing you or your children from using their cell phones after an arranged time, for example.

- *Set application limits*: App Limitations enable you to choose which group of applications you want to include a period limit to. Choose the category and then "add" before choosing a period limit and striking "plans."

- *Choose "always allowed" apps*: However, you might be willing to lock down your phone to avoid you utilizing it, that's no good if most of your way of getting in touch with people is via an application that gets locked away. Utilize this feature always to allow certain applications whatever limitations you apply.

- ***Content & Personal privacy limitations***: This section is also within the primary Screen Time configurations menu and particularly useful if you are a mother or father with kids who use iOS devices. Utilizing it, you can restrict all types of content and options, including iTunes and in-app buys, location services, advertising, etc. It's worth looking at.

Siri shortcuts

- ***Siri Shortcuts***: There are several little "help" the iPhone 7 offers via Siri Shortcuts. To start to see the ones recommended for you, go to *Configurations > Siri & Search* and choose what you think would be helpful from the automatically produced suggestions. Touch "all shortcuts" to see more. If you wish to install specific "shortcuts" for a variety of different applications that aren't recommended by the iPhone, you can do this by downloading the dedicated Siri Shortcuts.

iPhone 7 Control Centre Tips

- *Add new handles*: Just like the previous version of iOS, you can include and remove handles from Control Centre. Check out *Configurations > Control Centre > Customize Handles* and then choose which settings you would like to add.

- *Reorganize handles*: To improve the order of these settings, you've added, touch, and contain the three-bar menu on the right of whichever control you would like to move, then move it along the list to wherever you would like it to be.

- *Expand handles*: Some settings may become full screen, press harder on the control you want to expand, and it will fill the screen.

- *Activate screen recording*: Among the new options, you can include regulating Centre is Screen Recording. Be sure you add the control, then open up Control Centre and press the icon that appears like an excellent white circle in the thin white band. To any extent further, it'll record everything that occurs on your screen. Press the control again if you are done, and it will save a video to your Photos application automatically.

- *Adjust light/screen brightness*: You can activate your camera adobe flash, utilizing it as a torch by starting Control Centre and tapping on the torch icon. If you wish to adjust the lighting, power press the icon, then adapt the full-screen slider that shows up.

- *Quickly switch where a sound is played*: One cool feature is the capability to change where music is playing. While music is playing, through Apple Music, Spotify, or wherever, press on the music control or touch the tiny icon in the very best part of the music control; this introduces a pop-up screening available devices that you can play through; this may be linked earphones, a Bluetooth loudspeaker, Apple Television, your iPhone, or any AirPlay device.

- *Set an instant timer*: Rather than going to the

timer app, you can force press on the timer icon, then glide up or down on the full-screen to create a timer from about a minute to two hours long.

- **How to gain access to HomeKit devices**: Open up Control Centre and then tap on the tiny icon that appears like a home.

iPhone 7 Photos and Camera Tips

- **Enable/disable Smart HDR**: Among the new iPhone's camera advancements is HDR, which helps boost colors, light, and detail in hard light conditions. It's on by default, but if you would like to get it turned on or off, you manually can check out *Settings > Camera and discover the Smart HDR toggle change.*

- **Take a standard photograph with HDR**: Right under the Smart HDR toggle is a "Keep Normal Photo" option, which would save a regular, no HDR version of your picture as well as the Smart

HDR photo.

- **_Portrait Lights_**: To take Portrait Setting shots with artificial lights, first go to capture in Family portrait mode. Portrait Setting only works for people on the iPhone 7 when capturing with the rear-facing camera. To choose your Portrait Setting capturing style, press and hang on the screen where it says "DAYLIGHT" and then move your finger to the right.

- **_Edit Portrait Lights after taking pictures_**: Open up any Family portrait shot in Photos and then tap "edit." After another or two, you will see the light effect icon at the bottom of the image, touch it, and swipe just as you did when shooting the picture.

- **_Edit Portrait setting Depth_**: Using the new iPhone 7, you can modify the blur impact after shooting the Portrait shot. Check out Photos and choose the picture you want to regulate, then select "edit." You will see a depth slider at the bottom of the screen. Swipe to boost the blur strength, swipe left to diminish it.

- *How exactly to Merge People in Photos app*: Photos in iOS can check out your photos and identify people and places. If you discover that the application has chosen the same person, but says they vary, you can combine the albums collectively. To get this done, go directly to the Photos application > Albums and choose People & Places. Touch on the term "Select" at the very top right of the screen and then select the images of individuals you want to merge, then tap "merge."

- *Remove people in Photos app*: Head to Photos App, Albums, and choose People & Places. To eliminate tap on "Choose" and then tap on individuals, you do not want to see before tapping on "Remove" underneath still left of your iPhone screen.

iPhone 7: Keyboard Tips

- ***Go one-handed***: iOS 13's QuickType keypad enables you to type one-handed, which is fantastic on the larger devices like the iPhone 7 and XS Greatest extent. Press and contain the emoji or world icon and then keypad configurations. Select either the still left or right-sided keypad. It shrinks the keyboard and techniques it to 1 aspect of the screen. Get back to full size by tapping the tiny arrow.

- ***Use your keyboard as a trackpad***: Previously, with 3D Touch shows, you utilize the keyboard area as a trackpad to go the cursor on the screen. You'll still can, but it works just a little in a different way here, rather than pressure pressing anywhere on the keypad, press, and hangs on the spacebar instead.

Face ID Tips

- *Adding another in-person ID*: if you regularly change appearance now, you can put in a second In person ID to state the iPhone 7 getting puzzled. That is also really useful if you would like to add your lover to allow them to use your mobile phone while you're traveling, for example.

iPhone 7: Screen Tips

- *Standard or Zoomed screen*: Since iPhone 6 Plus, you've had the opportunity to select from two quality options. You can transform the screen settings from Standard or Zoomed on the iPhone 7 too. To change between your two - if you have changed your mind after set up - go to *Configurations > Screen & Lighting > Screen Focus and choose Standard or Zoomed.*

- *Enable True Tone screen*: If you didn't get it done

at the step, you could transform it anytime. To get the iPhone's screen to automatically change its color balance and heat to complement the background light in the area, check out Control Centre and push press the screen lighting slider. Now touch the True Firmness button. You can even go to *Configurations > Screen and Lighting and toggle the "True Shade" switch.*

iPhone 7 Battery Tips

- *Check your average battery consumption*: In iOS 13, you can check out Settings > Battery, and you will see two graphs. One shows the electric battery level; the other shows your screen on and screen off activity. You would find two tabs. One shows your last day; the other turns up to fourteen days; this way, you can view how energetic your phone battery strength and breakdowns screening your average screen on and off times show under the graphs.

- *Enable Low-Power Mode*: The reduced Power

Mode (Settings > Electric battery) enables you to reduce power consumption. The feature disables or lessens background application refresh, auto-downloads, email fetch, and more (when allowed). You can turn it on at any point, or you are prompted to carefully turn it on at the 20 and 10 % notification markers. You can even put in control to regulate Centre and get access to it quickly by swiping up to gain access to Control Centre and tapping on the electric battery icon.

- *Find electric battery guzzling apps*: iOS specifically lets you know which apps are employing the most power. Head to Configurations > Electric battery and then scroll right down to the section that provides you with an in-depth look at all of your battery-guzzling apps.

- *Check your battery via the Electric battery widget*: Inside the widgets in Today's view, some cards enable you to start to see the battery life staying in your iPhone, Apple Watch, and linked headphones. Just swipe from left to directly on your Home screen to access your Today view and scroll until you start to see the "Batteries" widget.

- *Charge wirelessly*: To utilize the iPhone's wifi charging capabilities, buy a radio charger. Any Qi charger will continue to work, but to charge more effectively, you will need one optimized for Apple's 7.5W charging.

- *Fast charge it*: When you have a 29W, 61W, or 87W USB Type-C power adapter for a MacBook, you can plug in your iPhone utilizing a Type-C to Lightning wire watching it charge quickly. Up to 50 % in thirty minutes.

Chapter 3

Amazing iPhone Features & Tips

This chapter would help you maximize the new iPhone 7 and iPhone 7 plus features, while also obtaining a refresher on other iPhone tips you might have forgotten.

Change the iPhone 7 Home Button

Among the first things, you'll notice with the iPhone 7 (well, maybe immediately after that missing headphone jack) is the fact that the *Home button* doesn't move whatsoever; instead, it's a track pad-like cutout that responds when you press onto it; the Home button uses haptic opinions to simulate the feel of the button.

You can change the Home button to three different degrees of feedback to get the one which feels easiest to your finger *(go to Configurations > General > Home Button to get the right degree of feedback)*.

Restart your iPhone 7

The fact that the *"Home button"* is unable to move means the technique for forcing an iPhone to restart changes with the iPhone 7 and iPhone 7 Plus; rather than holding down the *Home button* and *Power button* concurrently as you do with earlier iPhones, you now press and contain the power and volume buttons at precisely the same time; it's a relatively simple tip to understand.

Utilize the Depth of Field Impact with your iPhone

The iPhone 11 features two lenses on its back: inside the 12-megapixel cameras includes a focal amount of 28mm, as the other has a 56mm focal length, which allows the iPhone focus on items with less distortion than you get from a telephone with an only digital move. Using the latest version of iOS 10, you can take photos utilizing a depth-of-field impact that keeps the subject in sharp focus, while artfully blurring the background (which can also be called a ***bokeh impact*** in the photographic world.)

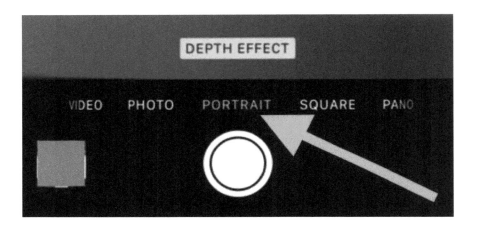

You access the result (called Family portrait setting by Apple) the same manner you'd have a panoramic shot or change between video but still photos. The family portrait appears as a choice in the carousel of different camera settings. Just swipe to choose it, and the iPhone will do all of those other works, with the 56mm zoom lens capturing a close-up of your subject matter as the other lens catches background information to be blurred by the iPhone's image processors.

Utilize the Optical Focus on the iPhone 7 Plus

Here's something you can do with your iPhone 7 plus right from the package: Use its dual-camera set up to focus on items; apple makes being able to access this feature as easy as possible.

From within the camera app, find the 1x button on the iPhone's display; touch that button to move directly into a 2x view; tapping the button again goes back to 1x.

To get more of a focus, tap and press the 1x button, and a semicircle would show; following that, you can pull the button to get right up to a 10x focus. Just remember that anything beyond 2x includes digital move, which can degrade image quality (though less than phones which have to rely entirely on digital focus, our screening has found.

However, if you're the type who lives and dies with pinch-to-zoom gestures, you can still use those to move, though, with no accuracy, you'd get from the other options for controlling your camera's focus.

Secure the Focus on the iPhone

The addition of Move features has added a fresh option to the Photos & Camera settings: Now you can lock at the camera zoom lens when you're recording video; this will prevent you from switching between your wide-angle and telephoto lens on your iPhone as you record video and also stop the flickering image that can result as you change between lenses.

In Settings, go for Photos & Camera, and then tap on "Record Video"; you'll find the Lock Camera Zoom lens option there next to a slider.

Enable iOS 10's Rest Finger to Unlock Phone Feature

iOS 10 changes how you uncover your iPhone with Touch Identification, needing you to press the Home button rather than just relaxing your finger there, which may be a bit of the shock, especially if the very first time you encounter this change is when you've improved to a fresh iPhone 7 or iPhone 7 Plus. Luckily, it's easy to return to the old way to do things, if you know where you can look.

Check out Settings* > *General* > *Convenience, and find the Home Button option; following that, you can move a slider to turn on the other Finger to open up features carefully.

Restoring iPhone 7 Backup from iCloud and iTunes

There is no need connecting your brand-new iPhone to your personal computer, as long as there is a mobile data connection designed for activation.

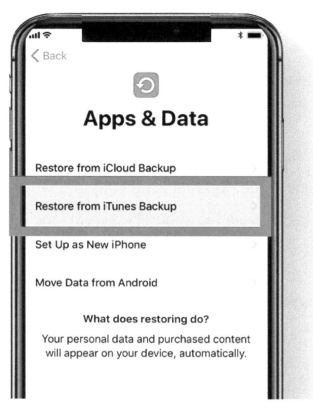

As you end the set-up wizard, you may navigate back by tapping the back arrow at the top left-hand side of the screen and scroll further to another display by tapping another button at the top right-hand corner.

You can commence by pressing down the power button at the top edge of your brand-new iPhone. You may want to keep it pressed down for about two seconds until you notice a vibration, meaning the iPhone is booting up.

Once it boots up finally, you can start initial set up by following the processes below;

- Swipe your finger over the display screen to start the set-up wizard.

- Choose the language of preference - English is usually at the top of the list, so there is no problem finding it. However, if you would like to apply a different language, scroll down to look for your desired *language,* and tap to select the preferred language.

- Choose your *country* - the *United States,* for instance, which may be close to the top of the list. If otherwise, scroll down the list and select the United States or any of your choice.

- You need to connect your iPhone to the internet to start its activation. You can test this via a link with a Wi-Fi network. Locate the name of your available network in the list shown, and then tap on it to select it.

- Enter the Wi-Fi security password (you will generally find this written on your router, which is probably known as the WPA Key, WEP Key, or

Password) and select Sign up. A tick indication shows you are connected, and a radio image appears near the top of the screen. The iPhone would now start activation with Apple automatically. It may take some time!

- In case your iPhone is a 4G version, you would be requested to check for updated internet configurations after inserting a new Sim card. You can test this anytime, so, for the present time, tap **Continue**.

- Location services would help you with mapping, weather applications, and more, giving you specific information centred wholly on what your location is. Select whether to use location service by tapping to *allow location services*.

- You would now be requested to create **Touch ID**, which is Apple's fingerprint identification. **Touch ID** allows you to unlock your iPhone with your fingerprint instead of your passcode or security password. To set up Tap Identification, put a finger or your thumb on the home button (but do not press it down!). To by-pass this for the moment, tap *setup Touch ID later*.

- If you are establishing Touch ID, the tutorial instruction on the screen will walk you through the set-up process. Put your finger on the home button, then remove it till the iPhone has properly scanned your fingerprint. Whenever your print is wholly scanned, you would notice a screen letting you know that tap recognition is successful. Tap **Continue**.

- You would be requested to enter a passcode to secure your iPhone. If you create **Touch ID**, you must use a passcode if, in any case, your fingerprint isn't acknowledged. Securing your computer data is an excellent idea, and the iPhone provides you with several options. Tap password option to choose your lock method.

- You can arrange a Custom Alphanumeric Code (that is a security password that uses characters and figures), a Custom Numeric Code (digit mainly useful, however, you can add as many numbers as you want!) or a 4-Digit Numeric Code. In case you didn't install or set up **Touch ID,** you may even have an option not to add a Security password. Tap on your selected Security option.

- I would recommend establishing a 4-digit numeric code, or Touch ID for security reasons, but all optional setup is done likewise. Input your selected Security password using the keyboard.

- Verify your Security password by inputting it again. If the Password does not match, you'll be requested to repeat! If indeed they do match, you'll continue to another display automatically.

At this time of the set-up process, you'll be asked whether you have used an iPhone before and probably upgrading it, you can restore all of your applications and information from an iCloud or iTunes backup by deciding on the best option. If this is your first iPhone, you would have to get it started as new, yet, in case you are moving from Android to an iPhone, you can transfer all your data by deciding and choosing the choice you want.

How to Move Data From an Android Phone

Apple has made it quite easy to move your data from a Google Android device to your new iPhone.

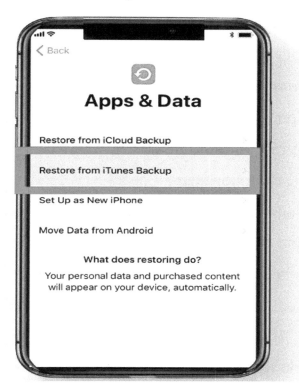

Proceed to the iOS app. I'll direct you about how to use the application to move your data!

- Using the iPhone, if you are on the applications & data screen of the set-up wizard, tap *move data from Google android*.

- Go to the Play Store on your Google android device and download the app recommended by the set-up wizard. When it is installed, open up the app, select **Continue,** and you'll be shown the ***Terms & Conditions*** to continue.

- On your Android device, tap ***Next*** to start linking your Devices. On your own iPhone, select ***Continue***.

- Your iPhone would show a 6-digit code that has to be received into the **Google android** device to set the two phones up.

- Your Google android device would screen all the data that'll be moved. By default, all options are ticked - so if there could be something you don't want to move, tap the related collection to deselect it. If you are prepared to continue, tap ***Next*** on your Google android device.

- As the change progresses, you would notice the iPhone display screen changes, showing you the position of the info transfer and progress report.

- When the transfer is completed, you will notice a confirmation screen on each device. On your Android Device, select ***Done*** to shut the app. On your own iPhone, tap ***Continue***.

- An ***Apple ID*** allows you to download apps,

supported by your iPhone and synchronize data through multiple devices, which makes it an essential account you should have on your iPhone! If you have been using an iPhone previously, or use iTunes to download music to your laptop, then you should have already become an *Apple ID* user. Register with your username and passwords (when you have lost or forgotten your Apple ID or password, you will see a link that may help you reset it). If you're not used to iPhone, select doesn't have an Apple ID to create one for free.

- The Terms & Conditions for your iPhone can be seen. Please go through them (tapping on more to study additional info), so when you are done, tap *Agree*.

- You'll be asked about synchronizing your data with iCloud. That's to ensure bookmarks, connections, and other items of data are supported securely with your other iPhone data. Tap *merge* to permit this or *don't merge* if you'll have a choice to keep your details elsewhere asides iCloud.

- **Apple pay** is Apple's secure payment system that stores encrypted credit or debit card data on your device and making use of your iPhone also with your fingerprint to make safe transactions online and with other apps. Select *Next* to continue.

- To *feature/add a card*, place it on a set surface and place the iPhone over it, so the card is put in the camera framework. The credit card info would be scanned automatically, and you would be requested to verify that the details on display correspond with your card. You'll also be asked to enter the *CVV* (safety code) from the personal strip behind the card. If you choose (or the camera cannot recognize your cards), you can enter credit card information by hand by tapping the hyperlink. You could bypass establishing **Apple Pay** by tapping *create later*.

- Another screen discusses the *iCloud keychain*, which is Apple's secure approach to sharing your preserved security password and payment information throughout all your Apple devices. You might use *iCloud security code* to validate your brand-new device and import present data, or you might be asked to continue registering your keychain if it's your first Apple device. In case you don't want to share vital data with other devices, you should go to *avoid iCloud keychain* or *don't restore passwords*.

- If you want to set up your Apple keychain, you'd be notified to either uses a Security password (the same one you'd set up on your iPhone or produce a different code. If you're making use of your iCloud security code, you should put it on your iPhone when prompted.

- This would confirm your ID when signing on to an iCloud safety code; a confirmation code would be delivered via SMS. You may want to hyperlink your smartphone text code (if you have never distributed one with Apple already) so that the code may be provided as a text. Then enter this code to your iPhone if requested, then select *Next.*

- You'll then be asked to create **Siri**. *Siri* is your own digital personal associate, which might search the internet, send communications, and check out data in your device and a lot more, all without having to flick via specific apps. Choose to create Siri by tapping the choice or start Siri later to skip this task for now.

- To set up and create SIRI, you would need to speak several phrases to the iPhone to review your conversation patterns and identify your voice.

- Once you say every term, a tick would be observed, showing that it's been known and comprehended. Another phrase may indicate that you should read aloud.

- Once you've completed the five phrases, you would notice a display notifying that Siri has been set up correctly. Tap *Continue*.

- The iPhone display alters the colour balance to help make the screen show up naturally under distinctive light conditions. You can switch this off in the screen settings after the iPhone has completed configuring it. Tap *continue* to continue with the setup.

- Has your iPhone been restored? Tap begin to transfer your computer data to your brand-new iPhone.

- You'll be prompted to ensure your brand-new iPhone has enough power to avoid the device turning off in the process of downloading applications and information. Tap *OK* to verify this recommendation.

- You would notice a notification show up on your apps to download in the background.

NB: *Setting up any new iPhone model: A similar method, as described above, applies.*

How to Restore iPhone 7 Back-up from iCloud or iTunes

If you want to restore your iPhone from an iTunes back-up, you may want to connect to iCloud and have the latest version of iTunes installed on it. If you are ready to begin this process, tap **restore** from iTunes back-up on your iPhone and connect it to your personal computer. Instructions about how to bring back your data can be followed on the laptop screen.

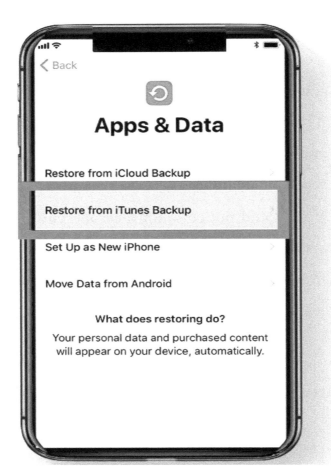

In case your old iPhone model was supported on iCloud, then follow the instructions below to restore your applications & data to your brand-new device:

- Tap *Restore* from iCloud back-up.
- Register with the Apple ID and Password that you applied to your old iPhone. If you fail to recollect the security password, there's a link that may help

you reset it.

- The Terms & Conditions screen would show. Tap the links to learn about specific areas in detail. When you are ready to proceed, select **Agree**.

- Your iPhone would need some moments to create your Apple ID and hook up with the iCloud server.

- You would notice a summary of available backups to download. The most up-to-date backup would be observed at the very top, with almost every other option below it. If you want to restore from a desirable backup, tap the screen for *all backups* to see the available choices.

- Tap on the back-up you want to restore to start installing.

- A progress bar would be shown, providing you with a demo of the advancement of the download. When the restore is completed, the device will restart.

- You would see a notification telling you that your iPhone is updated effectively. Tap *Continue*.

- To complete the iCloud set up on your recently restored iPhone, you should re-enter your iCloud

(Apple ID) password. Enter/review it and then tap *Next*.

- You'll be prompted to upgrade the security information related to your *Apple ID*. Tap on any stage to replace your computer data, or even to bypass this option. If you aren't ready to do this, then tap the *Next* button.

- **Apple pay** is Apple's secure payment system that stores encrypted credit or debit card data on your device and making use of your iPhone also with your fingerprint to make safe transactions online and with other apps. Select *Next* to continue.

- To *feature/add a card*, place it on a set surface and place the iPhone over it, so the card is put in the camera framework. The credit card info would be scanned automatically, and you would be requested to verify that the details on display correspond with your card. You'll also be asked to enter the *CVV* (safety code) from the personal strip behind the card. If you choose (or the camera cannot recognize your cards), you can enter credit card information by hand by tapping the hyperlink.

You could bypass establishing **Apple Pay** by tapping *create later*.

- Another screen discusses the *iCloud keychain*, which is Apple's secure approach to sharing your preserved security password and payment information throughout all your Apple devices. You might use *iCloud security code* to validate your brand-new device and import present data, or you might be asked to continue registering your keychain if it's your first Apple device. In case you don't want to share vital data with other devices, you should go to *avoid iCloud keychain* or *don't restore passwords*.

- If you selected to set up your Apple keychain, you'd be notified to either uses a Security password (the same one you'd set up on your iPhone) or provide a different code. If you're making use of your iCloud security code, you should put it on your iPhone when prompted.

- This would confirm your ID when signing on to an iCloud safety code; a confirmation code would be delivered via SMS. You may want to hyperlink your smartphone text code (if you have never distributed one with Apple already) so that the code may be provided as a text. Then enter this code to your iPhone if requested, then select *Next.*

- You'll then be asked to create **Siri**. *Siri* is your own digital personal associate, which might search the internet, send communications, and check out data in your device and a lot more, all without having to flick via specific apps. Choose to create Siri by tapping the choice or start Siri later to skip this task for now.

- To set up and create SIRI, you would need to speak several phrases to the iPhone to review your conversation patterns and identify your voice.

- Once you say every term, a tick would be observed, showing that it's been known and comprehended. Another phrase may indicate that you should read aloud.

- Once you've completed the five phrases, you would notice a display notifying that Siri has been set up correctly. Tap *Continue*.

- The iPhone display alters the colour balance to

help make the screen show up naturally under distinctive light conditions. You can switch this off in the screen settings after the iPhone has completed configuring it. Tap *continue* to continue with the setup.

- Has your iPhone been restored? Tap begin to transfer your computer data to your brand-new iPhone.

- You'll be prompted to ensure your brand-new iPhone has enough charge to avoid the device turning off in the process of downloading applications and information. Tap *OK* to verify this recommendation.

- You would notice a notification show up on your apps to download in the background.

Find the Camera Shortcut

This is another iOS 10-centric tip that could come as a surprise if you haven't explored the iOS Apple launched last fall. iOS 9's lock display used to include a camera icon that allowed you to gain access to your phone's camera and never have first to unlock it (perfect for grabbing an instant picture you don't want to miss while fumbling to unlock your phone and open the camera app). That icon's eliminated in iOS 10, though Apple has managed to get easier to leap right to your camera.

From your lock screen, swipe left. The camera application will start on your iPhone, prepared to take any picture you want with the iPhone 7's greatly improved camera.

Turn Off Raise to Wake

We usually think the addition of *"raise to wake"* (where your lock display screen springs alive the minute you hold up the phone) is among the best additions to iOS 10 and the new iPhones. Perhaps you choose your iPhone only turning on when you wish it to, which makes it easy enough to disable the raise-to-wake feature. Again, check out Settings, but this time, select Screen & Brightness (just underneath the region where you can modify your phone's auto-lock time); a slider enables you to turn Increase to Wake on or off.

Turn Your Keypad Right into a Track-

pad

This isn't a fresh feature for the iPhone 7 or 7 Plus, but it's still somewhat useful one for 3D Touch-capable iPhones; when you're keying in an email, or message and want to make the cursor to stay on a term, you could place your finger where you desire the cursor to be (but that option does not have precision, and it could be hard to see wherever your cursor is, as your finger is in the manner). Instead, execute a hard press on the on-screen keypad: the secrets will go away, and you've got a MacBook-style track-pad.

You will slip your finger around to take the cursor anywhere on display. After the cursor is hovering over the term you want, hard press again to choose that term; hard-pressing double selects the complete sentence.

Add Widgets to Your Screen

iOS 10 provides Today display screen a new home and new look for just about any iPhone, but you'll want to customize what appears on that display once you obtain a fresh iPhone 7 or iPhone 7 Plus. From either your lock display screen or home display, swipe to start so you can see the Today display screen. By default, it'll include widget displaying the current climate, upcoming calendar occasions, headlines from the news headlines app, Siri application recommendations, and Maps locations for forthcoming visits.

But you're not stuck with this view (scroll right down, underneath the "Today display" and tap *Edit* to customize what widgets show up); you can delete those that are there by default or add others with a click, and you're not limited to widgets from Apple's built-in apps: if a third-party application installed on your mobile phone has been up to date with an iOS 10 widget, it'll appear as a choice that you should add in the more fabulous Widgets section.

Avoid Water Damage and Mold

Both iPhone 7 and iPhone 7 Plus can withstand a splash of water. Apple says the new cell phones come with an IP67 ranking for the water level of resistance, indicating that you don't need to stress if your iPhone gets dunked in 1 meter (about 3ft) of water for thirty minutes. In our screening, we could spill water on the phone and even drop it in a pitcher of water with no sick effects.

Despite having the iPhone's new found water resistance, you're heading to want to wipe down your wet iPhone before utilizing it and prevent charging it after any unpredicted dips. Apple has generated another feature into its new mobile phones that warn you when any dampness is recognized. That's you should be aware of unplugging the phone and keep it switched off as the iPhone has an opportunity to dry out.

Change Your Video Resolution

You might not have even a 4K TV in your living room yet; however, many days, you almost certainly will. So when you need to do, your iPhone 7 can already capture video in the super high-definition format. Open up Configurations and go to Photos & Camera, then scroll right down to the Camera section. You'll see a Record Video option - touch it to choose from several different resolutions, starting in 720p at 30 fps, and going entirely up to 4K.

Take note, though, that extra resolution comes at the price of drive space; as iOS warns you, one minute of video at 4K can cost you 350MB - almost six times more than the same timeframe in the lowest (but high-definition!) quality.

Have a Live Photo

The iPhone 6s introduced the thought of Live Photos: animated pictures that you can snap with your iPhone's camera that add a couple of seconds of video before and following the picture itself. If you're improving to the iPhone 7 from an iPhone 6 or previously, you might need a refresher about how to take a Live Picture.

Live Photos are enabled by default; you can concur that it's fired up by locating the *bullseye icon* right above the viewfinder in the Camera app. If the icon is yellowish, Live Photos is on; faucet the icon if you would like to turn the feature off carefully.

With Live Photos allowed, your camera captures 1.5 seconds of video and sound before and once you take the shot. Once you touch the shutter button, the term "Live" can look for 1.5 seconds on the viewfinder to inform you the camera continues to be recording. If you await the "Live" to vanish before placing your camera down, you won't finish up with a blurry Live Image.

Disable Touch Feedback

Apple has bumped in the Taptic Engine - the hardware that the phone uses to produce vibrations. Due to the more exact capabilities of these devices, Apple's integrated touch responses into its whole operating-system. When you spin a dial, you'll actually "feel" it; same for tugging down the Notification Middle sheet, swiping to delete communications in Email, and a great many other actions.

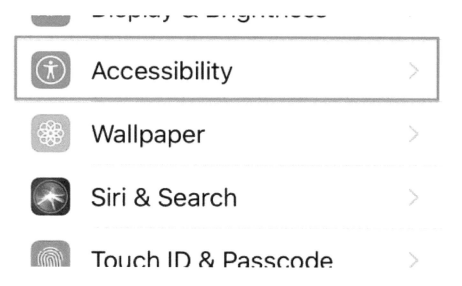

However, if those little blips and buzzes are distracting, don't be concerned: you can deactivate them. Turn up

Configurations and go directly to the recently christened Seems & Haptics section. Scroll entirely down to underneath, and you'll visit a new option for System Haptics. Change it to off, and you'll no more be bothered by those touchy-feely sensations.

Disable Flashy Messages Effects

Among the significant new top features of iOS 10 is, of course, the additions to Communications that enable you to send your text messages with a multitude of flashy bubble and display screen results; perhaps those results aren't for you, whether you're especially delicate to onscreen movement or don't look after them. That's cool: the glad tidings are you can disable them so that no balloons or confetti will ever accompany a congratulatory text message sent the right path.

Just get into *Settings > General > Accessibility > Reduce Motion* and change the feature. Not merely will this disable message results, but it'll also reduce motion-based results somewhere else in iOS. (Suggestion: If you're discovering that you can't send message results, it might be because you currently have this feature fired up.)

Enable the Magnifier

Sometimes it's convenient to have the ability to take a look at things up close, whether it's due to a visual problem or just out of attention. iOS 10 provides a new option to its Availability toolbox by presenting a magnifier. *Head to Configurations > General > Ease of access > Magnifier and switch the Magnifier change to On.*

To result in the magnifier, triple tap the *Home button* (you may want to adjust the Convenience Shortcut option in the Availability settings to ensure the Magnifier is selected); this starts up a camera user interface with a focus slider that enables you to zoom in a lot more carefully than the default camera. You can lock concentrate by *tapping the padlock button, activate the adobe flash to shed some light about them, or even snap a freeze framework if you don't want to carry the phone still.* Some high-contrast filter systems make it simpler to discern details, and which you can apply either to the live image or a frozen body.

Enable Color Filters

Regardless of how bright the display on the new iPhone 7 is, if you have problems with some color blindness, it could be challenging working with a device's screen. iOS 10 efforts to help you by adding in some new filtration system options to help those people who have trouble distinguishing specific colors.

Under Configurations > General > Ease of access > Screen Accommodations > Color Filter systems, you can choose from some different alternatives, including Grayscale, a Red/Green filtration system, a Green/Red Filtration system, and a Blue/Yellowish Filtration system to help people that have Protanopia, Deuteranopia, and Tritanopia respectively.

If none of these works, you can also set a color tint for your screen, choosing a specific Hue and Strength that you find helpful. Several color images on the display screen help you to get a concept of what sort of particular filtration system will impact the display.

Clear All Notifications Simultaneously

This becomes hook revamp in iOS 10; however, the best addition is specifically for users of the iPhone 6s and iPhone 7 cell phones. On prior iPhones, you'd to clear notifications on the day-by-day basis, every time tapping the 'x' button near the top of the section and then tapping Clear.

But on the 3D Touch-enabled phone like the iPhone 7 or 7 Plus, you merely pressure press on the 'x' near the top of the list, and you'll see a choice to Clear All Notifications. Touch that and all of your unread notifications will vanish, departing with a great clean Notification Middle.

Control Center Shortcuts

Talking about Control Center, 3D Touch starts up lots of helpful shortcuts there. Swipe upwards from underneath of the display on your iPhone 7 to talk about the panel. As before, the control keys in the bottom enable you to quickly access regular features, just like a torch, timer, calculator, and the camera; however, in iOS 10, force-pressing on each introduces additional options.

For instance, you can force press the torch button to talk about different intensities for the torch: shiny, medium, and low. Pressure pressing the timer enables you to quickly take up a timer for a common period, like an hour, twenty minutes, 5 minutes, or about a minute. Around the calculator, push press to duplicate the last computation result. As well as the camera icon enables you to quickly leap to the picture, slow-motion video, normal video, or selfie views in the Camera app.

Pay with Your iPhone

If you're upgrading to the iPhone 7 from anything sooner than the iPhone 6, this will be your first contact with *Apple Pay*, Apple's mobile payment system that enables you to purchase things by tapping your iPhone at any payment terminal that helps Near Field Marketing communications.

(You'll visit a useful Apple Pay logo design at stores that support Apple's payment system.)

To create Apple Pay, release the Wallet application on your iPhone and follow the steps for entering a payment card. (Apple keeps an updated set of taking part banks.) Furthermore, to making use of your mobile phone to make transactions, iOS 10 provides the capability to use Apple Purchase buying things from within the phone's Safari browser at participating sites.

See Your iCloud Storage Space Instantly

Wondering how many photos, documents, and email messages you have stashed in *iCloud*? Just check out Settings, touch on your *Accounts ID* near the top of the display screen, and choose *iCloud*. You will see an; at-a-glance view of your iCloud storage space usage. Touch it to observe how much room you have gone, manage your storage space, eliminating things, or buy additional storage space.

Chapter 4

Top Best iPhones Model Tips
Keyboard Tips

- *Go one-handed*: The QuickType keypad enables you to type one-handed, which is fantastic on the larger devices. Press and contain the little emoji icon and choose either the *left or right-sided keypad*; it shrinks the keypad and brings it to one part of the screen. Get back to full size by tapping the tiny arrow.

- *Pull the plug on one-handed*: if you never want the choice to visit one-handed, check out *Settings > General > Keypad and toggle the "One-handed keypad"* option off.

- *Use your keyboard as a trackpad*: Because the introduction of 3D Touch shows on iPhones, you may use the keyboard area as a trackpad to go the cursor onscreen. It works anywhere there's text message input, and will save you need to try and touch the precise location you want to begin editing. Just hard press anywhere on the keypad and move the cursor around.

- *Picking your Emoji color*: In recent iOS, Apple added lots of new emoji and specifically emoji, which have pores and skin tones. To gain access to them, go directly to the emoji keypad in any application and long press on the main one you want to use. If it has options, they'll show.

- *Adding third-party keyboards*: Set up the application (*SwiftKey or Gboard* are an example) and follow the instructions in the app. Sooner or later, it will request you to go to *Configurations > General > Keypad > Keyboards* and add the third-party keypad.

- *Being able to access additional keyboards beyond Emoji*: When you have more than three keyboards installed, the keyboard will show a globe icon next to the spacebar; virtually any app which has a keypad touch on that world icon and on the other hand to reveal another keypad you have installed.

- *Hiding or teaching auto recommendations on QuickType keypad*: The brand new Apple keypad shows word recommendations predicated on what you type. Unless you utilize this, you can conceal it to offer more space on display. Softly press and keep near the top of the auto-suggest pub and pull it towards the very best row of secrets. You may bring it back by dragging up from the very best of the keypad if you change your brain.

- *Disable keyboard capitalization*: Until iOS 9, whether you handled the shift key or not, all the letters on the keyboard were capitalized. Now, the keypad shows the characters in lowercase when change is off. But unless you want this, you can disable it by heading to *Configurations > Availability> Keypad* and toggling from the screen lowercase Secrets option.

- *Disable keyboard animations*: Apple's keyboard has a pop-up character animation that serves as feedback when you tap the secrets. You can shut it off (*Configurations> General> Key pad> Personality Preview*).

- *Text message replacement shortcuts*: As in every earlier year, one of iOS' most readily useful keyboard solutions is creating shortcodes that become full words or phrases. Head to *Configurations > General > Keypad > Text Alternative*. We think it is beneficial to have one for an address that fills in automatically if we misspell "addresses," adding a supplementary "s" by the end.

Maps Tips

- *How to manage preferred transport in Apple Maps*: If you discover you merely ever use Apple Maps when walking, you can place the preferred transportation type to be that. To improve it between Traveling, Walking, and General public Transportation, go to *Configurations > Maps* and select the one you want.

- *Us ARKit in FlyOver*: A couple of years ago, Apple developed its Maps app, filled with Flyover, digital 3D variations of major towns. You will shop around 3D metropolitan areas by merely moving your iPhone. Visit a major city - like London or NY - then tap the ***"FlyOver"*** option. Then all you have to do is move your device and show you around the town.

- *Use interior maps*: Now, you can use inside mapping to stay on course around major department stores. It's limited for the present time; nevertheless, you can check it out in AIRPORT TERMINAL. To use in Home maps, visit a backed location and pinch-to-zoom in before outdoor areas go dark gray. You will see inside the building.

- *Move between building levels on indoor maps*: Once you're in the building map, you will see lots in the right aspect of the display screen. Touch it, and then choose a floor level.

Apple Music Tips

- *How to cover Apple Music*: You can completely cover Apple's Apple Music service, to take action, go to Configurations > Music, and then toggle off Show Apple Music. Now when you attend the application, you are only going to see your music, as opposed to the music on the service.

- *How to gain access to your complete music collection*: To find out all the tunes, albums, and playlists that you added from the Apple Music catalog, as well as any music that you purchased from iTunes, including CDs that you ripped, touch the Library tabs from the app's menu club along underneath.

- *How exactly to edit your Collection categories*: To completely clean up your collection and specify which categories you'd prefer to see instantly, such as styles, artists, or track, tap the Edit button in the very best right of the Collection display, and then toggle on/off your requirements.

- *Where to find your downloaded music*: if you only want to start to see the music that's physically on your device, tap the Library tabs from the app's menu pub underneath the screen, and then tap *Downloaded Music*.

- *How exactly to create a fresh playlist*: Heading on a street trip and want to produce a playlist? It's easy. Touch the Library tabs from the app's menu club along underneath, then touch Playlists, and choose New Playlist. Following that, you can include a playlist name, explanation, music, and toggle on/off whether you want the general playlist public.

- *Where to find Apple's curated playlists*: The "FOR YOU PERSONALLY" tab within the menu pub/bar underneath is a location where you can go to and discover music recommendations hand-selected by the Apple Music team. Recommendations add a curated favorites blend, daily playlists, performers spotlights, and new produce, which focus on you and are customized to your music choices.

- *Where to find top music graphs*: Go directly to the Search tabs in the menu pub along underneath, and then tap "Top Graphs" to visit a regularly updated set of typically the most popular tracks on Apple Music.

- *Where to find top music graphs by genre*: By default, the very best Graphs section in the Search tab teaches you all styles. But you can pick a particular genre, such as Blues, by tapping the All Styles button in the very best right and selecting your genre from the list that shows up.

- *How to gain access to Connect*: Apple has ditched the Connect tabs in iOS 10 (it allowed you to check out performers and curators to be able to see their new products and articles). They have instead buried the feature in the new Search tab. Following that, select Top Graphs, and then scroll to underneath of the display screen to see music on Connect and videos on Connect.

- *Where to find videos*: Apple Music isn't nearly music. It's also about music videos and other video content. Go directly to the Browse tabs in the menu club along underneath, and then touch Videos to see new videos on Apple Music and top music videos.

- Where to find the Beats 1 radio train station: Apple Music offers a 24/7 live-streaming radio place called **Beats 1**. To gain access to it, tap the air tabs in the menu pub along underneath, and then touch the Beats 1 thumbnail.

Where to find r / c: Aside from Beats 1, Apple Music offers channels that derive from genres and various themes. You'll find them under the air tabs in the menu club along underneath. Following that, tap "R / C."

- *How to talk about a record*: Want to talk about a recording via Twitter, Facebook, or wherever? Touch on any record, and then choose the button with the "…" three dots at the very top. Following that, tap Share Recording and choose how you would like to talk about it.

- *How exactly to add a recording to your Play Next queue*: Apple Music can queue up albums you want to hear while on the run. Just add it to your Play Next list. Touch on any record, and then choose the button with the "…" three dots at the very top. Following that, touch "Play Next."

- *How exactly to add a recording to a playlist*: You can include an entire record to a fresh or old playlist. Just tap on the recording, and then choose the button with the "…" three dots at the very top. Following that, tap "Increase a Playlist," and then select which playlist (old or new) you want to include it too.

- *How exactly to download a record to your Collection for offline hearing*: Touch on the recording, and then choose the button with the "…" three dots at the very top. Following that, tap

Increase a Library. You'll then be cut back to the record screen. Touch the button with the "…" three dots again, and then choose the Download option. Oh, and later you will notice the option to eliminate it if you'd like.

- *How exactly to love/dislike a recording*: You can show Apple Music if you value or dislike a record such that it can better tailor music recommendations to you. Touch on any recording, and then choose the button with the "…" three dots. Following that, touch Love or Dislike, depending on your choice.

- *How to produce a train station from a track*: Touch on any music, and then from the music handles menu (tap it along underneath to make it expand into a full screen card) choose the button with the "…" Three dots in the low corner. Following that, tap Create Train station; this will generate a radio train station predicated on that specific tune.

- *How to talk about music*: Want to talk about a record via Twitter, Facebook, or wherever? Touch on any melody, and then from the music settings menu (touch it along underneath to make it broaden into a complete screen credit card), choose the button with the "..." three dots in the low corner. Following that, tap Share Record and then click how you would like to talk about it.

- *How to put in a track to your Play Next queue*: Apple Music can queue up tunes you want to hear while on the run. Just add it to your Play Next list. Touch on any track, and then from the music handles menu (tap it along underneath to make it increase into a complete screen card), choose the button with the "..." three dots in the low corner. Following that, touch "Play Next."

- *How to put in music to a playlist*: Touch on any music, and then from the music settings menu (tap it along underneath to make it expand into a complete screen credit card) choose the button with the "..." three dots in the low corner.

Following that, tap Increase a Playlist and then select which playlist (old or new).

- *How exactly to download a tune to your Collection for offline hearing*: Touch on any tune, and then from the music handles menu (touch it along underneath to make it expand into a complete screen card) choose the button with the "…" three dots in the low corner. Following that, tap Increase a Library. You'll then be cut back to the music control menu. Touch the button with the "…" three dots again, and then choose the Download option. Oh, and later you will notice the option to eliminate it if you'd like.

- *How exactly to love/dislike a melody*: You can show Apple Music if you value or dislike a melody, such that it can better tailor music recommendations to you. Touch on any track, and then from the music settings menu (tap it along underneath to make it broaden into a complete screen credit card), choose the button with the "…" three dots in the low corner. Following that, touch Love or Dislike, depending on your choice.

- *How exactly to see lyrics for a track*: Can't show the actual designer in a track is saying? Browse the lyrics in Apple Music. Touch on any music, and then from the music handles menu (tap it along underneath to make it increase into a complete screen card) choose the button with the "..." three dots in the low corner; following that, tap Lyrics.

- *Switch sound source for music*: Want to improve from your iPhone to a linked speaker? Touch on any tune, and then choose the red arrow button with radio waves (it rests below the volume slider, alongside the button with the "..." three dots. Following that, pick your sound source.

- *Share a musician*: Like tracks and albums, you can talk about a designer with a pal via internet sites and messaging apps. Just touch on any artist's web page (seek out a musician, then click his / her name to gain access to the web page, etc.), then tap the button with the "..." three dots next with their name, and choose Share Artist; following that, pick and choose how you'd prefer to share.

- *How to collection the alarm predicated on when you attend rest*: The Clock application can remind you to visit bed and then wake you up 8 hours later, for example. To create it, go directly to the Bedtime section in the Apple Clock application and arrange it from there.

- *How to routine Night Change mode*: Added in iOS 9.3, Evening Shift is an attribute that can automatically change the colors of your screen to the warmer end of the color spectrum at night. It isn't on by default, so to carefully turn it on, go to Settings > Screen & Lighting > Night Change. Here you arranged when you wish it scheduled to perform or "By hand allow it until tomorrow." You can even establish the "warmness" of the screen from "Less warm" to "More warm."

- *Schedule USUALLY DO NOT Disturb*: If you wish to make sure random electronic mails and

Facebook notifications don't wake you up in the night time, go to Configurations > USUALLY DO NOT Disturb and then toggle the Scheduled option before choosing a period for this to be on.

- *Setup ScreenTime*: You can now set limitations on application use as well as observe how enough time you've spent using apps. For many more upon this, check out our complete guide to ScreenTime.

Siri Tips

- **Translate**: Siri can translate a small number of dialects into American British (sadly no UK British region support yet). Just ask "Hey Siri, how will you say [Biscuit] in German/Spanish/Italian/Japanese/Chinese language."

- **Hey Siri**: To get Siri working by simply shouting at it rather than pressing a button, go to *Configurations > Siri & Search > Listen for "Hey*

Siri."

- **Disable Proactive Associate**: Unless you want Siri to suggest apps, people, locations, and more by using the new Limelight Search, you can always disable Siri Suggestions (in *Configurations > Siri and Search > Suggestions browsing*).

- **Tell Siri to keep in mind what you observe on display**: Siri can manage reminders, and can also remind you about whatever is shown on your device display screen - whether a website or note. Just say, *"Siri, remind me concerning this,"* and she'll scan the web page and add relevant details to your Reminders app.

- **Ask Siri to fetch a picture for you**: Siri is now able to search your photos predicated on their information and requirements. Ask her to discover a specific picture from 14 July 2019, for example, and she'll do that.

- **Shut up Siri**: Sometimes Siri is merely useful when she isn't speaking. Fortunately, an establishment called Voice Opinions (*Configurations> General> Siri*) enables you to decide when she may use her tone of voice. You are able to toggle the placing to always-on, hands-free only (which works only once using "Hey Siri" or linked to a Bluetooth device), or a fresh ring change option (which halts Siri from speaking whenever your ringer is changed to silent).

Safari Tips

- ***Stop websites monitoring you***: Head to *Settings > Safari* and then toggle the *"Ask Websites never to monitor me"* change to the on position.

- ***Gain access to saved passwords***: Because of iCloud, Safari can store your security password across all of your devices. Head to Configurations > App & Website Passwords then sign in making use of your Touch Identification scanner. Here you can view all the passwords that are saved, and manage them.

- *Find on a Web page in Safari*: To Find text message in a Safari web page, hit the Talk about button on a full page to visit a Find on Web page option (it areas a pop-up on the keyboard).

- *Disable frequently-visited sites in Safari*: Safari displays icons of your most visited websites each time you open up a fresh page. It enables you to delete specific ones by tapping and securing them, however now you can change them off completely by heading to *Configurations > Safari*; following that, *switch off Frequently Visited Sites*.

- *DuckDuckGo*: If you wish to place DuckDuckGo as your default internet search engine over Google, Yahoo, or Bing, go to *Configurations > Safari > INTERNET SEARCH ENGINE* and choose the private friendly internet search engine as the default.

- *Auto suggesting websites*: Like Safari on the desktop, you could have the iPhone or iPad Safari recommend suggested serp's as you type. It's on as default, but unless you want to buy, go to *Settings > Safari > INTERNET SEARCH ENGINE Recommendations* and toggle the feature off.

- ***Auto-suggesting apps***: Likewise, as you enter popular app brands into the Safari search Web address box, Apple will attempt and match that with applications you either have or may want. It's on as default, but if you would like to carefully turn if off, go to *Settings > Safari > Safari Recommendations*.

- ***Getting the hyperlink quickly***: Settings > Safari > Quick Website Search will determine whether Safari offers up website fits or not for you.

- ***Making websites weight faster or conserving your computer data***: Safari preloads the first strike of the search, which helps launch your choice quicker. The downside is that it might use up data. If you wish to transform it off, go to Configurations > Safari > Preload Top Strike and transform it off.

- ***Scan your credit card***: Instead of needing to type all of your details now, you can use the camera to scan your credit cards. With regards to getting into the credit card details either press to car fill up if you already are using that feature with Keychain, or press it and then choose Use Camera on another menu you get.

- ***Swipe forward and backward***: Swiping from the display to the display screen from the still left of the display dates back through your surfing background while swiping from the right of Safari moves ahead through your surfing around the background.

Handoff and Continuity Tips

Allowing Handoff between iOS devices: *Head to Total > Handoff* and then toggle the package.

- ***Being able to access Handoff apps***: Around the Lock Display press, the application icon underneath the left corner.

- *Allowing SMS mail messages on your Macintosh*: To get this done, you will need to enable the feature on your iPhone. Be sure you are operating iOS 8.1 or later and then go to *Settings > Text messages > TEXT Forwarding*. Find your Mac pc or iPad you want to permit access and set both devices with a security code. You'll now have the ability to see and send Texts via the desktop.

iCloud Tips

- *Start iCloud Drive*: Head to *Settings*, touch on your ID at the very top, then go to *iCloud > iCloud Drive*. Here you can control which applications get access to your iCloud Drive and whether they may use Cellular / Mobile Data.

- *Manage your Storage*: Settings, in that case, your *ID > iCloud > Manage Storage*. From here, you can view how much storage space you have, how much you have gone, and choose to buy more.

- *Family Posting*: Instead of having your iTunes

accounts on all of your family's iPhones and iPads, now you can set up Family Sharing for five people. Head to Configurations, then tap your ID at the very top and choose the *"Family Writing"* option.

- **Secure iCloud Keychain Access**: Head to Settings, in that case, your ID at the very *top iCloud > Keychain*, and toggle it on or off.

- ***Send the last location, and that means you will get it even though the phone is lost***: Apple's added an awesome hidden feature that will automatically send the last known location to Apple whenever your electric battery is critically low. Even if the electric battery dies as you've lost the phone behind the trunk of the couch, you can still at least get some idea where it surely got to.

- ***Gain access to iCloud Drive documents***: Go directly to the Documents app then touch "Search" then "locations" before choosing the iCloud Drive option. Here you will see all the documents and data files kept in your iCloud Drive.

Apple Pay Tips

- ***Pre-arm your payment***: To greatly help speed up your time and effort at the cashier, you can pre-arm your *Apple Pay* before you get to the counter. To get this done, get into Apple Pay, select the cards you want to use and then keep your finger on the Touch ID sensor. Once complete, you have one minute to use the equipped payment before it becomes off.

- ***Weigh multiple cards***: There is no limit to the volume of control cards Apple Pay can take, so keep launching them into Finances.

- ***How to gain access to Apple Pay from Lock display screen***: To gain access to Apple Pay on the Lock display, you can double-tap the *Home button*. Unless you want this feature, you can switch it off by heading to *Configurations > Pocket & Apple Pay and turn off "*Double-Click *Home Button."*

- ***How exactly to allow Apple Pay Obligations on***

Macintosh: You should use Apple Pay on your iPhone to verify payments on the nearby Mac. To make sure this is fired up, go to *Configurations > Budget & Apple Pay and start "Allow Obligations on Mac pc."*

- *How exactly to change the default Apple Pay credit card*: Head to *Settings > Finances & Apple Pay and choose the Default Cards* you want. If you just have one card, it'll automatically be the default credit card.

- *Choose an Apple Pay payment cards*: When paying with Apple Pay, now you can quickly choose which credit card you want to use simply by double-clicking the Home button while on the lock display screen. It'll talk about all your credit cards on your iPhone.

General Tips

- *Standard or Zoomed screen*: Since iPhone 6 Plus, you've had the opportunity to select from two quality options. You can transform the display establishing from Standard or Zoomed. To change between your two - if you have changed your mind after set up - go to *Configurations* > *Screen & Lighting* > *Display Focus and choose Standard or Zoomed.*

- **Set the display brightness**: Either go to Control Centre and adapt the screen brightness slider or go to *Settings* > *Display & Lighting.*

- **Text message Size and Daring Text**: To improve the default text message size and whether you want all fonts to be strong to help make them simpler to read, go to show & Brightness > Daring Text.

- **10-day forecast in weather**: Head to weather, and on any city swipe up. You now reach start to see the ten-day forecast as well as more information just like a mini weather forecast for your day, sunrise and sunset times, and the opportunity of rain.

- **Select a new wallpaper**: Apple has completely revamped its wallpaper offering for iOS. New wallpapers to be enjoyed in the Configurations > Wallpaper.

- ***Reach Wi-Fi configurations quickly with 3D Touch***: If you have an iPhone 6S, 6S Plus, or later, you can drive press on the Settings icon to reveal quick links to Bluetooth, Wi-Fi, and Electric battery configurations; the move helps it to be really quick to leap to the cellular settings.

- ***Disable contact photos***: Now, you can toggle contact photos *on or off* on iPhone 6 and later. To improve the settings, which is On by default, go to *Configurations > Communications > Show Contact Photos.*

- ***Get back to apps***: When you open up a web link or touch a notification when using an app, you will be delivered to a fresh app to be able to view the info in full fine detail. You'll also visit a new "Back to..." button at the very top remaining of the just-opened app, providing you with the chance to tap it and instantly return the application you were utilizing.

- ***Monitor your reproductive health***: Medical application has finally added a Reproductive Health tab, with options for basal body's temperature, cervical mucus quality, menstruation and ovulation calendar, and more.

- ***Delete an alarm***: Apple's swipe-to-delete gesture now works in the Clock app. To delete a security alarm, swipe still left on the security alarm.

- ***Search in Settings***: The Settings application has a search field at the very top, which may be revealed by pulling down on the Settings menu; utilize it to get the switches you will need.

- ***Enable Low-Power Mode***: The brand new Low Power Mode (Settings > battery) enables you to reduce power consumption. The feature disables or reduces background application refresh, auto-downloads, email fetch, and more (when allowed). You can change it on at any point, or you are prompted to carefully turn it on at the 20% and

10% notification markers. You can even put in control to regulate Centre, and get access to it quickly by swiping up to gain access to CC and tapping on the electric battery icon.

- ***Find electric battery guzzling apps***: iOS specifically lets you know which apps are employing the most juice. Head to Configurations > Electric battery and then scroll right down to the new section that provides you with an in-depth look at all of your battery-guzzling apps.

- ***Make use of a six-digit passcode***: Apple has always given you the opportunity to established a four-digit passcode, however, now it includes a six-number option, indicating hackers will have a 1 in 1 million potential for breaking it, rather than 1 in 10,000. Just go to *Configurations > Touch ID & Passcode > Change Passcode*, and then choose "Passcode Options".

- ***Change how your display screen responds to taps***:

A fresh section under Ease of access in Settings enables you to change how your display responds to taps. You can show your iPhone to ignore repeated details. You can even boost the duration of taps before recognized, plus much more.

- *Check your battery via the battery widget*: Inside the widgets in today's view, some cards enable you to start to see the battery life lasting longer on your iPhone, Apple Watch, and W1 chip-equipped headphones. Unless you such as this widget, touch the Edit button at the bottom of the display screen and then tap the delete button.

Chapter 5

How to Group Applications

Creating folders on your iPhone is a sensible way to reduce mess on your home screen. Grouping apps collectively can also make it simpler to use your phone - if all your music applications are in the same place, you would not have to be searching through folders or looking at your mobile phone when you wish to utilize them.

How you create folders isn't immediately apparent, but once you understand the secret, it's simple — some tips about what you should know about how to make a folder on your iPhone.

How to Create Folders and Group Apps on the iPhone

- To make a folder, you will need at least two applications to place into the folder. Determine which two you want to use.

- Gently touch and hold one of the applications until all applications on the screen start shaking (this is the same process that you utilize to re-arrange apps).

  NOTE: Making folders on the iPhone 6S and iPhone 7, the iPhone 8 and iPhone X, and iPhone 11 and 11 Pro, is just a little trickier. That's because the 3D Touchscreen on those models responds differently to different presses on the screen. When you have one particular cell phones, don't press too much or you'll result in a menu or shortcut. Only a light touch and hold will do.

- Pull one of the applications at the top of the other. When the first application appears to merge into the second one, take your finger from the screen. Dropping one form into the other creates the folder.

- What goes on next depends upon what version of the iOS you're working with or using.

- In iOS 7 and higher, the folder and its own recommended name take up the whole screen.

- In iOS 4-6, you Typically the two applications and a name for the folder in a strip over the screen

- Every folder has a name assigned to it by default (more on this in a moment); nevertheless, you can transform that name by touching the x icon to clear the recommended name and then type the name you want.

- If you wish to add more applications to the folder, touch the wallpaper to close the folder. Then pull more apps into the new folder.

- When you've added all the applications you want

and edited the name, click on the Home button on the leading Centre of the iPhone as well as your changes would be saved (precisely like when re-arranging icons).

TIPS: *When you have an iPhone X, 11, or newer, there is no Home button to click. Instead, you should tap* **Done** *on the right part of the screen.*

How Default iPhone Folder Titles Are Suggested

When you initially create a folder, the iPhone assigns a suggested name to it. That name is chosen predicated on the App Store category that the applications in the folder result from; for instance if the applications result from the Video games category, the recommended name of the folder is Video games. You should use the suggested name or add your own using the instructions in steps above.

How to Edit Folders on Your iPhone

If you have already created a folder on your iPhone, you

might edit it by changing the name, adding or removing apps, and more. Here's how:

- To edit a pre-existing folder, touch and hold the folder until it starts to move.

- Touch it another time, and the folder will open up, and its material will fill up the screen.

- You may make the next changes

- Edit the folder's name by tapping on the written text.

- Add more applications by dragging them in.

- Remove applications from the folder by dragging them away.

- Click on the Home button or the Done button to save lots of your changes.

How to Remove Apps From Folders on iPhone

If you wish to remove an application from a folder on your iPhone or iPod touch, follow these steps:

- Touch and hold the folder that you would like to eliminate the application from.

- When the applications and folders start wiggling, remove your finger from the screen.

- Touch the folder you want to eliminate the application.

- Drag the application from the folder and onto the home screen.

- Click on the Home or Done button to save lots of the new set up.

How to Add Folders to the iPhone Dock

The four applications over the bottom of the iPhone reside in what's called the Dock. You can include folders to the dock if you'd like. To achieve that:

- Move one of the applications currently in the dock away by tapping, keeping, and dragging it to the primary section of the home screen.

- Move a folder into space.

- Press the Home or Done button, depending on your iPhone model, to save lots of the change.

How to Delete a Folder on the iPhone

Deleting a folder is comparable to eliminating an app. Some tips about what you must do:

- Pull all the applications from the folder and onto the home screen.

- When you do that, the folder disappears.

- Press the home or Done button to save lots of the change, and you're done.

Chapter 6

How to start Dark Setting on your iPhone in iOS 13

First, check out *'Configurations'* and then look for *'Screen & Lighting.'* Once there, you'll see an all-new interface that places dark setting front side and centre. You will toggle between *'Light'* and *'Dark'* mode with only a tap, assuming you want to activate it manually; however, its implementation within iOS is just a little smarter than either 'on' or 'off.'

Under the two main options, you'll also visit a toggle marked *'Automatic'* which, as you may be able to think, switches dark setting on alone, linked with sunset and sunrise. Additionally, you then have the choice to define specific times for dark settings to allow and disable.

Dark mode has shown to be one of the very most hyped features approaching to cellular devices in 2019. It isn't just a capability destined for iOS 13 either, it's a significant feature in Google android ten plus some devices have previously instigated their own undertake dark setting - cell phones like the Asus ZenFone 6 and the OnePlus 7 Pro.

What does Dark Mode in iOS 13 do?

A part of dark mode's charm originates from the decrease in power usage it brings, particularly on devices that use OLED shows, like the iPhone X, XS, and XS Max. Beyond power intake, however, darker interface shades also lessen eye strain, particularly when being viewed in dark surroundings. In some cases, alternative UI and font colours are also associated with alleviating conditions like Scotopic Level of sensitivity Syndrome - an affliction commonly within people that have dyslexia, which makes text visibility and comprehension difficult.

How to Upgrade Applications on your iPhone in iOS 13

If you're used to manually updating your applications on either an iPhone, iPad or iPod touch by going to the updates tabs in the App Store, then iOS 13 has made some changes.

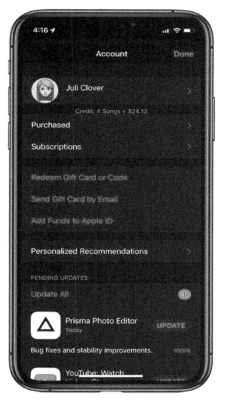

That tabs has eliminated and has been changed by *Arcade*. If you don't anticipate using the new Apple Arcade membership video gaming service, then there's no chance to eliminate this.

Here's how to revise your applications in iOS 13:

- Start the App Store on your iPhone.

- Tap the round consumer icon at the right-hand corner.

- Scroll down, and you'll see a list of all of your applications that either have updates available or have been recently updated.

- If an application comes with an update available, you can hit the button to start it manually

Do applications automatically upgrade in iOS 13?

It appears clear that the reason behind Apple moving this program is because applications tend to update themselves quietly in the background, removing the necessity for anybody to manage application updates manually. The downside with this is that it could be challenging to learn what new features have found its way to applications if you're not looking at the release notes.

Chapter 7

How to Fix Common iPhone 7 Problems

Is your iPhone 7 camera no longer working? Are you working with a faulty microphone? These issues and more are prevalent with this product, and you will reach a remedy with a few troubleshooting tips.

Factors behind Common iPhone 7 Problems

Software bugs or application malfunctions cause some

typically common iPhone 7 issues. Others may be triggered by physical obstructions or miscommunication between devices. The iPhone concern you're experiencing depends on the root problem. A little bit of troubleshooting is to be done.

Basic iPhone 7 Troubleshooting Tips

Although each issue will have its group of unique troubleshooting tips, you can solve general iPhone issues by:

- Performing an instant iPhone restart: A restart could jump-start your iPhone back to health.

- Upgrading your iPhone's software: If you are not using the most up to date iOS, there may be a bug you're experiencing. Upgrade your iPhone and try again.

- Resetting your iPhone's settings: As a final vacation resort, you can reset your iPhone's basic settings or come back to your iPhone to factory settings if everything else fails.

Resetting your iPhone to factory settings may cause you to lose all your data. Only perform this after exhausting all your options, including calling Apple Support.

iPhone 7 Getting Hot

Your iPhone can overheat due to several factors, from overuse to being left in the hot sunlight. Additionally, it may get hot credited to a concern with the iPhone's software or an application you're using. Contrary to popular belief, your iPhone cover could even be at fault, so are there a couple of things you can test whenever your iPhone is overheating?

- *Remove your iPhone's case*: Many cases could cause overheating. Take it off for a couple of days to find out if this resolves your overheating concern.

- *Check to ensure iPhone applications aren't crashing in the background*: Crashing applications can cause your iPhone to overheat gradually. Head to *Settings > Personal privacy > Analytics > Analytics Data* to see which applications crash frequently.

- *Look for a crashing app? Delete it and reinstall it or delete it and discover an alternative*: Check for applications that drain your iPhone 7's battery. You'll find a summary of these applications in your Settings under battery usage. If there's an application draining the life span from your iPhone, you will see it. Delete it and discover an alternative.

- *Check your network connection*: Is your iPhone looking for network signal?; this may cause overheating. Try turning your mobile phone to airplane setting or pull the plug on Wi-Fi to find out if heat is reduced.

- *Turn off background application refresh*: When all your apps continue steadily to refresh at the same time, your iPhone 7's CPU can get into overdrive.

Make sure you're using an Apple-certified phone control: If you are not, the control may be faulty, leading to your iPhone to overheat.

iPhone 7 Camera, not Working Well

Blurry camera? Dark screen when starting the camera app? An iPhone camera that won't work properly may be triggered by physical obstructions or software issues within the Camera app.

- *Remove your case and any attachments*: An instance might stop your camera, and a film may cause your camera to be blurry. After eliminating cases and accessories, test the camera to find out if the problem is solved.

- *Both iPhone 7 and the iPhone 7 Plus offer image stabilization*: Metallic instances or zoom lens accessories can hinder this feature.

- *Clean your camera lens*: Blurry video cameras are often the consequence of filthy camera lenses. Utilize a microfiber fabric to pull out the lens.

- *Check the display*: If you want to use the display and it will not work, touch the lightning bolt and ensure that your adobe flash is defined to on.

- *Toggle backward and forward between back camera and front side camera*: This simple function sometimes pulls the camera out of the lag or glitch.

- *Close the Camera application and reopen it*: This may be all you have, to leap start your camera back to health.

iPhone 7 Microphone Faulty

Your iPhone 7 features four microphones: two on underneath, one close to the headphone jack, and one by the loudspeaker grill. In case your microphone isn't working, a blockage or software glitch may be the reason.

- *Clean your microphones*: Utilizing a microfiber towel or a smooth toothbrush, softly clean the microphones of your iPhone 7. Obstructions such as dirt can result in a muffled tone.

- *Remove any instances or attachments*: These

accessories may obstruct your microphones.

- *Disconnect Bluetooth devices*: Bluetooth devices that are linked to your iPhone may cause you to believe they're no longer working. Disable any Bluetooth devices and then try your mic again.

- *Update the application you're using*: If you notice your microphone isn't dealing with a definite app, try upgrading it to repair any software glitches.

- *Check application permissions*: You can even check the app's microphone permissions. If an application doesn't have usage of your microphone, it will not work. Head to *Settings > Personal privacy > Microphone* and toggle the change to turn it on carefully.

iPhone 7 Headphone Adapter not Working

When you buy an iPhone 7, you will discover lightning to 3.5mm adapter in your box that you will need to use when plugging in wired headphones. An adapter may fail to work credited to a filthy headphone jack, software concern, or a faulty adapter, but there are many things you can test to repair headphone jack problems.

- *Connect another couple of earphones*: The issue might not be your adapter whatsoever. Get one of these different groups of earphones to see if indeed they work. If so, it is time to replace others.

- *Use an Apple-certified adapter*: If you want to use an adapter you bought from a third-party after misplacing your Apple-certified adapter, it might not work with well with your device.

- *Clean your headphone slot*: A dirty slot full of dirt and particles won't work properly. Work with a can of compressed air to lightly blow out the interface. Or, operate a smooth toothbrush over the port.

- *Check your volume*: It could be that your volume was muted unintentionally. Use your iPhone control keys to raise the volume. When you tune your volume up, does the pop-up package say earphones? If not, your earphones might not be completely connected. Try getting rid of your earphones and placing them back firmly.

- *Switch Bluetooth off*: Your iPhone might want to play audio through another device linked through Bluetooth. Transform it off and use your earphones again. A similar thing might occur as a consequence of AirDrop; disable AirDrop in your iPhone Settings and use your earphones again.

iPhone 7 Bluetooth not Working

Is your Bluetooth refusing to pair? Will your iPhone not recognize your Bluetooth device? Bluetooth devices sometimes go wrong after critical software improvements or credited to faulty devices. So, if your Bluetooth is no longer working, troubleshooting it could help.

- *Switch your iPhone Bluetooth off and back on*: After improvements, your iPhone Bluetooth might need a restart to work properly. Plus, you will need to ensure your Bluetooth was on.

- *Move your device nearer to your iPhone*: In case your Bluetooth device is too far from your iPhone, it will not set or work properly.

- *Disconnect Bluetooth devices from other resources*: If you're linked to your Bluetooth device from another computer or source, it could hinder your iPhone pairing.

- *Restart your Bluetooth device*: This task will vary with respect to the device you're using. Check your device's consumer manual, carry out some research online, or call your device's producer to find how to restart these devices.

- *Try connecting another Bluetooth device to your iPhone*: To learn if the problem is with your iPhone or these devices, try linking another Bluetooth device. If it links, the initial device reaches fault.

- *Clear Bluetooth connections*: You may want to set your Bluetooth devices up as though these were new. To take action, you must delete Bluetooth contacts from your iPhone and established them again.

- *Reset your networking settings*: Network mistakes can wreak havoc on iPhone features such as Bluetooth. After reset, you can test reconnecting your device.

Chapter 8

5 Ways of Fixing iPhone Screenshots Problem

Going for a screenshot on your iPhone is usually quick and painless, with the technique varying predicated on your unique model. On previous versions that have a Home button, it's only a matter of pressing that and the on/off button concurrently. When you have an iPhone 11, iPhone 11 Pro, iPhone 11 Pro Max, iPhone X, XS, XS Max, or XR, then you will have to press the medial side button and 'volume up' at the same time to fully capture the subject of your display.

Reason behind iPhone Screenshot Problems

Sometimes things aren't working needlessly to say, and the typical method for going for a screenshot simply isn't doing the secret; perhaps one of your control keys is stuck, or possibly there's another problem with your device avoiding what is said to be basic features from working. Don't fret, as our troubleshooting guide below will walk you through some option options for snapping that iPhone screenshot.

- Find Your Screenshots

Before we dive into fixes or alternatives, maybe the screenshots feature is working. Open up the Photos application and see if indeed they arrive in the Photos section of the Photos app. You can even tap Albums (bottom level of display screen in the Photos app) and swipe until you start to see the Press Types and touch the Screenshots label.

- Start a Forced Reboot of the iPhone

Before proceeding further, you need to force reboot your device and try going for a screenshot once it's powered back on. For older models that have a *Home button*, take the next steps to force a reboot of your iPhone.

Press and hold the Home button down

Next, *press and hold the Rest/Wake button* at the top or

side of your device; don't let go of the *Home button* while carrying this out. After about ten seconds, you'll observe that your screen will turn black. Sustain your hand on both control keys before Apple logo design is displayed, of which point you can release and await the reboot to complete.

For newer models that don't have a Home button, the procedure is slightly different, and it's imperative to check out directions in the precise order.

Press and release the volume down button

Press and hold the Volume button for approximately ten seconds before the screen turns dark. Maintain your hand on this button before Apple logo design is displayed, of which point you can release and await the reboot to complete. After you have forced a reboot, try going for a screenshot once more. If you are still struggling to do so, keep on to another portion of this troubleshooting guide.

Taking Screenshots via the AssistiveTouch Feature

The iPhone's Assistive Touch features were devoted spot to help users with accessibility issues, permitting them to control their device through easier-to-navigate pinches, gestures, swipes, and voice-activated commands. AssistiveTouch can also are available in handy if you are having difficulty taking screenshots through traditional methods. It could be enabled by pursuing these steps.

Touch the Settings icon, situated on your iPhone's Home Display

The iOS Settings interface should now be shown. Choose the General option.

- A screenshot of the iOS Settings interface

- THE OVERALL settings will now appear. Touch Accessibility.

- A screenshot of the iOS General Settings screen

- Some accessibility-related options should now be listed. Scroll down until you find the one tagged AssistiveTouch, within the Conversation section. Select this program.

- On the next display, tap the button accompanying the AssistiveTouch option such that it turns from white to green (off to on).

A screenshot of the iOS AssistiveTouch settings

Next, go for Customize Top Level Menu.

Touch the plus (+) button, located towards underneath the right-hand part of the display screen. A screenshot of the iOS Customize Top Level Menu screen A fresh icon, also an advantage sign will now be put into this screen. Touch this button.

A screenshot of the iOS Customize Top Level Menu screen

A summary of accessibility features should now appear. Scroll down and choose the one tagged Screenshot, making sure they have a blue check tag next to it.

Tap Done, situated in the top right-hand part of the display. You should now visit a Screenshot option put into your Top Level Menu.

A screenshot of the iOS Customize Top Level Menu screen

You'll observe that a grayish circular button is overlaying your iPhone screen. Touch this new button anytime to open up the AssistiveTouch user interface.

A screenshot of the iOS AssistiveTouch interface

The AssistiveTouch button can be moved by dragging and shedding it to a fresh location on the screen when it ever gets on the right path.

To fully capture the items of your display screen, simply tap the Screenshot icon. The brand new image will be instantly preserved to your Camera Move.

Taking Screenshots with 3D Touch

If you're like the majority of people, you almost certainly don't make enough benefit from your iPhone's 3D Touch-enabled features. This pressure-sensitive efficiency gives you to perform everyday jobs quickly, but the technique is focusing on how to result in it properly to fit the bill.

You can also configure 3D Touch to consider screenshots. Remember that AssistiveTouch must be allowed first, which may be done by following steps above. 3D Touch is available with iPhone 6s or later.

- Go back to the AssistiveTouch Settings screen.

- Choose the 3D Touch option, positioned in the CUSTOM Activities section.

A screenshot of the iOS AssistiveTouch Settings screen

A summary of actions that may be linked with 3D Touch should now be shown; choose the one tagged Screenshot, making sure they have a blue check tag next to it. Now you can take screenshots by simply tapping and briefly holding the AssistiveTouch circular button, eliminating a supplementary tap along the way.

Other Options

If you have tried all the above and remain struggling to take screenshots on your iPhone for reasons unknown, you can test one of the next last-resort measures.

Chapter 9

12 Methods of Fixing iPhone Poor Sound

Unless you hear any audio on your iPhone, you may take several steps to troubleshoot the problem. The problem may be common with various models of your iPhone, or it could only happen with one app. Listed below are 12 steps for troubleshooting when there is no audio on the iPhone.

- *Test Thoroughly Your iPhone's Speaker*

Open up the Settings application and choose Touch & Haptics (on some devices, choose Noises). Under Ringers and Notifications, move the slider to increase the volume; if you hear audio, the iPhone loudspeaker works. If you don't hear audio, the device might need a hardware repair; contact Apple Support.

- *Adjust the Band/Silent Switch*

The Band/Silent switch, also known as the mute switch, has two positions.

When the switch is pushed toward the trunk of these devices, the colour orange appears and indicates that the switch is defined to silent mode. Drive the change toward the display to enable audio.

- *Turn Off DO NOT Disturb*

"DO NOT Disturb," silences many noises and alerts. Transform it off unless you hear any audio. Open the Settings app, and tap "DO NOT Disturb," then move the slider to the Off position.

- *Change or Disable Bluetooth Settings*

Whenever your iPhone is linked to a Bluetooth sound device, it transmits sound to these devices rather than to the speaker on the iPhone. To carefully turn off Bluetooth so that noises play from the iPhone, open up the Settings app, tap Bluetooth, then move the slider to the Off position.

- *Adjust Volume Control keys While within an App*

Sometimes the audio volume in an application may be too low to hear; open up an app, such as Music, Podcasts, or any other application with sound. Utilize the hardware volume buttons privately of the iPhone to carefully turn up the volume.

It might also be that the audio environment in the application is turned too low; open up the Music or Podcasts app, then go directly to the web page with the Play/Pause button. Move the slider to increase the volume.

- *Check Third-Party App Audio Settings*

Many third-party applications offer personalized volume and mute sound settings. For instance, some video games offer separate Settings for volume, music, sound files, ambient sound, and more. In the app, look for sound or sound settings. Switch off any personalized mute options, allow audio, and change the volume sliders to increase volume. With regards to the app, either move sliders up, move sliders to the right, or touch an icon to make it energetic.

- *Check Notification Settings for Your App*

Check the iPhone notification audio settings for the application if you anticipate to listen to notification noises but don't. Head to *Settings* > *Notifications*, then scroll through the list to get the app. Touch the name of the app, then move the Notifications and Seems sliders to the On position.

Some apps, such as Reminders and Communications, enable you to choose notification audio. If this audio is defined to none, the alert is silent.

- *Try Headphones*

Find the headphone that was included with the iPhone. For old iPhone models, plug the earphones into the headset slot. For newer iPhone models, plug the headphone into the lightning interface (the charging wire also connects to the slot). Pay attention to sound with the earphones when using an application that has sound. On the other hand, plug in and then take away the headphones, then listen for audio.

- *Restart or Reset Your Device*

If you still don't hear any audio, restart the iPhone. To restart, turn the iPhone off and then back on. If a restart doesn't solve the problem, get one of these hard reset, which clears additional Settings without affecting all of your applications or data.

- *Look for App Updates*

In rare circumstances, having less sound may be the consequence of an application developer's error. Head to *App Store > Update* to check on if an application update is designed for an application. Touch Update next for an application to download and install the existing version then tests to find out if the audio works needlessly to say. If you see only applications in the Updated Recently section, no additional updates can be found.

- *Look for System Updates*

A system upgrade might fix an audio problem. Head to *Settings > General > Software Update* to check for just about any system software improvements from Apple. Download and install the available enhancements.

- *Reset All Settings*

If none of the above-mentioned steps handle your audio issue, reset the iPhone Settings; this resets the audio, screen, and network Settings to the iPhone defaults.

Head to *Settings > General > Reset > Reset All* Settings. Enter your iPhone passcode; if prompted, then tap *Reset All Settings*. Wait a few moments for the iPhone to reset and reboot, then test to find out if the audio works needlessly to say.

Chapter 10

5 Methods to Fix an iPhone That Keeps Shutting Down

Whether we need these to communicate, entertain us, or make sure we awaken on time every day, we rely on our iPhones to work correctly regularly. So an iPhone that keeps shutting off for no apparent reason is a problem.

What can cause an iPhone to keep Shutting Down

There are a variety of things that might lead to this issue, including faulty applications and water damage and mold, but, in almost all cases, the problem is the battery. There are many ways to show for sure that the battery is the problem: the battery health feature included in the iOS, if your iPhone shuts down at 30% electric battery, and an instrument provided by Apple. Many of these options are protected in this specific article.

There are a few easy software actions you can take to

attempt to fix an iPhone that retains shutting off.

- Hard Reset Your iPhone

When you're having troubles like your iPhone arbitrarily shutting off, the first and easiest step to fixing it is almost always restarting the phone. In cases like this, though, you should employ a particular kind of restart, called a *hard reset*. A difficult reset differs from a typical restart since it deeper resets the operating-system and memory space on the phone (but don't be concerned: you will not lose any data). If the reason for the restarts can be an application with a flaw that triggers it to drain the electric battery faster than it will, this may clear the problem. Some tips about what you must do:

1. *The steps differ predicated on what iPhone model you have*:

- With the iPhone 8, iPhone X, and iPhone 11, click and release the volume up button. Click and release the volume down button. Click and contain the Side button.

- On the iPhone 7, hold down the volume down and Side button at the same time.

- On all the iPhone models, hold down the Home button and on/off/side button at the same time.

2. Keep pressing the buttons before the screen moves dark, and the Apple logo design appears.

3. Release the control keys and allow the iPhone to set up like normal.

- Update iPhone OPERATING-SYSTEM

In some instances of the iPhone randomly shutting off, the problem is in the operating system. If the hard reset didn't work and you own a version of the iOS sooner than 13, you should revise to the latest version of the operating system.

How to update iTunes to the latest version.

If you try those steps as well as your iPhone can't update its OS, follow these steps:

1. Tap *Settings*

2. Tap *Notifications*

3. Tap each application that's outlined in this section and make its *Allow Notifications slider* to off/white.

4. Update the operating-system

5. When the upgrade is complete, and the phone has restarted, repeat steps 1 and 2, and then change notifications back on for every application whose notifications you switched off in step3.

- *Check Your Electric battery Health (iOS)*

If you're working iOS 13 or more on your iPhone, there is a feature specifically made to help pinpoint issues with your electric battery. Electric battery Health provides two critical information: the utmost charging capacity of your electric battery and exactly how your battery's power has effects on your phone's performance.

To see your phone's Electric battery Health, follow these steps:

- Tap *Settings.*

- Tap *Battery.*

- Tap *Battery pack Health*

THE utmost Capacity menu shows the full total control capacity your electric battery can hold, the bigger, the better. In case your Maximum Capacity is surprisingly low, that could be an indication of the problem with the electric battery.

The Maximum Performance Ability menu lets you know if the performance of your iPhone has been automatically reduced due to problems with the electric battery. If you see anything apart from Peak Performance Capacity, that could be an indication that your electric battery has issues. The Electric battery Health section will also let you know if your electric battery is at a spot where it requires to be changed.

- *Restore iPhone from Back-up with DFU*

In case your iPhone continues to be shutting down unexpectedly, you are going to need to get one of these bigger steps: a **DFU** restores of your iPhone. DFU, which means **Disk Firmware Upgrade**, creates a brand new installing of all software on the iPhone, not only the operating system, which is a more extensive kind of reset. To get this done, you are going to need a pc with iTunes installed onto it that you can sync your iPhone. Once you have got that, follow these steps:

1. Connect your iPhone to the computer via USB.

2. In iTunes, make a backup of your iPhone by clicking *BACKUP Now* in the primary iTunes window.

3. With this done, you will need to place your iPhone into *DFU Mode*. How you do that depends on the model you have:

For iPhone 8, iPhone X, and iPhone 11, quickly press and release the volume up button, then your volume down button, press and contain the Side button. Keep pressing the medial side button and, when the display turns dark, press and keep volume down. After five seconds, forget about the medial side button, but keep pressing volume down. Whenever your iPhone shows up in iTunes, forget about the button.

For iPhone 7, press and maintain the on/off button and volume down button at the same time. When a window arises in iTunes that says iTunes has recognized an iPhone in a recovery setting, forget about the volume down button. If the iPhone's display is black at this time, you're in *DFU Mode*.

For all the models, the steps will be identical to the iPhone 7, except you press down the on/off and Home buttons rather than the volume down button.

1. Regain your iPhone from the volume up you did in step 2.

• *Contact Apple for battery Replacement*

If none of the other activities you've tried up to now has solved the problem, which may be because the problem has been your iPhone's hardware, not software. Maybe the electric battery in your iPhone is faulty or by the end of its life; this may affect any model of iPhone, but Apple has found a specific problem with some batteries in the iPhone 6S. This has even created an instrument that enables you to check your iPhone's serial volume to see whether it's got that problem. If the website confirms that your iPhone battery has that concern, follow the steps detailed on that web page to obtain a repair.

Even though you don't possess an iPhone 6S, a defective battery or other hardware failures might be the reason for your issue. Apple is your very best bet so that you can get help, so contact the support to get technical support.

Chapter 11

How to unlock its Photographic Potential

Taking photos in the iPhone's default camera application is pretty simple and straightforward - in fact, almost too simple for individuals who need to get a little more creative using their shots. Well, that's all transformed on the iPhone 7, which not only brings a fresh wide-angle zoom lens but a pleasant assisting of new software features that you should explore.

The difficulty is, a few of these aren't immediately apparent, and it's not necessarily clear just how to take benefit of the excess photographic power stored in your shiny new iPhone.

That's why we've come up with this guide for the iPhone digital cameras, to get a solid foothold and springtime towards Instagram greatness. Continue reading and get snapping.

1. *Figure out how to look beyond your frame*

When shooting the typical (26mm comparative) zoom lens, the iPhone use the wide-angle zoom lens showing you what's happening beyond your frame, a little just like a range-finder camera. Those digital cameras have always been popular with professional road photographers because they enable you to nail the precise moment when a fascinating character walks into the frame.

You shouldn't do anything to create this up - endure your iPhone with the camera application open and point it towards the scene to view it in action. Look for a photogenic background like a vacant road, then use the wide-angle preview to time as soon as your subject matter enters the shot. Want to keep the wide-angle view of your picture carefully.

2. *Adjust your compositions*

Here's another fun new feature on the iPhone that's great if you can't quite determine the ultimate way to take a picture. You'll need to go to the main configurations, wherein the Camera section; you'll find an option called "*Composition.*" If you enable "Photos Catch Outside the Framework," the camera will record two photos at the same time - one using the wide-angle zoom lens, and another using the typical angle.

There are always a few facts to consider when working with this nifty trick. First is that you'll have to take in the HEIF format, which isn't always dealt with well by non-iOS devices. Also, the broader position picture will be erased if it's not used within thirty days, so you'll have to be reasonably quick with your editing and enhancing.

To get the wide-angle view of the shot, tap *'Edit'* within the photo, then your cropping icon, then press the three dots button in the very best right and choose "Use Content Beyond your Frame."

3. *Manage HDR*

The iPhone include Smart HDR, which is started up by default; this automatically detects the light levels in your picture and protect both shows and shadows for a far more balanced image.

More often than not, you will see occasions when challenging conditions lead to a graphic, which is nearly right. If you'd favour less processed photos to edit within an application like Lightroom, check out the configurations menu, find the Camera section, then switch off Smart HDR.

The great thing concerning this is it doesn't eliminate using Smart HDR for several scenes - in the Camera application, you'll now see an HDR button at the very top to turn it On/Off. It just means your default capturing will be without Smart HDR's sometimes overzealous processing.

4. _Reach grips with Night Mode_

Night mode is a new feature for the iPhone and it's something we've been waiting around to see in a while. It's not an ardent setting you can opt for - instead, it'll activate automatically when the iPhone detects that ambient light conditions are on the reduced side.

Nevertheless, you can still have little control over it once it is used; tap the night time setting icon at the left, and you may use a split to choose a faster shutter speed if it's brighter than the telephone realizes, or leave it on Car - or you can also choose to turn it off entirely carefully.

It's worth keeping your iPhone constant on the surface, or perhaps a tripod if you have one, as the telephone will recognize this and raise the shutter rate to 30 mere seconds, which is potentially ideal for night sky photos.

5. _Grasp the ultra-wide-angle lens_

The iPhone will be the first ones with a super wide-angle

lens. If you haven't used one before, their 13mm equivalent field of view will come in super-handy for several different subjects, but particularly landscape and architecture, where you want to fit in as much of the scene as possible.

If you wish to exceed dramatic building pictures, one common technique utilized by professional scenery photographers is to juxtapose one close object with a distant object - for example, some close by plants with a long way background subject.

You could also want to use it in a while composing in portrait orientation, for a fascinating new look that wouldn't have been possible before with older iPhones.

6. *Portrait setting is not only for humans*

Even though iPhone XR had a great camera, you couldn't use the inbuilt Family portrait mode for anything apart from human subjects. Bad information for pet-lovers, or merely those who wish to create a shallow depth of field results with any subject.

That's all transformed for the iPhone, which uses its two digital cameras to help you to take shallow depth-of-field impact images for many different subjects, and has been specially optimised for domestic pets. To begin with, all you have to do is swipe to *Family portrait mode* and point the camera the four-legged friend. It'll tell you if you're too near to the subject and instruct you to move away. The details are nearly perfect, but they're perfect - particularly if you're looking on a little screen.

7. *Locate those lacking settings*

Through the keynote release of the iPhone, it was announced that the native camera application would be simplified to help you consider the key method of shooting your images.

That's great and produces a much cleaner interface, but it can imply that some configurations are now just a little concealed away. If you think where they've eliminated, touch the arrow near the top of the display, and you'll find a range of different alternatives, including aspect percentage, adobe flash, night setting (if it's dark enough), timer and digital filter systems.

8. *Try the new 16:9 aspect ratio*

This is an attribute that is new for the iPhone, adding a new aspect ratio to the prevailing 4:3 and square (1:1) options. Using a 16:9 aspect percentage is ways to get more full shots which ingest more of the scene, and also eventually screen very nicely on the iPhone display screen.

You'll need to activate it from the menu - the default is 4:3. It's well worth also using the 16:9 aspect proportion with the ultra-wide position to get some good great breathtaking type shots.

Chapter 12

40 iPhone Tips & Tricks

Inside the iPhone lies an array of hidden features you might not have even known were around. We've selected our favorite time-saving, life-enhancing guidelines for every model of iPhone, Apple wants to show how exactly easy its products are to use, and the iPhone exemplifies that viewpoint more, perhaps than every other.

This chapter is about taking another step with your iPhone and discovering everything it can do that you didn't find out about. From advanced security to electric battery management and custom notifications, they are our methods for iPhone users.

1. Increase a slow iPhone

Computing devices have a tendency to decelerate as time passes, as components degrade, storage fill with old documents and overlooked/unused apps, and new software is increasingly created for more modern and faster processors.

You can defer the inevitable by following some simple guidelines, including:

- Every once in a while, you should power off your device completely; this clears out the memory space.

- It's also advisable to enter the habit of deleting applications and files you do not use (photos are a common problem for storage space) and archive the latter in the cloud and local backup.

- It's also well worth going right through the configurations and checking which application refreshes in the background, thereby burning up precious control power.

- Upgrade iOS on your device.

Remember that updating iOS has historically been a combined blessing in regards to accelerating your iPhone, but with iOS 13, it has changed.

iOS 13 is especially centered on performance. Apple stated it could make old devices faster, and inside our tests, it seems to have done so.

More tips are available on How to increase a slow iPhone in this book and other books by Engolee Publishing House.

2. *Start Dark Mode*

If your iOS 13 on your iPhone (at the time of writing, it's available as a general public beta; it'll launch standard in Sept 2019), you can change on the system-wide Dark Setting very quickly. Thus giving all the pre-installed applications and any third-party applications that have built-in compatibility a dark or dark-grey background that's more calming to read at night.

To carefully turn on Dark Setting, open up the Settings application, and tap Screen & Brightness. Near the top of the next display, you will see Light and Dark options hand and hand - tap the main one you want to use. You can even set Dark Setting to seriously automatically at times, such as from dusk until dawn.

If you haven't yet upgraded to iOS 13, you may still find some workarounds. You can test Invert Colours setting,

Low Light setting, or Night Change; each one of these offers a few of the advantages of Dark Setting and learning much more inside our dedicated article How exactly to use Dark Setting on iPhone.

3. *Improve your passcode security*

You can unlock your iPhone with your fingerprint or face, depending on which model you have; however, your iPhone is secure if nobody can think of your passcode. If it's as simple as 1234, you're requesting trouble.

iOS now prompts users to make a six-digit passcode rather than the four-digit passcode (here's how to carefully turn a six-digit passcode back to four digits), but there's a more advanced way to make your iOS device better: using an alphanumeric passcode; this means that you may use both characters and numbers in your password, providing you an almost unlimited variety of possible passwords, instead of the roughly 1,000,000 possible six-digit passcodes that could be hacked with the right equipment.

It's simple enough to improve your passcode for an

alphanumeric one:

- Open up the *Settings app*.

- Tap *'Touch Identification and Passcode'* (or 'Face Identification and Passcode' on X-series iPhones), then Change Passcode.

- When prompted to enter a new passcode, tap *'Passcode Options'* and choose *'Custom Alphanumeric Code.'*

- Now enter your brand-new passcode. Make certain it's one you can keep in mind.

- Here's choosing a good security password.

- Gleam a new way of securing your iPhone in iOS 12.

- This security change means nobody can plug a tool into the iPhone so that they can hack involved with it. It kicks one hour after your iPhone was locked (if you don't deselect the placing).

- You'll find the environment in Configurations >

Touch Identification & Passcode.

- Scroll right down to Allow Gain access to When Locked section, and you'll see USB Accessories.

- Ensure that it's deselected if you don't want devices to have an admission.

- Create custom iMessages for phone calls you can't answer.

- Create custom iMessages for phone calls you can't answer

Sometimes it isn't the right time for a phone call; even though you could just allow phone calls you do not want to consider going to voicemail, sometimes you want to clarify why you are not picking right up. iOS enables you to react to a call with a text quickly.

Based on which version of iOS you're operating, you either swipe upwards on the phone icon that appears next to the uncover slider and choose to Respond With Text message or touch the button labeled Message above the Slip To Answer slider.

By default, you'll receive three pre-written options ("Sorry, I cannot chat right now," "I'm on my way" and "MAY I call you later?"), plus a button that enables you to enter text message there and then.

However, you can customize the instant messages:

Head to Settings > Phone > Respond With Text message.

You can't have significantly more than three responses; however: if you would like to add a fresh one, you need to sacrifice one of the existing options. Tap the main one you're prepared to reduce and enter the new response.

4. *Join an organization FaceTime call*

This feature wasn't ready with time for the decontrol of iOS 13, but soon you'll be able to partake in an organization FaceTime call with up to 32 participants.

To produce a group FaceTime video call, you have to enter several contacts into the address package when initiating the talk.

The interface is just a little different: the tiles showing each participant (there may be up to 32) vary in proportions and prominence depending on how recently it sees your face spoke.

Double-tapping a tile brings to see your face to leading in your view.

You can even launch an organization FaceTime call from within Text messages if a thread gets particularly beyond control.

5. Skip phone calls with *Remind Me personally Later*

On the other hand, you can get iOS to remind you to call back later. Much like the auto-replies, how you do this depends on your version of iOS: probably, you tap the *Remind Me button* above the glide, but in previous versions, you'd to swipe up-wards before you could go for **Remind Me Later**.

You can prefer to get reminded within an hour, 'When I Leave' or (where applicable) *'When I Get Home.'* Ensure that your address details are current in Contacts, which means that your iPhone understands where home is. The timings depend on your GPS navigation movements.

6. *Create custom ringtones and alert shades in iTunes*

You can create ringtones for your iPhone predicated on any music monitor in your iTunes collection. We viewed this comprehensive here, but last but not least: produce a brief, sub-30-second duplicate version of the monitor; convert the document kind of this monitor from .m4a to .m4r; re-import the monitor to iTunes as a ringtone; sync the ringtone with your iPhone.

On top of that, you can create unique custom iPhone ringtones from your audio creations, which is particularly user-friendly if you undertake the creative focus on the iPhone itself. Produce a 30-second monitor in GB and; go directly to the Talk about options and choose Ringtone; then, assign it to a contact or notification.

7. *How to place custom vibrations on your iPhone*

Wish to know who's getting in touch with you without taking your phone away from your pocket? That's easy - assign a ringtone to a contact. But how about carrying it out all silently? You can not only assign a custom ringtone or text message firmness to a connection, you can also provide them with a custom vibration design.

- Open up Phone or Connections.

- Decide on contact.

- Touch the *Edit button* at the top-right part.

- Scroll right down to find the ringtone field; below, it is a vibration field.

- Tap *Vibration,* and you will see a variety of built-in vibration patterns you can choose from.

- Further down is the capability to put in a custom design: touch *Create New Vibration*, and you will tap on the display screen to generate your tempo.

- If you are satisfied (touch the Play button to see what it'll feel just like), tap Save to create the pattern.

- If that's insufficient, get back to the contact and also assign a custom vibration design for texts.

8. Customize the Control Centre

It was quite a while coming; however, in iOS 13 Apple finally allowed us to customize the toggles and options that occur in the Control Centre.

Head to Settings > Control Centre > Customize Settings. The settings that can be seen are listed at the very top, under the Include, touch the red minus indication to eliminate one, or tap and keep to pull them around and change the order.

Available controls that aren't currently included are the following, under the heading More Controls. Touch the green plus indication to include one.

9. Customize your Emoji

Owners of X-series iPhones (the iPhone X, XS, XS Max, and XR) will currently have enjoyed the pleasures of Emoji: the face catch animations you can create and send to your pals.

But did you know, since the start of iOS 13, you've had the opportunity to make Emoji of yours? They are called

Memoji, plus they can appear to be you, or your preferred celebrity, or just about anyone you choose.

When mailing an Emoji, the first stage is to find the dog, robot, poultry, poop, etc. But if you go directly to the far left of the selection pane, you will notice a plus indication with the New Memoji underneath. Touch this, and you'll be strolled through the (many) different customization steps accessible to you.

We address this technique in more depth here: How exactly to produce a custom Memoji.

10. Save Electric Battery with Low Power Mode

Whenever your iPhone drops below 20 percent power, a note will pop-up to warn you of the fact and also to offer to begin Low Power Mode. Nevertheless, you may use this handy setting if you want to make your electric battery last just a little longer.

Change to Low Power Setting by tapping *Settings > Electric battery > Low Power Setting.*

Low Power Setting reduces power usage by turning off lots of iPhone features. For instance, it'll reduce animations, reduce the time before the display darkens, fetch Email less frequently, switch off Hey Siri, and background application refresh; it generally remembers to eke out your electric battery life for just a little longer.

You might not spot the difference (although you might not get an essential email or social media message if you don't look for it). Overall, though, the iPhone works as normal, and the electric battery can last for a lot longer.

If you found this suggestion useful, you could also like our advice on how best to improve iPhone electric battery life.

11. Maximize Electric Battery Life

Talking about eking out more electric battery life, you can examine your battery utilization on your iOS device to find out if your behaviour could improve things.

Apple enables you to see which of your applications are using in the most electric battery on your device.

Head to *Settings > Electric battery.*

Scroll listed below to the section that presents the Last a day, and the final 4 Days.

Here you will see information regarding which applications used the most battery.

Apple offers up Insights and Recommendations to save you electric battery life in the section above; this may include turning down the display screen brightness or allowing auto-lock.

12. Tremble to undo

That one can be considered a little awkward sometimes, but it could be a bit of the lifesaver.

If you have just typed an extended-phrase and accidentally deleted it or made various other catastrophic mistakes, you can provide your iPhone with a tremble to talk about the undo/redo dialogue container.

Just make sure you're securing to your iPhone firmly before you tremble it!

13. Touch top

Just scrolled down an extremely long list in Notes, or worked your weary way through a huge amount of emails? Rather than laboriously scrolling back to the very best, you can leap there immediately by tapping towards the top of the iPhone's display.

We'd rank this tip with the double-space full stop: it's fairly widely known, however for everybody else, it's a game-changer.

And it's not only Records and Mail; touch top generally works in most iPhone apps. Some apps, cleverly, offer an undo upon this function, for those who tap it unintentionally and lose your Home in an extended article. The wonderful Instapaper arises a Go back to Position control, for example - and if the menu pubs have vanished, you have to tap the very best of the display screen double to activate the feature, to begin with.

Experiment to find out if the application you're using offers various other variance on or development of the handy feature.

14. Set up Do Not Disturb mode

Are you using the *Do Not Disturb* feature? It's ideal for insulating you from interruptions where you want to work or get some rest.

"Do Not Disturb" can be activated from the Control Centre; swipe up-wards from underneath of the display, and touch the crescent moon icon.

A matching moon icon will appear in the very best pub of your iPhone display screen. With *Do Not Disturb* triggered, incoming phone calls and notifications will be silenced.

For a far more advanced selection of options, go to *Settings > Do Not Disturb*; this consists of the power (under the label Planned) to create 'silent hours' every day or night time. You can even allow exceptions: people who'll be permitted to contact you despite having this setting activated, and in iOS 13, it's now possible to create *Do Not Disturb* for one-off events, rather than at precisely the same time every day.

To take action, hard press on the crescent moon icon in the control Centre and choose from your options: For one hour, Until tonight, Until I leave this location.

On the related note, you might be interested to learn how to tell if someone is using Do Not Disturb.

15. *Using, Do Not Disturb While Driving*

"Do Not Disturb" has some version settings, such as Do Not Disturb During Bedtime in the iOS 13 upgrade. But the most well-known is the version launched in iOS 11 to lessen distractions when travelling. It blocks incoming notifications (nevertheless, you can arrange an automated reply for chosen contacts only such as "I'm generating right now, are certain to get back in a little bit") and blocks calls too unless there is a hands-free package.

Head to *Settings* > *Do Not Disturb* and then, under *Do Not Disturb While Traveling*, tap **Activate**.

You will see there are three configurations: Automatically (which tries to work through when you're travelling from your motion, and which we wouldn't recommend, given just how many times we've seen this activate on trains), When Linked to Car Bluetooth, and Manually. Choose whichever option fits you.

Get back to the Do not Disturb web page of Settings, and you will start to see the automated replies on the bottom of the display. Select who you need to get this reply, and edit the reply by tapping Auto-Reply and then tapping the message.

16. Take photos while shooting videos

You're making use of your iPhone to film a magical instant, and you wish you could snap a picture at the same time. Don't stop saving! Just tap the camera button, which shows up onscreen as well as the shutter button as you film.

You are not using the iPhone's actual picture sensor; you are getting the somewhat less impressive video detectors instead. However, the photos should still come out quite nicely.

17. Portrait Lighting

If you an iPhone 8 Plus, an iPhone X, an iPhone XS, XS Max, iPhone 11, iPhone 11 Pro or iPhone 11 Pro Max you can gain access to a photographic feature called Family portrait Light (the XR has some Family portrait Lighting features, however, not all). We find Family portrait Lighting just a little inconsistent, but it will often produce some attractive results with hardly any effort.

Open up the Camera app, and swipe over the bottom revolving menu, so you're in *Family portrait Mode.*

Just above this label, you will see a hexagonal icon and the label *DAYLIGHT*, which indicates you are about to have a standard *Family Portrait Mode shot*, with the arty bokeh background blur.

If you tap the DAYLIGHT icon, however, it'll pop-up slightly, and you will see it's on the circular menu. Swipe across, and you could scroll through the four other available choices: Studio room Light, which brightens in the subject's face and other 'high factors' and is normally the most dependable setting; Contour Light, which darkens the shadows and sometimes produces a good impact, but often makes people look scruffy or unshaven; and two variations of Stage Light (color and mono), which slice out the subject and place her or him against a dark background.

The Portrait Lights are just a little better in iOS 13, but we still find the mono settings to be a bit unreliable as it pertains to curly hair. Note that you don't need to apply these results while or before taking the shot. Open up any photo which includes the label Family portrait at the very top left, and you will be in a position to apply them retrospectively. Touch Edit, then touch the hexagon icon, and you will be in a position to scroll through your options as above.

A fresh feature on the iPhone 11, iPhone 11 Pro, iPhone XS, and XS Max gives you to adapt the blur after going for a picture. It's permitted by the individual levels in photos. Whenever we get to try the iPhone XS, we'll fill up you in about how it works.

18. Switch path in Panorama mode

You can transform the path of your Panorama picture in the Camera application by tapping the arrow that appears in the centre of the display screen in the Panorama setting.

19. Use your headphones to have a selfie

Selfies continue being extremely popular, as we're sure you've noticed if the quality of your selfies is a problem, try this useful trick.

A right proportion of iPhone owners know that you can activate the camera shutter by pressing one of the volume buttons (volume up or volume down - doesn't matter which) rather than the onscreen button; this will produce less camera tremble.

But a still better option for selfies - and one which is much less well known - is by using the volume button with an attached couple of headphones.

When the camera application is open on your iPhone, you may use the volume button with an attached couple of headphones to have a photo. Not merely will this reduce tremble even more than using the iPhone's volume button, but it additionally means you may take a far more natural-looking picture from further away or have a photo hands-free.

20. Make an iPhone safe for kids

Kids love iPhones, but there are actions you can take to ensure children aren't able to access unsuitable content on the devices.

Head to Settings > General > Restrictions, and you may limit the usage of specified apps, stop in-app buys, and place a long time for appropriate content; all this is protected in How exactly to set up parental controls with an iPhone.

It's also advisable to check out the likelihood of Family Sharing, an attribute which allows you to talk about applications and content in the middle of your family's devices and never have to purchase them more often than once.

The arrival of iOS 13 provides further parental controls utilizing Screen Time, which enables you to set 'allowances' for the use of certain applications or types of app, warnings when time is running out, and finally a block. (They can ask for more time, but you'll get the ultimate decision.)

21. Stop iPhone addiction

Speaking of Display Time, it's a new feature in iOS 13 that will help you be less dependent on your iPhone. To learn the amount of your time you are wasting on your iPhone, go to *Settings > Display Time.*

Here you will see details about how long you utilize each app, how often you viewed your mobile phone, and what applications you spent the most time with. Touch on your device in the very best section to start to see the Display screen Time breakdown. You can try the break down for today, or going back seven days.

You can set Downtime, with only specific applications being available between certain hours, say after 9 pm. You'll get a reminder right before your Downtime begins. You can decide which apps are allowed during Downtime in the Always Allowed section.

It's also possible to create App Limitations (although

these limitations reset every day at nighttime). For instance, you could limit your SOCIAL MEDIA apps, which means you can only utilize them for just one hour daily.

You can set a Screen Time security password to use if you want a few moments more.

22. *Quickly add symbols*

You might have been making use of your iPhone's keyboard for a long time without realizing that it is easier than you considered to add icons to your communications.

Rather than tapping once on the 123 buttons, once on your selected symbol and then once more on the ABC button to return to the traditional keyboard layout, you can do the whole lot in a single gesture.

Tap the 123 buttons, slip your finger to choose the sign you want to place, then release. Once it has been added, your keypad will automatically revert; one tap rather than three: that's some serious time cost savings right there.

Oh, even though we're talking icons: keep your finger on

any notice or mark for another or two, and you will see what other (usually related) icons that the button can provide instead. The buck key offers pound, euro, and yen icons, for example. *If you often type words with accents this is also an instant and easy way to see an accented option.*

There are numerous additional symbols hidden inside your keyboard that you might do not have discovered. Experiment!

23. One-handed keyboard

This feature is feasible if you are on iOS 11 or later version.

Head to Settings > General > Keyboards, and tap One-Handed Keypad. Select Left or Right.

iOS's QuickType system-wide keypad is clever at guessing what you're trying to create, and in many situations will auto-correct your clumsily typed screed into something a lot more accurate.

It gets on top of that, however, when you begin customizing it such that it has learned your private favorite shortcuts and abbreviations and the entire phrases you would like it to expand those abbreviations into.

You may decide that "omg" should be converted into "Oh my God," for example. "omw" should become "On my way." Etc.

You can create a personalized shortcut:

- Head to *Settings > General, scroll down, and touch Keyboard.*

- Select Text Alternative, you will see what text message replacements you now have set up.

To add a fresh one, tap the plus indication. Enter the required full term ("MACBOOK-PRO 2020 with Touch pad" might be considered a good one for a technology journalist), the shortened version that you would like to expand into the longer expression ("MBP," say), and touch Save.

24. *Never complete a password, address, or account info*

If you wish to save time and also reap the benefits of devoid of to memorize passwords or username and passwords, be sure you start auto-fill. It is possible for your iPhone, iPad, even your Mac pc, to enter your name, address, email, contact number, passwords, and more automatically.

Head to Settings > Safari > Autofill.

You'll need to ensure the info you desire to be filled in is correctly entered in your phone in a variety of places - read this short article for help establishing passwords, control cards, titles, and addresses to allow them to be auto-filled on your iPhone.

Finally, in iOS 12 or later, whenever a security code arrives in a text, it'll automatically be accessible as an AutoFill suggestion - and that means you won't have even to open the Messages application to start to see the code.

25. *Get yourself a thesaurus*

There is a thesaurus option in iOS; nevertheless, you need to allow it. To take action, go to *Configurations > General > Dictionary*. Now Select English British *"Oxford Thesaurus of British"* (or if you are American, the *"Oxford American Writer's Thesaurus"*).

As long as you're here, you can download translations, such as French-English and Spanish-English too. Now decide on a phrase by tapping it.

Choose RESEARCH from your options (you may want to touch on the arrow to uncover extra options). Now you will notice suggestions of option words, as well as the dictionary description.

26. Rich formatting

While it isn't universally supported, you may use the great format in several iOS applications, including Mail, Records, and third-party applications such as WhatsApp, to be sure about the parts of text stick out; but while you can use, it is also effortless to miss.

Just open an application that supports rich formatting,

highlight the written text you would like to edit by double-tapping it, and choose the formatting menu, labelled BIU; following that, select your selected effect, and it will be employed to the selected text message.

Touch the arrow to see additional results such as struck-through text messages.

27. Quick-delete in the Calculator app

If you are using the calculator application a lot, you may like this helpful and little-known time-saving technique.

The *Calculator app*, like real-world calculators, does not have a delete button, which may be annoying if you have just typed out an extended number and made a blunder right by the end.

Thankfully you can swipe over the volume in the dark area at the very top - still left or right, no matter - and for every swipe, an individual digit will be taken off the finish of the physique.

28. Stop music with a timer

This is an excellent trick for anybody who enjoys drifting

off to sleep with music. The problem with that is it'll be playing when you awaken each day, and you might have just drained the majority of your electric battery along the way. Using the concealed *'Stop Playing' timer*, you can pick how long you want the music to try out for as you drift off to rest.

Open up the *Clock app's Timer tabs*. (You can get just right to this from Control Centre: tap the stylized clock face.) Choose how long you want your timer to last for and then touch *'When Timer Ends.'* Scroll right down to underneath of the menu and choose 'Stop Playing.'

Press start on the timer and then begin taking part in your music from the Music app. When the timer ends, the music will fade to an end. This technique will also work for audiobooks and other press.

In iOS 13 or later version, you have the excess option of searching for a monitor with a lyric - whatever stage it is that is trapped in your mind because you heard it on the air this morning.

Just open the Music application and enter what in the

Search field. It will work even though you don't have all that, but the much longer the term you enter, the much more likely it is going to offer you a correct result.

You can even ask Siri the same question without typing anything.

29. Get an iPhone's display to blink when you get a note

If you discover that the vibration or audio that your phone makes when you get a note is not necessarily enough to attract your attention, there's another component that you can include to the alert: light. By heading to *Configurations > General > Convenience* and scrolling right down to the 'Hearing' section, you can change on *'LED Display for Notifications.'*

Now each time you get a notification, the flash next to your iPhone's rear-facing camera will blink.

30. Find words or phrases on the web page

You can find a specific word or expression on a website in Safari on the iPhone. While on the required page, tap the URL/search bar and enter the desired term. You'll see a summary of search results from the net, App Store, etc., but at the bottom of this list, you will see "on this web page," with the number of matches.

Touch it, and you will see that the email address details are highlighted in yellow. Touch the arrows at the bottom of the display to scroll through the situations.

31. Use AirPods as a hearing aid

When you have a set of AirPods, you may use the Live Listen feature in iOS 12 or later version to carefully turn your AirPods into a hearing help.

Head to Settings > Control Centre > Customize Handles.

Touch on Hearing (under More Settings) to include it to your Control Centre. Now when you select this option in control Centre, it'll magnify voices through your AirPods.

We can't wait around to try out this out so that people can spy on what our friends say behind our backs.

32. Save a website to Books

You can turn webpages into PDFs and add them right to your Books app; that is handy if you are reading an extended web record, or mainly if you've found an HTML publication online and want to keep a duplicate of it.

When you touch Share, scroll over the applications to find Copy to Books. Touch it, and the net web page will be converted and put into your reserve collection.

(Note that this program appears only when you have Booked on your iPhone! Unless you can still Save as PDF and add it to your Documents).

33. Change Siri's accent

British speakers have had the opportunity to improve Siri's voice from male to feminine with the decision of 3 accents since iOS 11; iOS 12 added the decision of Irish or South African too.

Head to Settings > Siri & Search > Siri Tone of voice.

Here you can transform an English speaking voice from

Male to Female, or change the accent to American, Australian, British, Irish or South African. Talking about accents, Siri can result in several different dialects for you.

In iOS 13 and later version gained the capability to translate words and phrases into even more languages - there are up to 50 different combinations. We have an ardent article teaching how to translate using Siri.

It ought to be a straightforward case of saying: "Hey Siri, how do you say Good Night time in Spanish," for example.

34. Ask Siri to do mathematics for you

Regardless of how good a mathematician you may be, having Siri readily available to assist with organic and straightforward mathematics questions is always useful.

Open Siri and recite your equation to it. If the volume is complicated, be sure you say it at a somewhat slower speed, so Siri doesn't misunderstand. We found Siri can also properly separate, multiply, subtract and add, along with some slightly more complicated equations.

35. Create shortcuts for common tasks

In iOS 12 and later, you can group jobs and cause them with an individual Siri command. You will have to download the Shortcuts application from the App Store.

Open up the *Siri Shortcuts application* and touch on *Gallery* to visit a gallery of ready-made shortcuts, such as *Calculate Suggestion, Log water, Make PDF, or Remind Me at Home.*

Once you have the application on your iPhone, you will notice recommendations of shortcuts you might like to use when you swipe down on your Home display screen - Shortcuts are available below your Siri Suggestions of applications you might want to use.

Just tap on the suggestion - which is predicated on something you frequently do, such as send an organization text message, and you'll be taken a right to a message.

36. Measure things

The brand new Measure application in iOS 13 can make it easy to gauge the dimensions of objects. All you have to do is track the edges of the thing and it'll let you know how long they may be.

Open the application, and you'll start to see the option to go the iPhone to start; eventually, a circle can be seen and the choice to add a spot.

The Measure application is also the new home of the particular level app; this level can be utilized if you would like to ensure that bookshelf you're adding is flawlessly level.

The iPhone uses its Gyroscope to look for the level of the height the iPhone is positioned on; you should have the chance to calibrate it on a set surface before evaluating the situation.

37. Enable Nighttime Shift

Night Change dims the white shades of your screen, to make it easier on your eye in low-light conditions. You can routine Night Shift to occur at the same time every day, or you can manually allow it until tomorrow.

You can even adjust the color temperature such that it is pretty much warm.

Head to Settings > Screen & Lighting > Night Change.

38. Have your iPhone read aloud your texts

If you require or want your iPhone to learn out your text messages, you'll be able to allow Speak Selection.

To begin with, navigate to *Configurations > General > Availability and toggle the choice 'Speak Selection.'*

If you're to long-press on the speech bubble inside your Messages, you'll now find the choice to 'Speak' - the choice is particularly useful if you have an extended text or decide to begin travelling and want to hear the written text while in hands-free setting.

39. See whenever you receive a message

Inside the Messages app, you can swipe forth to the left to expose the time-stamps of every individual message.

Usually, you can see what date with what time the first message was sent; however, to reveal every individual message from then on, you will have to go through the timestamps by swiping quickly; this is beneficial to either know very well what time the last call was received at or even to find out if your friend was lying about arriving promptly!

40. Call from within Messages

If you are chatting via Messages and then decide it might be useful to talk instead, you can merely touch on the icon for the individual you're texting to see options for a sound or FaceTime call. You can begin an organization FaceTime call from an organization Communications chat too - suppose

CHAPTER 13

Secret iPhone Camera Features Strange to You

Do you want to make the full use of your iPhone camera when you take photographs? As it's easy to take a photo with your iPhone, the excellent and crucial iPhone digital camera features are hidden from regular iPhone users. So, in this section, you'll find out the concealed iPhone camera features that every iPhone users must use.

- Swipe Left for Swift Access to Your iPhone Camera. How often have you seen or witness an incredible scene in front of your eyes, only to discover that it's gone at the time you're prepared to take a photo? You can improve your possibilities of taking a perfect shot if you know how to use your camera effectively.

- In case your iPhone is locked, you can press the home button to wake up your phone, and then swipe left through the lock display.

- The camera would open immediately, and you won't even need to enter your password to unlock your iPhone. This trick would make you begin capturing in less than a second!

- However, what if you're already making use of the iPhone, and also you want to access the digital camera quickly, swipe up from the lower part of the screen to open the Control Centre as shown below.

From here, select the camera icon in the bottom right, and you're ready to start taking pictures!

How to Set Focus and Exposure

If you haven't set focus and exposure, the iPhone can do it for you automatically. Usually, it can be a reasonably good job. Furthermore, that's how most iPhone users take almost all their photographs.

There are a few times, though, when autofocus fails - or when you wish to Focus on something in addition to the apparent subject.

That's when you'll want to create focus manually. That is super easy to do - Tap the location on the display where you'd prefer to set Focus, and the camera deals with others.

What distinction does the *focus* make? If you go through the picture above, the Focus is defined on the blossom in the foreground. The topic is bright and shiny, as the bloom petals and leaves in the background are blurred.

When you Tap on the screen to set Focus, the camera automatically sets the exposure. The exposure refers to improving the brightness of an image. So it's essential to get the exposure right if you are taking your picture.

*NB: When you wish to set **Focus**, check out the display to find out if the lighting of the image appears suitable. If it seems too vibrant or too darkish, you can change exposure before taking the picture.*

After you've Tapped on the screen to create focus and exposure, the exposure slider with a sun icon would be observed. Swipe up to help make the picture brighter or right down to make the image darker.

Efficaciously setting focus and exposure is one of the primary element skills that a photographer must master. When it takes merely a few Taps to modify focus and exposure, you must do it effectively to Focus on the most crucial components of the complete picture.

The task is that every photograph takes a specific method of focus and exposure setting. Things that work notably for landscapes don't work almost as properly for night or tour photos.

How to Lock Focus and Exposure with AE/AF Lock

The iPhone also allows you to lock each one of the appealing points; focus and exposure. So why would you need to close those functions while going for a picture?

- The principle motive is if anything changes in the scene, including a moving subject or altered lighting, your focus and exposure would stay unchanged.

- That's why it's a great idea to lock Focus and exposure when you're expecting motion within the picture. For instance, *Focus and exposure* lock could be beneficial in street picture taking.

- You might frame the shot, and set the focus and

exposure earlier, then obviously watch out for a person to pass-by before taking your photo.

- Once you've locked the focus and exposure, you might take several pictures of the same image and never have to set focus and exposure each time you want to consider photos. To unlock Focus and exposure, select anywhere on the screen.

- To lock focus and exposure, Tap and retain your hands on the display screen for mere multiple seconds at the stage where you want to create the centre point. A yellowish package with AE/AF lock can look near the top of the display.

Note: You can nevertheless swipe up or down on display to regulate exposure manually.

*Now regardless of what happens within the framework or how you fling the iPhone 7, iPhone 7 Pro, and iPhone 7 Pro Max, the **Focus and Exposure** would still be unchanged.*

How to Take HDR Photos

HDR, which means *High Active Range*, is another

incredible picture tool that is included in the camera of your iPhone.

HDR picture taking with the iPhone combines three unique exposures of precisely the same image to produce one nicely exposed picture.

It's exquisite for high comparison moments with shiny and darkish areas since it allows you to capture extra components in both shadows and the highlights fully.

Some small adjustments within an editing application such as Snapseed can indeed draw out the colours and detail that were captured in the **HDR photograph**, although it still comes with fantastic well-balanced exposure.

- You'll find the HDR setting on the left side of the camera app. Tapping on HDR provides you with three options: Motion, ON, or OFF.
- Notably, it's high-quality to use HDR for panorama or landscape pictures and scenes where the sky occupies a significant area of the photograph. This enables the taking of extra fine detail in both the brighter sky and the darker foreground.

- There are a few downsides to HDR, especially in conditions of pictures of motion. Because HDR is a variety of three sequentially captured photos, you might encounter "ghosts" if the picture is changing quickly. HDR images also require a long period to capture, which means that your hands may shake even while the shutter is open up.

- It's additionally essential to state that non-HDR pictures will sometimes look much better than HDR ones, that's the reason it's a good idea to save lots of each variation of the image. To make sure that each variant is stored, go to configurations > photos & camera, and ensure Save Normal Picture is **ON** in the ***HDR section***.

- It's also well worth mentioning that the default iPhone camera application comes with an alternatively subtle ***HDR impact,*** a sophisticated camera application that can create much more powerful HDR results and provide you with complete control over the catch.

How to Take Snapshot in Burst Mode

- Burst mode is one of the very most useful capturing features in the iPhone camera app. It enables you to take ten images in only one second, which makes it easy to capture the suitable movement shot with reduced blur entirely.

- If you wish to activate a *burst setting*, press down the shutter button for half a second or longer, and the iPhone begins capturing one after another. When you've shot a burst of snap photos, after that, you can choose the lovely images from the

Set and delete others.

- Burst setting is worth using each time there's any movement or unpredictability in the picture.

Remember utilizing it when photographing kids, animals, birds, and splashing water.

It's also excellent for taking pictures on magical occasions in street picture taking. Likewise, try the utilization of burst setting to capture the correct stride or present.

How to Take Pictures with Volume Buttons

Perhaps you have ever overlooked or missed the iPhone's tiny on-display shutter button? If so, change to the utilization of volume control keys beside your iPhone.

Either of these buttons can be utilized for shutter release, and the tactile opinions you get from pressing this button is a great deal more pleasurable than pressing an electronic switch.

Additionally, this enables you to carry the iPhone with two hands, just as you'd grab a typical digital camera.

The only drawback of the approach is that you'll require pressing the Volume button pretty hard, which might produce camera shake. That's especially essential in a low-mild or less lighted environment, where any movement of your iPhone would lead to the blurry picture.

How to take Photographs with your Apple Headphones

Remember those white apple headphones that were included with your iPhone, on purchase can be utilized for photo taking. It additionally has *Volume buttons*, and you may use these control keys to consider photos!

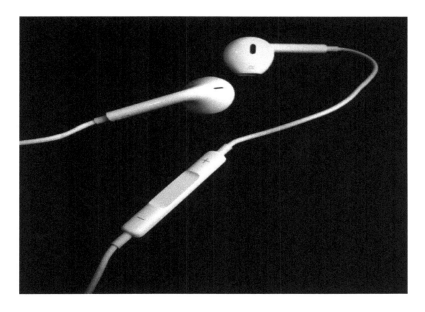

This feature is tremendously useful when you need to take discreet pictures of people you don't recognize or know in person, as you could pretend to be paying focused attention to music or making a call while you're taking pictures.

This method additionally is available when your iPhone is on a tripod. As you release the shutter with your headphones, you can get rid of any unintentional digital camera movement, which is quite essential for night time pictures, long exposure images, etc.

CHAPTER 14

How to Use iPhone Portrait Mode to Make Blurry Background

The **iPhone portrait mode** is the correct device to make brilliant looking portrait photographs with your iPhone. The portrait setting allows you to produce a shallow depth of field in your pictures quickly. This leads to an excellent blurry background that could typically be performed with a **DSLR camera**. With this section, you'll see how to use the iPhone portrait setting to make a professional-looking iPhone photo with a beautiful background blur.

What's Portrait Mode?

Portrait mode is a distinctive capturing mode available in the native camera application of an iPhone. It creates the use of a unique **Depth Impact Tool** to make a shallow Depth of field in your pictures.

Shallow depth of field means that only a little area of the photo is within focus as the other is blurred. More often than not, you'll need your most significant concern at the mercy of appearing in razor-sharp focus as the background shows up blurred.

This soft and tender blurry background is categorized as "**bokeh**," which originates from the Japanese language.

Why Should You Use Shallow Depth of Field?

Portrait photographers often utilize the **shallow depth of field**. Why? Since it places the focus on the average person and creates a sensitive, dreamy background in it. Blurring the context is also truly useful when taking in locations with a busy, messy, or distracting background. The blurring makes the context secondary, getting the viewer's attention back to the main subject matter in the foreground.

Shallow Depth of Field isn't something you'd use for every kind of picture. You typically wouldn't want a blurry Background in scenery or architectural photo as you'd want to see everything vividly from foreground to Background.

However, in portrait pictures, a Shallow Depth of Field can make a significant distinction to the result of your photo. By blurring the background, you may make your subject matter stand out.

How to Make Background Blur on iPhone

Sometimes back, the iPhone camera hasn't allowed you to have any control over the depth of field for your pictures. You've had the choice to have everything in Focus - unless your most significant subject matter comes very near the zoom lens; in such case, the background seems blurred.

However, with portrait setting on the new iPhone, now you can pick and choose what's in focus and what isn't. This gives you unprecedented control over your iPhone, permitting you to mimic the appearance of DSLR cameras that can catch a shallow depth of field.

While portrait mode is most beneficial when planning on taking pictures of humans, pets, nature, etc., it can be utilized to blur the background behind any subject.

Many things appear better when there's a soft, dreamy background in it - especially if that background could distract the viewer from the primary subject.

How to use iPhone Portrait Mode

- Developing a shallow **Depth of Field** with Portrait mode on the iPhone is super easy. You can start by starting the default camera app, then swipe through the taking pictures modes (video, picture, etc.) until Portrait is highlighted in yellow.

- The very first thing you'll notice when you switch

to Portrait Setting is that everything gets enlarged. That's because the camera automatically switches to the iPhone's 2x Telephoto Zoom lens. The telephoto zoom lens typically creates more flattering portrait images than the huge-angle zoom lens that could distort cosmetic features.

- You'll additionally spot the words **Depth Impact** appears at the bottom of the screen. Moreover, your telephone will help you give on-screen instructions in case you don't have things framed up optimally for an enjoyable portrait shot. For instance, you'll possibly see Move Farther Away or even more Light Required:

- The moment you're at the right distance from your subject, the words **Depth Effect** would be highlighted in yellow. You'll also see four yellow crop marks, indicating the face of your subject:

- You're now ready to take, so select the shutter button to consider your picture. After making the picture, you'll observe that two variations of the image can look in the camera app. One image will have the ***Depth Impact*** (blurred Background), and the other won't.

- Evaluating those two versions of the image

sincerely suggests how nice a portrait picture shows up when it has a **Shallow Depth of Field**.

- If for reasons unknown you're not sure which of both pictures had the **Depth impact**, it'll be labelled in your image Set as shown below:

Tips For Creating Background Blur

When taking photos with the iPhone portrait mode, it's essential to think about your background plus your subject. The type of Background you choose against its distance from your subject matter, will each have a significant effect on the final image.

The **Depth Effect** in Portrait mode is most effective when your subject matter is not the background. The further away the topic is from the background, the more delightful blur you'll get. Spot the difference in the background blur of the two pictures:

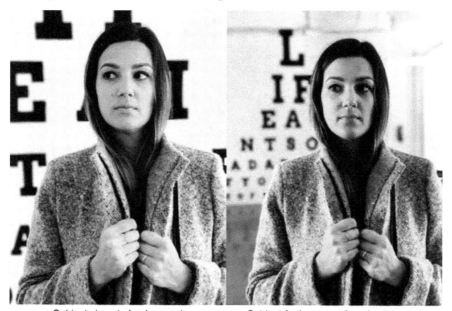

Subject close to background   Subject farther away from background

So; if your Background doesn't show up blurry enough when taking photos in a portrait setting, move your subject matter further from the background.

It's additionally essential to have something in the background so that there are a few components for the camera to blur.

Conclusively; the iPhone has continuously been a first-rate device for most types of picture taking - such as landscape, structures, and street picture taking. However, now the iPhone provides the potential to take amazing, high-quality portrait photos.

The telephoto zoom lens on the iPhone is more flattering for shooting people than the typical wide-angle zoom lens.

As well as the **Magical Depth Impact tool** on the iPhone Portrait Mode creates a lovely background blur - simulating the shallow depth of field that could formerly only be performed with a DSLR camera.

Taking photos with the iPhone portrait mode is a delight.

Moreover, your subject will be thrilled when you suggest to them how beautiful they show up in your photos.

Don't forget; even while Portrait mode is the perfect setting when planning on taking pictures of individuals, pets, nature, etc., you can use it on any subject matter in which you require to make an attractive *background blur*.

CHAPTER 15

How to Shoot Unique iPhone Photos

Hipstamatic is an elegant iPhone camera application for growing unique photos with a retro or vintage appearance. It comes with an outstanding selection of analogue film, zoom lens, and flash results, which enable you to easily change an ordinary picture into something exceedingly thrilling, stunning or dramatic. Besides, it comes with an accessible improving and editing Set for fine-tuning your photographs in post-processing. With this section, you'll learn the step-by-step instructions when planning on taking pictures and editing and enhancing lovely images using the Hipstamatic app.

Hipstamatic Zoom Lens & Film Combos

Hipstamatic is most beneficially known because of its potential to make a vast selection of retro-styled pictures based on numerous filters. The filter systems are applied when you take the photo; nevertheless, you can always change the ultimate result by just selecting different filter systems once you've used the shot.

The Hipstamatic filters get into three categories that are: zoom lens type, film type, and flash type. Before you proceed with going for a picture in Hipstamatic, you should select which zoom lens, film, and flash you want to use.

The lens decides the colours and tones in your photo. The film determines the framework or vignette across the advantage of the image (and occasionally also changes the colours of the image). The flash helps in creating distinctive lights.

The lens, film, and flash mixtures in Hipstamatic are known as "***combos.***" Through the utilization of diverse combinations of the zoom lens, film, and flash, you can create an enormous variety of image styles - from faded superior results to high comparison dark and white pictures.

To give an example of how Hipstamatic can change an ordinary picture into something a lot more aesthetically attractive, check the photographs below. The first picture is the original photo without Hipstamatic filter systems applied:

Subsequent are a few examples of the same scene captured with the use of specific Hipstamatic lens and film combos:

When taking a picture with Hipstamatic, you can either permit the app to select a combo for you or try different mixtures of your desire until you locate an impact you like.

Hipstamatic includes a core set of lenses, film and flash options, and many more can be found as in-app purchases.

Selecting A Camera Interface

Hipstamatic has two different camera settings/interfaces included in the application. You may use the vintage camera user interface that mimics the appearance and feel of old film cameras:

You can likewise Utilize the *Pro camera interface,* which has a modern and professional feel. This camera mode is excellent if you want a bit of manual control while taking pictures:

If you wish to select from both camera settings, Tap both opposing arrows icon (arrows are either facing each other or aside depending on which digital camera setting you are employing).

How to Take Pictures with Hipstamatic Vintage Camera

You are going to learn how to consider pictures using the vintage camera mode in Hipstamatic. Be sure you've chosen the primary camera interface. If you're presently in the pro camera setting, select the opposing arrows to change to a traditional setting.

When working with Classic mode, you can change between your front and back views of the camera by Tapping the flip icon (curved arrow) in the bottom right of the screen.

How to Take a Picture with Basic Camera

- When you point the camera at a picture, you'll view it in the *sq. Viewfinder*. When capturing, you can choose from viewfinder alternatives.
- You can both view the picture with no filter

systems (lenses, movies, etc.) applied, alternatively, you can see in real-time, what the actual photograph can look like following when the shot has been taken using your chosen filters (you'll understand how to select lens, movies, etc. later as you read further).

- To change between those two viewfinder options, Tap the small dark switch in the bottom right of the viewfinder (as shown below):

When the switch is at the **OFF** function (completely black colour), you won't start to see the picture with all of your selected filters applied, but, when the photograph is used, the filters will be employed to the image when the switch is within the ON position (yellow eyeball icon will be shown).

I endorse getting the viewfinder change in the ON position, and that means you can easily see the impact of the existing zoom lens, film, and flash combo.

When you've composed your shot, take the picture by Tapping the yellow shutter button at the very top right.

NB: You can additionally enlarge the viewfinder by double-Tapping the viewfinder windows. You'll be able to select the viewer once to consider the shot.

If you wish to start to see the picture you've taken, Tap the square image thumbnail icon in the bottom still left of the screen. The image gallery can look displaying a preview of the photos you've shot with Hipstamatic, as shown below.

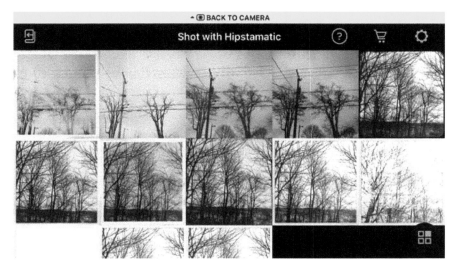

If you wish to see a much larger model of a specific photo, select the picture you want to see.

When viewing the entire sized image, you'll see which film/zoom lens/flash combo used, as well as the location where the picture was taken.

How to Decide on a Zoom lens/Film/Flash Combo

- For you to specify the appearance and design of your picture, you'll need to pick from the several options of lens and film (and flash if preferred).

- You can either decide on a preset combo from the favorites screen, or you create your combo from scrape. Taking into consideration the preset combo, first of all, begin by Tapping the circular icon (the next from the cheapest right-hand part) as shown in the red group below:

- Swipe across to see the number of cameras with diverse zoom lens/film/flash combos, however; don't Tap on the cameras yet. Every camera comes with an example photo showing the type of picture style that unique combo will generate.

- Tap and keep a camera to see more information in what configurations to be Utilized, then select the x to come back to the standard display screen.

- To select a specific combo from the favorites screen, Tap on the camera combo you want to use. On the other hand, you can allow the app to shuffle the combo on every occasion arbitrarily you are taking picture shot, providing you with a definite effect for every chance. If you like this option, select the shuffle icon (two arrows at the top right) and pick your chosen option:

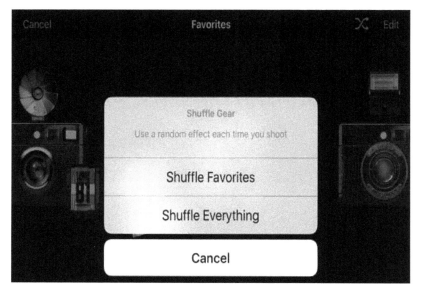

- When you've chosen a camera combo from the listed favorites, or the shuffle option, you'll be taken back to the camera to be able to begin capturing.

- You can additionally create your own lens/film/flash combos and upload these to the report on favorites. To achieve that, Tap the spherical icon (second from right hands side) at the bottom of the screen to access the preferences display.

- Swipe over the cameras to the much right, then select the newest favorites (+) icon.

- The proceeding screen will show a preview image with three icons beneath it. From still left to right, these icons are **Zoom lens, Film, Flash.**

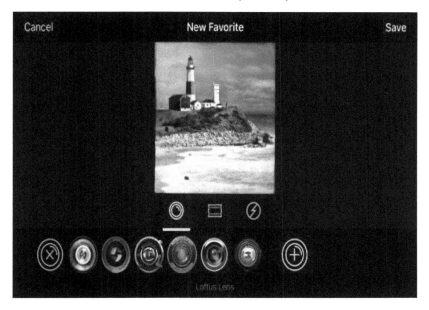

- Begin by selecting the type of zoom lens that you want to use - recollect that the zoom lens adjusts the colors and shades of your picture when you choose the particular lens at the bottom of the screen, the preview image changes showing what impact that zoom lens could have on your photo.

- When you've chosen the lens that you like, Tap the Film icon (middle icon) under the picture preview. The film determines the framework or vignette round the advantage of the image, and additionally, it may change the firmness. Pick the film style that you want from underneath of the display:

- Next, select the flash icon (right-hand icon) under the image preview. The flashes put in a particular lightning impact on your picture. If you wish to apply flash, choose your decision from underneath of the display, typically, select No Flash.

- You'll discover that there's an advantage (+) indication for the zoom lens, film and flash options - Tapping this icon goes to the Hipstamatic store where you can buy new lenses, movies, and flashes to increase your Sets.

- When you're pleased with your selected combo, Tap Save at the very top right part of the screen. On the next screen, you can enter a name for your combo, then select Done:

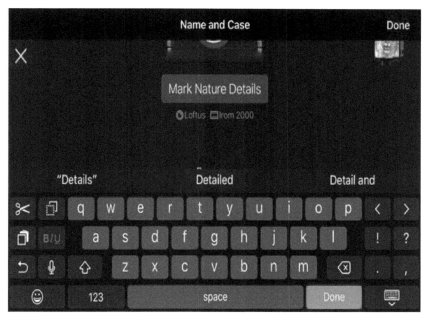

- Your newly added combo can look in the set of Favourites. To use this combo, select onto it, and also you'll be taken back to the camera and that means you can begin snapping:

- There's one other method of choosing a combo of a zoom lens, film and flash for capturing. Remember, there's a back view and front side view in traditional camera setting - on the back camera view, Tap the **Turn icon** (curved arrow in the bottom right) that may change you to the leading camera view.

- To select a particular zoom lens, swipe over the large zoom lens in the center of the display till you start to see the zoom lens you desire.

- To choose a film, select the film icon at the still left of the display screen. Swipe up or down on the rolls of the film until you find the lens you wish.

- To find out more records regarding a specific film, as well as test pictures, Tap the motion of the film - select Done to exit the film information.

- When you've selected the film you want to use, Tap the camera body at the right of the screen to return to the leading camera view.

- To select away a flash, select the **Flash icon** (second from lower still left) then swipe over the distinctive flash options. If you don't want to use flash, choose the No Flash option. Tap Done to come back to the leading camera view.

- If you wish to buy more lenses, movies, and flashes to increase your Sets, Tap the **SHOPPING CART SOFTWARE** icon (second from bottom level right). You will see the presented products or click on a particular item if you wish to exit the shopping cart software, Tap **Done**.

- When you're content with the zoom lens/film/flash combo which you've selected, select the **Flip icon** (curved arrow in the bottom right) to come back to the back camera view, then start taking pictures!

How to Switch Flash ON & OFF

When you're capturing with the back camera view, you'll observe a black colour slider below the sq. Viewfinder. This will help you to select if the flash should be brought ON or not if you are going for a picture.

Whenever the flash slider reaches the center, the flash is powered down.

When the flash slider is moved left, your selected flash

effect will be applied to the photo; however, the flash at the front end of your iPhone X Series won't fire on.

When the flash slider is moved to the right, your selected flash effect will be employed to the photograph, and the flash at the front end of your iPhone X Series will fire to provide more light on your subject.

How to Change Shutter Speed

- At the very top right of the camera, the display is the **shutter speed dial**. Modifying the shutter rate does a couple of things - it changes the exposure of the image (how gleaming it seems) and impacts how motion is captured.

- The lower the Volume on the dial, the slower the shutter speed. A slow shutter acceleration results in a brighter image, and an effortless shutter swiftness leads into a darker picture. You might use this feature to produce artistically shiny photos or very darkish moody pictures.

- Inside a case where you're capturing a scene with moving subjects, a natural shutter rate will freeze movement, and a sluggish shutter rate will capture the action as a blur.

How to Create Multiple Exposures

Hipstamatic gives you to generate thrilling dual exposure pictures. You take two different pictures, and then your camera combines them. That is a fun strategy to apply and can result in some exciting artwork and abstract images.

- To begin with, creating this kind of photograph, slide the **Multiple Exposure switch** (at the top left-hand side of the camera display) left such that it turns yellowish:

- Take your first picture by Tapping the yellow

shutter button at the right. You will notice that the multiple exposure switch has moved to the right such that only half of the yellow square is seen:

- Position your camera at a different subject matter or view, then take the next shot. You'll start to see the "**Multi Revealing**" message show up as the app combines both images.

- If you wish to view the two times exposure image on your gallery, select the square model thumbnail icon at the bottom left of the screen. Tap the yellow pub near the top of the gallery to come back to the camera.

- Given that you're familiar with the functions of the vintage camera user interface, let's consider the procedure of taking pictures with the ***Pro camera mode***.

How to Take Pictures with Hipstamatic Pro Camera

Hipstamatic pro camera mode gives more advanced camera application that gives you more manual control when shooting pictures.

- If you're presently using the Vintage camera mode, change to the pro camera user interface by just Tapping both opposing arrows at the low area of the screen as shown below:

- The pro digital camera interface appears very

distinctive to the classic interface which doesn't have any retro styling, but has a larger square viewfinder with icons around the edges:

- Let's begin the usage of those camera icons to customize the final picture. In case you're using the camera in landscape orientation, as shown above, the top-right icon allows you to change the **Aspect Ratio**:

- The Aspect ratio decides the width and height of images. Choosing the 1:1 aspect percentage will result in an excellent square image, as the 16:9 proportion will be full than its elevation. The next icon in the red circle below gives you to choose different flash options, including *Flash On, Flash Auto,* and *Constant Light*:

The icon under the flash icon will help you to switch to the front camera to be able to have a self-portrait. While in the bottom right of the display will be the two opposing arrows that may take you back to the **Classic vintage style** camera.

The icon in the bottom left of the screen gives you to choose which zoom lens/film/flash combo you should employ - similar from what you did with the entire classic camera mode:

After Tapping the icon, you can progressively swipe

through the various combos until you locate an effect that suits your interest, or Tap the plus (+) icon to create a new combo. Tap on the combo you want to apply to return to the camera:

The **"M"** icon (at the right-hand side of the shutter button as shown below) stands for **Manual**, and it permits you to fine-tune the camera settings before taking your shot:

When you Tap the **Manual (m)** icon, a bar of icons will appear in its place:

The **round target icon** allows you to adjust the focus manually. The **magnifying glass icon** helps you to zoom in. Each of these settings is modified by making use of the slider at the bottom of the display screen.

The **+/- icon** turns on the exposure slider which lets you alter the brightness up or down for brighter or darker photographs:

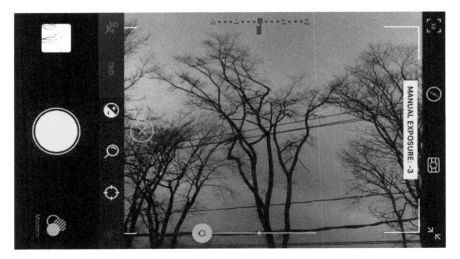

For the fun part! The **ISO** and **Shutter Speed** (running man icon) settings allow you to manage and control exposure and how motion appears in your photograph:

- If you wish to create motion blur when photographing an instant running subject matter, you'll need a *slow shutter speed* and a *minimal ISO* (a minimum ISO facilitates preventing the picture from being over-exposed).

- To begin with, select the **ISO icon**, and use the slider to lessen the ISO to the lowest selection of number feasible. Then Tap the Shutter Rate icon (operating man) and move the slider to reduce the shutter rate to ensure that the picture appears almost too bright.

- The reason behind this is that; the brighter the picture, the slower the shutter acceleration, which equals higher movement blur of moving topics.

- If you're capturing in fantastic daytime conditions, you will learn that your sluggish shutter images appear too vibrant. That is why it's typically more comfortable to take at dawn or nightfall, or on darkish overcast times, to fully capture excellent show shutter photos.

- The final camera function is White Balance (lamp icon) that allows you to change the shade temperature on the scale from blue to yellow:

- The white balance enables you to warm up or keep down the colors, either to get perfect color balance or for creative impact. You can pull the slider left to help make the colors warmer (i.e., more yellow), and move to the right to make sure they are more refreshing (i.e., extra blue):

This is undoubtedly a proper setting for indoor capturing situations where the scene is illuminated by using artificial light with a yellow coloration cast. You can merely pull the white balance slider till you're pleased with the color firmness shown in the viewfinder:

How to Edit Pictures in Hipstamatic

Hipstamatic isn't taken into account as a professionally graded picture editor. It merely has a significant number of user-friendly improving features that will help you get the images simply perfect, such as the potential to choose a different combo such as zoom lens, film, and flash you can use when planning on taking pictures.

- To access the modifying mode, whether or not you're using the vintage camera or the pro camera, select the sq. Image thumbnail, which ultimately shows the previous picture taken:

- In the image gallery, Tap the picture you need to edit, then Tap the edit icon (3 circles) at the lowest part of the display screen as shown below:

- Swipe through the preset combos at the bottom of the screen, Tapping on any that you prefer to see what impact it is wearing your image. Once you've chosen a preset that you want, use the slider to change the strength of the result till you're content with the final result. Tap **Save** when you're done editing.

- Much like the one-Tap presets, there are a few other modifying alternatives that you can use to improve your picture. Tap the edit icon (three circles), then select the choice icon (three sliders) situated merely above the configurations icon.

- Below your image, you'll visit a row of icons that may be used to fine-tune and edit the photo.

- Conclusively, Hipstamatic gives you to create an array of picture patterns, which include retro, classic, and dark and white.

- The application has two different kinds of camera settings (classic and pro), to be able to select to shoot using whichever interface you like. Each parameter can help you choose a zoom lens/film/flash combo, to enable you always to create the complete appearance and feel that you envisioned.

- The editing tools in the application enable you to fine-tune the picture when you've taken the shot, with the choice to decorate and improve the effect you used - or completely change the totality of the picture. With such a great deal of unique visual combos presented within this app, you can create excellent images, indeed with an incredible artistic edge.

CHAPTER 16

The 4 Best Camera Application For iPhone

Looking for the best camera application for an iPhone Series? Even while the default iPhone camera application has some fantastic capabilities, sometimes you'll want a more sophisticated camera. However, with so many camera applications available online, it might be tough to discover which to use. This assessment of the five best iPhone camera applications will help you to find the right app for you.

VSCO: How to Use VSCO

You might already be familiar with the VSCO application as it's more popular because of its picture improving functions and beautiful movie-like filters. However, this free application also has an effectively integrated camera with many guide settings.

- If you are capturing in VSCO, you could have manual control of *Focus, Exposure, White*

Stability, as well as *ISO and Shutter Speed*. Depending on how new your iPhone, you may even have the ability to shoot in *Natural Mode*.

- To gain access to the camera in VSCO, open up the application and swipe down with your finger. Once you are in the camera setting, you'll see numerous icons underneath (or the medial side, if you're making use of your phone horizontally) which may enable you to customize the camera configurations.

However, the above are just a few of the customizable options. If you swipe on the icons with your finger, you'll see there are very few extra "hiding" solely off display.

A significant number of the advanced camera features toggle among distinctive alternatives (flash, the grid, raw, and the funny "face overlay" choice), while some think of a slider for excellent fine-tuning settings with *exposure, white balance, focus, iso, and shutter rate.*

For example, if you select on the solar icon, the exposure slider will be observed at the lower part of the display screen, as shown below.

- Pull the slider to change the exposure (brightness) of your picture. In case you want to return to the default automated exposure, select on the "A."

- The **White Balance (WB)** setting is utilized for actualizing the right colors on your pictures by either starting to warm up or trying to cool off the colors. Use the slider to change the color heat in your image.

- You can view below two variations of the same image - one with a more relaxed white balance setting (bluer) and one with a warmer white balance setting (more orange). The color temp will have a significant effect on the overall temper of your picture.

The ISO setting controls the digital camera's sensitivity to light, and for that reason affects the exposure (brightness) of the photograph. The better the ISO Volume, the brighter the exposure maybe. However, retain in mind that high ISO configurations can result in grainy images.

Shutter Speed settings the exposure time for the picture. Lengthy exposures are perfect for night picture taking, blurring movement, and taking light trails.

When capturing lengthy exposure images, be sure you hold the camera still actually to avoid any camera tremble that brings about blurry pictures. Make use of a tripod for the product quality results.

While you're dealing with those types of manual settings in VSCO, you're essentially making the utilization of your iPhone as if you would use a manual DSLR camera.

VSCO can be an excellent application to use if you're merely starting or a dummy by using third-party camera apps. It's available for download from the application store and has a great selection of manual handles that will put in a level of course and creativeness to your pictures.

MANUAL: How to Use Manual

- If manual camera settings are what you're after, the aptly named manual application ($3.99) is just about the best replacement camera application for your iPhone. Quickly, you can transform the Shutter Speed, ISO, and exposure values to attain the creative impact you need.

- Unlike VSCO, you have the decision to manually control the camera settings, which include **Focus, White Balance, ISO, Shutter Speed,** and **Brightness (*called EV*).**

- The interface is quite intuitive. When you release the app, all the configurations are in automated mode. If you wish to change to manual control, select and hold on to the ISO or Shutter Speed, and you'll be able to access your configurations. Moreover, if you would like to restore to the automated setting, Tap the "A."

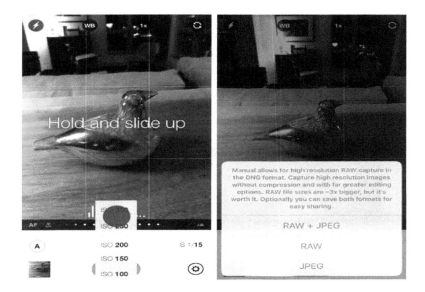

- You can even decide if you would like to snap images in Raw Layout, JPEG Layout, or both. Natural capture enables you to store images without compression, ensuring an excellent picture that provides you with more significant potential for improvement during editing. However, retain in mind that Natural photos take up plenty of more space for storage on your phone.

- There's a specific setting that may be great, which is the slow shutter speed.

- Another superb feature of the manual application is that you can by hand Focus on your subject. Just slip your finger left or directly on the Focus bar at the lowest area of the screen till your subject matter sometimes appears in perfect Focus. If you wish to go back to the auto-focus setting, select the AF button.

This app also offers a particular focusing device, rendering it more straightforward to focus manually. Once you start sliding the Focus bar, a middle square magnifies the subject, and that means you can test your important Focus thoroughly. This standard concentrating feature is particularly useful while taking up close or macro issues.

Having the ability to control those advanced manual settings provides you with more excellent alternatives as an iPhone X Series photographer, letting you create the best available picture, even in complex taking conditions.

CAMERA+: How to Use Camera+

Camera+ is a superb camera and picture enhancing app combined. It is the first advanced camera app I've seen great photographers using on iPhone, and you may set the middle point, and exposure one following the other, as the timer for the camera, could be arranged for 30 mere seconds.

- The camera+ programmer has continued to enhance the app over time, and it's now stronger than ever. All the classic features are just like they were; nevertheless, you could now use digital camera+ much as if you use the manual app. You can even shoot in Natural mode and extra control of your last photograph.

- In camera+ it's the simplest. It is easy to switch the center point, exposure, and white balance to creatively impact the feeling of your snap photos.

- To create the Focus and exposure individually, select on display with two fingertips at the same instant of your time. You'll visit an individual exposure factor (orange group) and Focus (red square). Pull the Focus and contact with distinctive elements of the picture until it appears the just as what you would like it to appear to be.

- If you wish to alter the shutter speed and ISO configurations, Tap the group icon above the shutter release button. A -panel will slip up, letting you by hand change the settings.

- The shutter speed setting appears on the left and the ISO at the right; swipe through each establishing to alternate them. To escape the manual configurations and came back to the default setting, you could either Tap the automated button or dual Tap the screen.

- Typically you will never need to disturb yourself about **white balance** because the iPhone does a notable activity of fabricating all the colorations to appear genuine. However, you can personally override the white balance placing to provide your photos with a different feel.

- You might use the shutter speed and ISO settings in camera+ to obtain computer images extraordinary impact evergreen exposures. In the example underneath, an image of a pool that experienced a lovely tree sculpture was captured.

The primary picture (above) converted into shot using the iPhone's default camera app. It made an appearance pretty good; nevertheless, the reflections and ripples in the water had been some distraction.

So let look at case research where the camera+ is utilized to shoot an extended exposure of the picture, as shown below. You will observe how the sluggish shutter speed has made water show up silky smooth. It makes the water significantly less distracting, and on the other hand, your vision is attracted to the tree.

Underneath you might observe how this impact in digital camera+. Indeed, when you have an iPhone, or later versions would be, digital camera+ will continue to work with either of the telephone's lens. Because of this shot, it was turned to the telephoto zoom lens (group icon near to top left) because the photographer couldn't get near to the tree without getting damp!

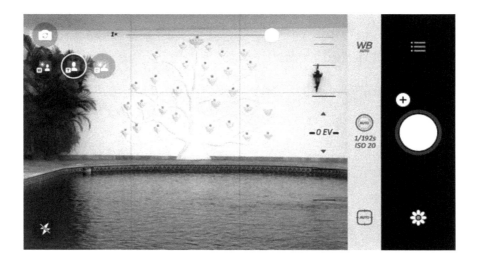

Moreover, subsequently, Tap the automatic button to show the manual controls. The shutter speed was set to an entirely long 8 seconds (with the iPhone set up on a tripod) and reduced the ISO value as little as reasonable (which on camera+ was 0.01) to make sure the photo didn't end up over-exposed (too brilliantly bright).

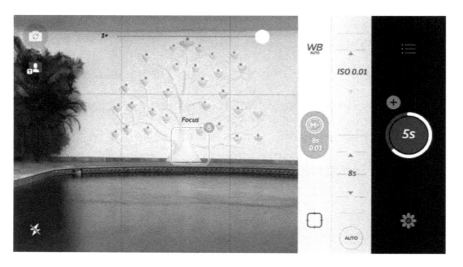

In the end, the spherical shutter button was tapped and watched because the picture was exposed over 8 seconds. Among many of these camera apps, camera+ is very powerful and can be a bit overwhelming. So I will recommend that you attempt out one function at a time and get accustomed to it before moving on to the next.

ProCAMERA: How to Use ProCAMERA

The ProCamera app, especially the latest version, gives you a remarkable number of control over your settings while taking pictures.

- Asides the usual manual controls like shutter speed, ISO and white balance, the application also includes advanced features like **RAW capture**, a **live histogram**, an **anti-shake feature**, and the capability to access either camera lens in the iPhone or later version of iPhone such as iPhone 7, iPhone 8, iPhone XS, iPhone XR, iPhone 11 etc.

- In case you're shooting in low light (or with the

telephoto zoom lens, when camera shake is more of a threat) and you don't have a tripod, attempt shooting with the use of the anti-shake mode.

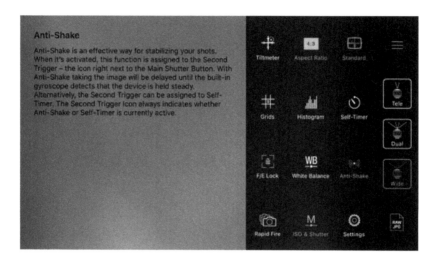

- This mode uses your iPhone's integrated intervalometer to gauge how much the telephone is moving. After that, it waits till you're securing to the camera at a sharp point before it requires a photo. That is a significant-excellent characteristic!

Once you want to modify shutter speed and ISO, you have options. The first option is by using a fully manual setting where you control both *ISO and Shutter Speed*.

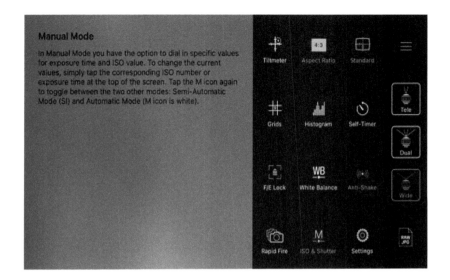

Manual Mode

In Manual Mode you have the option to dial in specific values for exposure time and ISO value. To change the current values, simply tap the corresponding ISO number or exposure time at the top of the screen. Tap the M icon again to toggle between the two other modes: Semi-Automatic Mode (SI) and Automatic Mode (M icon is white).

- The task with manual mode is you need to balance the shutter speed, and ISO settings are to be sure you get the exposure accurate (not too darkish not too shiny). In the event you're not used to the use of the settings, you will get this complicated to get right.

- Therefore, the second choice is to make by using **SI mode**, which enables you to change either the Shutter Speed or the ISO, and the application adjusts the option establishing to calculate the perfect exposure. This setting is exceptional if you're not used to the utilization of manual exposure settings.

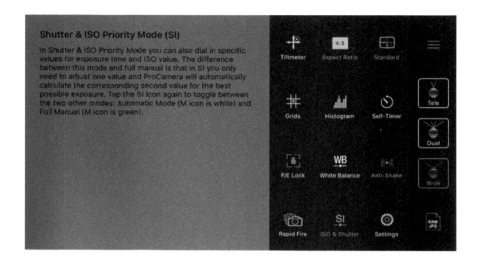

Shutter & ISO Priority Mode (SI)

In Shutter & ISO Priority Mode you can also dial in specific values for exposure time and ISO value. The difference between this mode and full manual is that in SI you only need to adjust one value and ProCamera will automatically calculate the corresponding second value for the best possible exposure. Tap the SI Icon again to toggle between the two other modes: Automatic Mode (M icon is white) and Full Manual (M icon is green).

ProCamera additionally can customize the self-timer for any amount of time as much as 30 seconds, which is very beneficial.

For this image, the iPhone was set on a tripod, then set the timer delay to 20 seconds to provide sufficient time to walk into the shot for the photographer to be seen in the photograph.

- Another great function of the self-timer would be that the flash blinks each second until it requires the picture. It implies you don't need to be surprised at how time has exceeded and set up image has been used. After the blinking halts, you'll know you can get back to the iPhone to have a look at your shot indeed.

Finally, there are a variety of in-app purchases you may make if you want to try their HDR or low-light cameras. You can get from them a free trial to see what they do; however, you'll get a watermark on your picture until you purchase the application, which can make an optional setting available.

Chapter 17

15 Recommended iPhone Applications

Spark: Best Email App for iPhone 7

If you centre on iOS apps, you would understand that email has taken on something similar to the role of the antagonist in the wonderful world of iOS. App designers appear to know that everyone needs a better email platform, and they want an application to resolve their issues. Controlling email is just a little less stressful if you are using *Spark* as you would find features to suit your needs, such as; sending, snoozing email messages, and a good inbox that only notifies you of important email messages.

Below are the things you'd like about this application:

- The app is simple to use and socially friendly.

- Swipe-based interaction allows for one-handed operation.

What You may not like about it:

- No filter systems for automatically sorting email messages.

- The app does not have a way of controlling messages in batches.

Things: *The best "To-do manager" for the iPhone 7*

To-do manager applications are a packed field, and the application called *"Things"* isn't the only good one, and it is also not the only *to-do manager* on this list, but it's a carefully reliable tool, seated between control and hardy. The application provides the ideal levels of both control and hardy, without mind-boggling users to dials and without dropping essential features.

Things you'd like about this application:

- This app has a simplified interface that reduces stress when adding and completing the task.

- Tasks can be added from iOS with the sheet extension.

What you may not like are:

- Repeating tasks and deadlines can be buggy.

- Tasks can't be put into the calendar automatically.

<u>OmniCentre</u>: Best GTD-compatible To-Do App for iPhone 7

Like *"Things,"* **OmniCentre** is a favourite and well-designed to-do manager; however, they have a different group of priorities. Where **Things** attempts to remain simple and straightforward, **OmniCentre** is feature-rich and robust.

The application fully integrates with the **"Getting Things Done"** approach to task management called **GTD**, and this method stimulates users to jot down any duties they have, as well as almost all their associated information and scheduling. GTD users would finish up spending a great deal of time on leading end arranging work; because of this, the software takes a robust feature collection to implement all areas of the GTD process.

Things you'd like about this application:

- Most effective to-do list manager available.

- Can participate in virtually any task management style.

What you may not like:

- Sacrifices simpleness and usability for power and versatility.

Agenda: Best iPhone 7 App for Busy Notice Takers

Agenda requires a different spin on the notes application than almost every other application; its also known as *"date centred notice taking app."* Records are structured by task and day, and the times are a large part of the Agenda. Instead of merely collecting your jotting into a collection, Agenda creates a to-do list from *"things,"* with tight time integration, Agenda makes an operating journaling app and an able to-do manager and general iPhone 7 note-taking app. The day and note mixture seems apparent, but Agenda is the first iOS note-taking application to perform this mixture effectively.

It's a "to-do manager" and also a note-taking application with some calendar features, which enables seeing every information in a single place with one perspective and only one app. The application is also highly practical in the freeform, which may be uncommon in flagship apps. The beauty of the app *"Agenda"* comes out when using Pencil support, but for the present time, we'll have to turn to the iPad Pro for the feature.

Things you'd like about this application:

- Note-taking small tweaks can improve many workflows.

- The time-based organization fits most users; mental types of information organization.

What you may not like:

- Slow app release can limit how quickly you can write down a note.

1Password: Best iPhone 7 App for Security password Management

Using the auto-fill in iOS 13, *1Password* is as near to perfect as we have in a password manager. The Face ID authentication isn't unique to the iPhone 7 alone, but access Face ID makes the application better and simpler to use, which is an uncommon combination of accomplishments to reach concurrently.

Things you'd like about this application:

- Finding and copying usernames and passwords is extremely easy.

- Secure document storage space means *1Password* can gather all of your secure information in a single place.

- Auto-fill support finally makes security password management as easy as typing your security password.

What you may not like:

- No free version.

- The paid version uses membership pricing.

Twitterific: *Best Tweets App For iPhone 7*

Twitter is probably not the most exceptional sociable media system, but it's still one of the very most popular internet sites around, and like many internet sites, Twitter's default application is disappointingly bad.

Unfortunately, Twitter does lately nerf third-party Twitter clients. Third-party applications won't receive real-time stream notifications, significantly reducing the effectiveness of the applications; this move seems to pressure users to go to the native app, but considering its many defects, Twitterific and applications like it remain better.

Things you'd like about this application:

- Improves Twitter's visual demonstration dramatically.

- Includes smart and powerful features that make Twitter simpler to use.

What you may not like:

- Some organizational options are initially unintuitive.

- Twitter has purposefully knee-capped a good number of third-party apps, and Twitterific is no defence to those results.

Overcast: Best iPhone 7 App for Podcasts

Overcast is the best application you may use to hear podcasts. The app's user interface is considered carefully for maximal consumer performance, with features like "Smart Rate" which helps to intelligently manages a podcast's playback speed to shorten silences without accelerating speech, while Tone of voice Boost offers a pre-built EQ curve made to amplify voices, which is ideal for a loud hearing environment.

Things you'd like about this application:

- Thoughtfully designed interface for sorting and hearing podcasts.

- Features like Smart Speed and Queue playlists are invaluable once you're used to them.

- Active developer centred on avoiding an unhealthy user experience concerning monetization.

What you may not like;

- It most definitely doesn't seem to go nicely with the iOS lock screen.

<u>*Apollo*</u>*: Best iPhone 7 App for Reddit*

If you're thinking about *Reddit*, you would want to see the website beyond the third-party app. The application has improved, sure, but it's still kilometres behind third-party offerings.

Apollo is the best of the number as it pertains to Reddit clients, conquering out past champions like "Narwhal." Development is continuous and ongoing, with many improvements from the dev in the app's subreddit.

The swipe-based navigation would continue to work on any iPhone, of course, but it dovetails nicely with the iPhone application switching behaviour. The real black setting is also a delicacy for OLED screens.

Things you'd like about this application:

- Effortlessly handles an enormous variety of media.

- Well developed UI makes navigation easy.

- No ads in virtually any version of the app.

What you may not like:

- Sometimes is suffering from annoying and lingering bugs.

Focos: Best iPhone 7 App for Editing and enhancing Portrait Setting Photos

By default, the iPhone Family portrait Mode is a one-and-done process; you take the picture, and the blur is applied. iOS doesn't give a built-in way for editing and enhancing the Picture Setting effect following the fact. Focos fills the space, creating a tool to tweak both degrees of shadow and the blur face mask. It mimics the result you'd see when modifying a zoom lens' physical aperture. More magically, you can also change the centre point following the shot by recreating the blurred cover up on the different object, or by hand adjusting the result on the image's depth face mask instantly.

Things you'd like about this application:

- The most effective approach to manipulating Portrait Mode's depth-of-field effect.

- The depth map is a distinctive feature to help visualize blur.

What you may not like:

- Simple to make images look over-processed.

- Only about the centre, 50% of the blur range looks natural.

Halide: Best iPhone 7 App for Natural Photos

Distinctively, *Halide* sticks essential info in the iPhone "ear." It embeds a live histogram for image evaluation; could it be precious? Nearly, but Halide is a near-perfect picture taking software besides that offering feature.

The settings are ideally positioned and configured, the RAW catch is pixel-perfect, and navigation within the application is easy and immediately understandable. If you are seriously interested in taking photos on your iPhone 7, *Halide* is the best camera application for iOS.

Things you'd like about this application:

- Low handling power for iPhone photos.

- The broadest toolset of any iOS image editing and enhancing the app.

What you may not like:

- It can overwhelm first-time users using its degree of control.

Euclidean Lands: The Top-rated AR Puzzle Game for iPhone 7

Augmented reality applications haven't yet found their killer use. But AR gambling takes great benefit from lots of the iPhone features.

Euclidean Lands is a short fun puzzler that calls for the full benefit of AR's potential. Similar to Monument Valley, players manipulate the play space to produce new pathways through puzzle designs, guiding their avatar to the finish of the maze. The overall game begins easy; nevertheless, you might be scratching your head just a little by the end.

Things you'd like in this application:

- Challenging and attractive puzzle levels that take benefit of AR's unique features.

What you may not like:

- Disappointingly short.

- The core game auto technician feels very familiar.

Giphy World: **Best AR Messaging App for iPhone 7**

Plenty of applications have tried to usurp Snapchat as an AR messaging system. While Snapchat might maintain a weakened condition because of self-inflicted damage, it isn't eliminated yet. But if it can decrease, Giphy World is a great replacement.

Things you'd like about this application:

- Simple to create fun and funny images from provided assets.

- Content isn't locked inside the Giphy app.

What you may not like:

- Object place and processing speed are inferior compared to Snapchat's.

Jig Space: **Best Usage of AR for Education on iPhone 7**

Learning with holograms is one particular thing you

regularly see in sci-fi movies; with *Jig Space* and ***augmented*** actuality, that kind of thing is now possible in our daily lives. You should use the application to find out about various topics, including what sort of lock works, manipulating every part of the system, and looking at it from alternative perspectives. Jig Space requires the benefit of AR's three sizes effectively, and the low-poly models AR has bound not to harm the grade of the visualizations.

Things you'd like about this application:

- Takes benefit of AR's advantages for a good cause.

- A substantial assortment of "jigs" charges is free.

What you may not like:

- Accompanying captions are occasionally disappointingly shallow.

<u>*Nighttime Sky*</u>*: Best Late-Night Outside Companion App*

Directing out constellations is much more fun if you are

not making them up as you decide to go. *Evening Sky* was the main augmented-reality style application to seem on iOS. It shows just how for others on the system wanting to mimic its success, but it's remained dominant nevertheless.

Things you'd like about this application:

- It enhances the natural world with technology.

- It improves the star-gazing experience for both children and adults.

What you may not like:

- Large image units mean large camera motions are stiff and jerky.

Inkhunter: Most Readily Useful AR Gimmick on iOS

There's something distinctively exotic about checking out new tattoos by yourself. *Inkhunter* uses the energy of augmented truth to generate short-term digital symbols you can construct on the body and screenshot. You should use the built-in adobe flash, pull your designs, or import property from somewhere else to project on your skin.

Things you'd like about this application:

- Fun and book application idea that's useful.

What you may not like:

- Is suffering from AR's existing restrictions in surface matching.

INDEX

CPSIA information can be obtained
at www.ICGtesting.com
Printed in the USA
LVHW080522080222
710483LV00009B/290

Let's Talk About Sex
and Muslim Love

Essays on Intimacy and Romantic Relationships in Islam

~

Umm Zakiyyah

Let's Talk About Sex and Muslim Love: Essays on Intimacy and Romantic Relationships in Islam
By Umm Zakiyyah

ISBN: 978-1-942985-06-8
Library of Congress Control Number: 2016946256

Order information at ummzakiyyah.com/store

Verses from Qur'an adapted from Saheeh International, Darussalam, and Yusuf Ali translations.

Published by Al-Walaa Publications
Camp Springs, Maryland USA

Cover photo from Shutterstock © by Anna Omelchenko

TABLE OF CONTENTS

Glossary of Arabic Terms

Alhamdulillah: literally "all praise is for God"

Allah: the Arabic word for "God"

amaanah: a trust and responsibility

Ameen: Amen; stated at the end of a prayer as a means to beg that it be answered

As-salaamu'alaikum: literally "peace be upon you"; the Islamic greeting of peace

ayah: Qur'anic verse or spiritual sign

bi'idhnillaah: "with the help (or permission) of God"

du'aa: informal prayer or supplication to God

du'aat: plural for *daa'ee*, Islamic preacher

dunya: this worldly life (in contrast to the Hereafter)

emaan: faith or Islamic belief

hayaa': a healthy sense of shame or shyness

insha'Allah: God-willing or "if God wills"

Istikhaarah: the prayer made when making a decision

Jannah: Paradise; also referred to as "Heaven" in some translations

khula': marriage dissolution initiated by the wife

khutbah: Friday sermon or formal religious talk before a congregation

kufr: disbelief in Islam

maashaAllah: literally "it was God's will" (also spelled *mashaAllah*)

mahr: dowry or marriage gift given to the woman upon marriage

mahram: a close relative, specifically one to whom marriage is forbidden

masjid: mosque, the Muslim place of worship

nafs: the self

naseehah: sincere Islamic advice

sahih: authentic (also spelled *saheeh*)

sallallaahu'alayhi wa sallam: "peace and blessings be upon him"

Shaytaan: Satan or devil

sihr: often translated as "magic," but more specifically refers to humans formally seeking the aid of jinn for some specified worldly outcome

Sunnah: prophetic guidance and life example

tawakkul: complete trust in God

tawbah: sincere repentance and returning to a life of obedience to God

tawfeeq: spiritual fortitude and lasting, sincere commitment

ummah: world Muslim community

zina: fornication or adultery

Author's Note

*"Faith has more than sixty branches,
and* hayaa' *is a part of faith."*
—Prophet Muhammad, peace be upon him (Bukhari)

~

Sex, intimacy, and love remain taboo topics in many Muslim circles today, even when the discussion is limited to the teachings of the Qur'an and authentic prophetic statements. As such, varying views abound regarding how these subjects should be broached. On one end of the spectrum are Muslims who believe such intimate subjects should not be discussed at all, even in the contexts of marriage and religion, and on the other end are Muslims who unapologetically trespass Islamic bounds in both discussion and practice. Thus, naturally, the concept of *hayaa'* (which is often translated as Islamic modesty) has become both controversial and confusing for practicing Muslims.

This book is a collection of essays and reflections that I have written on the topics of sex, intimacy, marriage, and love amongst Muslims in modern times. These essays include blogs, discussions, and articles published from 2010 through 2016 via onislam.net, muslimmatters.org, saudilife.net, SISTERS Magazine, and ummzakiyyah.com.

As these essays are mainly personal and spiritual reflections based on my and others' experiences as practicing Muslims in today's society, they draw mostly on anecdotal and fictional accounts to illustrate a point or highlight an unfortunate reality. As some pieces are didactic or persuasive in nature, where appropriate, I mention the Islamic point of view along with Qur'anic and prophetic evidences. However, this collection does not represent an exhaustive or scholarly analysis of these sensitive topics in Islam.

My aim is to inspire in Muslims both spiritual and personal reflection in light of modern reality, *bi'idhnillaah.* I also hope to offer a practical religious framework in which to spark healthy, necessary discussions of these topics. Prayerfully, this collection will be of further benefit to those sincerely interested in understanding the Muslim perspective on sexual intimacy and physical attraction.

PART I
Confronting the Taboo

"I'm not sure what we're so afraid of.
Perhaps, because discussing something so intimate
forces us to face what we fear most—ourselves."
—from the journal of Umm Zakiyyah

1
Let's Talk About Sex
Solutions in Confronting the Taboo

~

"In my family," my colleague told me proudly, "we had so much *hayaa'* that my mother and all the girls would come to every prayer, even when we were menstruating. If we couldn't pray, we would get dressed for prayer and sit in the row behind the men so that when our father and brothers finished praying, they would see us sitting there and have no idea that we weren't able to pray because of our menses."

Hayaa' is an Arabic word that is often translated as modesty, but it has the broader meaning of "a respectable sense of shame." In Islam, true *hayaa'* does not involve women being ashamed of their normal bodily functions nor does it involve women putting on pretenses to appease males or to maintain a false image. But unfortunately, in many cultures of predominately Muslim countries, the term has been so misconstrued that not only does it refer almost exclusively to the actions of women, it also defies the guidelines of Islam itself.

Prophet Muhammad (peace be upon him) said, "Faith has more than sixty branches, and *hayaa'* is a part of faith" (Bukhari).

Abandoning False Modesty: We Are All New Muslims

Perhaps, one effective way to overcome the false modesty that is rampant in many Muslim families and communities is for us all to embrace the idea that, on some level, we are all learning about Islam for the first time. Whether we accepted Islam on our own or were born into a Muslim family, living as a Muslim must be a conscious choice. Thus, if Muslims genuinely wish to live according to the guidelines of Islam, we must take time to study the religion for ourselves and filter from our minds and hearts false teachings, whether the falsehood came from anti-Muslim media propaganda or from the sincere efforts of our parents and cultural community who thought they were teaching us Islam.

Talking Sex: Embracing True *Hayaa'*

Sex is likely the most misunderstood subject pertaining to *hayaa'* in Islam. Perhaps the misunderstanding has occurred because by nature sex is such an intimately private act, or perhaps the misunderstanding has occurred because when sex is engaged in outside the marriage bond, personal and social disasters can result, thus making sex one of the most feared and avoided topics in many Muslim communities. However, the one whose very life embodied Islamic *hayaa'* in the most exemplary form, Prophet Muhammad himself, did not fear or avoid this subject. In fact, in an effort to teach the proper understanding of this subject and the Islamic guidelines of physical and spiritual purity, he customarily discussed sex with both men and women, even when both men and women were present.

Concerning men's sexual intimacy with women, Prophet Muhammad (peace be upon him) said, "When a man sits amidst her four parts and then exerts pressure on her, *ghusl* (a ritual bath) becomes obligatory upon him" (Bukhari and Muslim). Also, the Companions of the Prophet customarily asked about this subject, as in the famous narration when Umar ibn Khattab asked the Prophet about entering a woman from behind (through her vaginal area), and Allah revealed a verse on the subject (Sunan Al-Tirmidhi, 2980).

Additionally, the female Companions also asked the Prophet about this subject. The female Companion Umm Sulaym said, "O Messenger of Allah, surely, Allah is not shy of the truth. Is it necessary for a woman to take a ritual bath after she has a wet dream?" The Messenger of Allah (peace be upon him) replied, "Yes, if she notices a discharge." The female Companion Umm Salama then covered her face and asked, "O Messenger of Allah! Does a woman have a discharge?" He replied: "Yes, let your right hand be in dust, how does the son resemble his mother?" (Bukhari).

If Allah, His Messenger, and the male and female Companions were not shy to discuss truth, even in the subject of sex, why then are we? Do we imagine that our personal and cultural *hayaa'* is greater than their personal and spiritual *hayaa'*?

Glorified Ignorance and the Dangers of False Modesty

"I thought I was dying," my friend told me as she recalled her first menses. "I had no idea what was happening to me." Another friend told me how a family member ran from her husband on wedding night because she had absolutely no idea what he wanted from her and why he was removing his clothes. One of my female teenage students asked me, "Why do some girls sit outside the prayer area when it's time to pray? And what are pads for? What do you do with them?" And this student already had the physical signs of puberty, which means she could start menstruating literally at any moment.

Though some of us might find these incidents "cute" or funny, the truth is that they represent a very dangerous trend of "glorified ignorance" in some Muslim communities. The glorified ignorance trend defines modesty as an exclusively female trait, and the more ignorant a woman is about her body and sexuality, the more revered and "evident" her modesty is. However, men are expected to be anything but modest, often to the extent that they are expected and even encouraged to blatantly disobey Allah's command to come not even close to *zina* (fornication or adultery).

What has resulted is cultures of controlled, subjugated, and oppressed women, where the honor of the family or tribe rests with the "glorified ignorance" and asexuality of the women adhering to cultural codes of modesty. But even in members of these cultures who have immigrated to the West and sought to abandon misogynistic definitions of honor and modesty, the negative effects of culturally reinforced false modesty continue to disrupt marriages.

Often, both men and women remain sexually unsatisfied because while a woman's ignorance of her body and sexuality might be sexually arousing to some men on wedding night, this glorified ignorance gets old and tiresome over time, especially for those who wish to stay within the limits set by Allah and derive sexual satisfaction from only their spouse. Tragically, the women themselves suffer psychologically, as many feel ashamed of their sexual desires and view it as "inappropriate" to speak about what arouses them or to initiate any sexual contact.

Unmarried girls (and sometimes boys) from cultures that glorify ignorance often pray while they are in *janaabah* (a state of ritual impurity) because when they have a wet dream, they have no idea they need to make *ghusl* before praying. Many of them do not even know what sexual ejaculation or orgasms are. And naturally, if a young married woman from a culture of glorified ignorance has no idea about sex on her wedding night, it is only natural that, after her husband enters her, she won't know that she has to take a ritual bath before praying again.

Moreover, some Muslim girls are shunning Islamic relationships altogether in favor of the "less judgmental" non-Muslim culture of male-female interaction. "I would rather deal with non-Muslim guys," a teenage girl told me. "At least with them, I won't feel judged for what I think or feel."

There Is No "The Talk"

"Did you have 'the talk' with your teenagers yet?" is a common question non-Muslim parents ask in the West in reference to sitting down and having a serious conversation with young adult children about sex, birth control, and male-female relationships. The implication is that talking to our children about sexual intimacy is a "one shot deal." Here, we muster up the courage to finally sit our children down to hear us pour our hearts out about anything and everything related to sex, and then afterwards we sigh relief that it's all over so we can go back to sleep—literally and figuratively.

However, true sex education does not work like this. And incidentally, the Western culture of "the talk" isn't much different from the culture of glorified ignorance and false modesty. Both assume sex to be a shameful topic to be avoided if at all possible; thus, both potentially result in sexual irresponsibility and dangerous ignorance in young adults.

So no, there is no "the talk." Like any part of life, the topic of sex must be addressed on multiple occasions and in many different discussions. It's almost never a "one shot deal."

Sex Is a Part of Life

If we are to get beyond the taboos we've imposed on ourselves and our children regarding the topic of sex, we must accept and embrace the reality that sex is a natural part of life. We can achieve this by first acknowledging our own psychological and cultural barriers on the subject, whether we are indigenous Westerners who have accepted Islam or adults from predominately Muslim countries who have been practicing Islam for generations.

Steps to Confronting the Taboo

1. **As with any challenge in life, the first step to overcoming our internal hurdles regarding the topic of sex is to supplicate to the Creator and ask His assistance.** Many of us have never considered mentioning the topic of sex to Allah Himself, but this is part of the problem. If we cannot raise our hands to the Creator and ask His help in understanding this part of His creation, how do we imagine we will be able to help ourselves? As the female Companion Umm Sulaym said, Allah is not shy of the truth. So let's ask His help in understanding this truth and in embracing the proper way to overcome our false modesty.

2. **After supplicating to Allah for help, we should seek both worldly and religious knowledge on the topic.** Fortunately, in both secular and authentic religious contexts, there are many

books, articles, and lectures on the topic. As we learn, we can share the information with our children and have discussions about what we are learning.

3. **Ask questions, questions, and more questions.** In overcoming this taboo, we cannot be shy to ask questions when necessary, and we cannot be shy to ask our children questions regarding what they already know and think about the subject, especially given that the topic of sex is not at all taboo in many teenage circles—in the West and in predominately Muslim countries.

4. **Admit your shortcomings.** While it's not okay to glorify ignorance about sex, it *is* okay to not know everything. So when you or your children stumble upon something you are not familiar with, then go to trustworthy sources to find the answers.

5. **And finally, don't let go of your natural *hayaa'*.** Having a sense of shame is necessary, as *hayaa'* is part of our faith. With sex, we have *hayaa'* by discussing things in a proper context and decent manner so that both we and our children continue to have healthy shyness and discretion in our personal and religious lives. As with everything in Islam, maintaining a balance is most important. We do not avoid the topic of sex altogether, and we do not indulge in it unnecessarily; Islamic *hayaa'* is somewhere in between.

In this way, we won't feel unnecessary shame or false modesty when someone suggests, "Let's talk about sex."

This essay was first published via onislam.net

2
"Good Muslims Don't Think About Sex"
Part 1

~

"You won't believe what just happened," the assistant teacher said as she entered the staff room of the Muslim school where I worked. She was elder to me and had immigrated to America from a predominantly Muslim country.

The other teachers and I smiled knowingly as we looked toward her. We had grown accustomed to the comical stories that happened daily between teachers and students, especially in the elementary section.

"The teacher asked the second-grade girls what they want to be when they grow up," she continued as she pulled out a chair and sat down at the table where we were sitting. "And one-by-one, each girl talked about what she wanted to be."

We chuckled, anticipating that one of the students had said something the teacher hadn't expected.

"Some girls said, 'I want to be a doctor when I grow up,'" she said, mimicking the child-like voice of the students. "Some said, 'I want to be a nurse,' and one girl said, 'I want to be a firefighter.'"

We laughed heartily at that one, as it was not customary for a Muslim girl to dream of such a career.

"And then one girl said the strangest thing," the assistant teacher said. We grew quiet, light smiles on our faces as we awaited the punch line to the story. She twisted her face and raised her voice slightly to underscore the oddity of the girl's statement: "'When I grow up,'" she mocked, "'I want to be a mommy.'"

There was laughter from me and other teachers. "Aww, *maashaAllah*[1]," I said, still smiling. "That's so cute." Other teachers nodded in agreement and shared the same sentiment.

"Cute?" the assistant teacher repeated as she glared at me, her eyebrows furrowed in disapproval. The darkness of her expression quieted me, as it did the others, and we looked at her in confusion.

My smile faded as I met the woman's gaze and searched my mind for what I had said wrong. "Yes," I said tentatively, thinking perhaps the

---

[1] Literally "It was what God willed," often said in pleasure or admiration of something.

12

assistant teacher had misunderstood me. "That's really cute that she wants to be like her mother."

"No," the woman disagreed, her face contorted at she looked pointedly at me. "That's not cute. That's *disgusting.*"

Silence fell over the staff room at the intensity of her last word. Even those who were not participating in the conversation stopped their own discussions to turn toward us.

"If she wants to be a mommy when she grows up," she said, disgust still in her voice, "all she'll do every day is think about sex."

Americans Have No *Hayaa'*?

Though it has been nearly ten years since the discussion, I remember the conversation in the staff room as if it were yesterday. I remember how no matter how much I, as well as others, tried to explain to the woman that the little girl's dream had nothing at all to do with sex, the woman was persistent: the poor little girl had been so corrupted by "American thinking" that her only dreams for the future lay in fantasizing about sex day after day until she could bring it into fruition by becoming a mother in real life.

At the time, I was speechless in shock. Did this woman really imagine that a seven-year-old girl's desire to be a mother came from anything other than a pure, innocent admiration of the girl's own mother?

"Well," the assistant teacher had said to me in frustration at the end of the conversation, "either you have *hayaa'* [modesty or a sense of shame] or you don't."

I stared at her in disbelief. Was she saying what I thought she was?

"And if you don't have *hayaa'*," she said, "there's no way for you to understand where I'm coming from."

My mouth fell open, and even some of the teachers from the woman's home country spoke up in disagreement with her.

The assistant teacher shrugged smugly. "That's the problem with Americans. They don't have *hayaa'*."

"You can't say that," some teachers protested, shaking their heads emphatically in disagreement.

"Oh really?" the woman said, her voice suggesting that she would prove to all of us that Americans had absolutely no modesty or sense of shame.

"There was one American woman who was Muslim," the assistant teacher said, "and when she was pregnant, she actually told her children!"

Some of us laughed at the ridiculousness of the assistant teacher's perspective.

"And do you know what she did?" the assistant teacher asked, her tone suggesting that this would surely make us understand. "She let her child touch her stomach and feel the baby moving."

Silence fell over the staff room. Was this woman serious?

"And what's wrong with that?" I asked.

"Because now the child is going to be thinking about her parents having sex!"

Let's Not Talk About Sex

I left the staff room that day in a daze. I could not fathom what cultural and personal experiences could lead a person to obsess about staying away from the topic of sex so much that she saw it in places where it wasn't…and then imagined that her phobia of sex was actually an indication of a high level of modesty and Islamic spirituality.

"I'm an indigenous American," I told the woman that day, "and most of my extended family are Christians. I went to public school and heard and saw many inappropriate things," I said. "But I'm telling you, I've never in my life heard of an American thinking that a little girl wanting to be a mother or parents telling their child they're expecting a baby has anything at all to do with sex."

I shook my head. "If anything," I said, "it shows how *your* culture obsesses about sex."

Who Thinks of Such Things?

I wish I could say that the conversation with the assistant teacher was the last time I heard Islamic modesty connected with avoiding the topic of sex at all costs. But it wasn't. Time after time I continued to hear about "let's not talk about sex" so much that I felt as if I'd never heard sex talked about as much as I had from the "anti-sex" Muslim circles. In Islamic classes, in fatwas, in discussions of women's dress—you name it—these Muslims couldn't get enough of discussing how to not think about sex, which of course meant that they thought about it more than the average person.

I myself have left certain Muslim classes and religious gatherings to protect myself from the corruption I feared I would suffer if I remained around such immodest, inappropriate thinking in the name of Islamic modesty.

14

"My goodness! Who thinks of such things?" I found myself often saying after hearing of yet another way Muslims should dress or carry themselves—that went far beyond what Allah commanded—just to avoid inciting *others* to think about sex.

How Did We Come To This?

Only Allah knows. But my experiences in different Muslim cultures and communities in America and abroad have given me a glimpse into what might be happening to this *ummah* as it relates to the beautiful blessing that Allah has given the husband and wife in the form of sex and intimacy.

This essay was first published via onislam.net

3
Is Sexual Attraction Sin?
"Good Muslims Don't Think About Sex"
Part 2

~

"As you grow," my father said, "your bodies will start to change."

Listening attentively, my brothers and sisters and I sat on the carpet of the living room opposite our parents. It was just after dawn, and our family was having the morning class that my parents held for us each day after Fajr, the first of the five daily prayers.

"And as your bodies change," he said, "the boys and girls at school will start to look really good to you." There were a few suppressed giggles and shy glances from the younger ones. "And you'll begin to feel different things happening inside of you. And when this happens," my father said, "be thankful to Allah. This means you are healthy and that Allah is preparing your body to enjoy your husband or wife when you get married."

As early as I can remember, this morning class was part of my family's daily routine. My mother would get up early in the morning and come to our rooms to wake me and my brothers and sisters to let us know it was time to pray. Sometimes, if we were feeling lazy or resistant, she would sprinkle water on our faces. Then we would crawl out of bed, often still with our blankets wrapped around us, and we'd drag ourselves to the bathroom for *wudhoo'*, the ritual ablution in preparation for prayer.

After praying Fajr as a family, my father—or occasionally one of the older children—would read something from the Qur'an, and we would each share our reflections on the reading and how it could benefit us practically in our lives, even if we were only four or five years old. Then my father and mother would discuss different topics that they felt would help us with our struggles in public school and with what we'd likely face later in life.

Though we didn't quite grasp it at the time, today's topic was sex and marriage. My father and mother talked to us about how the physical desires we felt for the opposite sex were not only natural and healthy, but blessings for which to be grateful to Allah. They told us that there was nothing wrong or shameful in these desires or feelings—even if we were attracted to someone who was not permissible for us at the time—because physical desires themselves are not sinful, they said. It was only a question of how you responded to them that determined right or wrong.

"You Have No Right to Mention Marriage"

I think my first genuine culture shock regarding how many Muslims view sex and marriage came when I was, for the first time, part of a Muslim community that was made up primarily of people who had immigrated to America from predominantly Muslim countries. Previously, most of my interactions on a community level had been with fellow indigenous Americans. But now, as a full-time teacher in a Muslim school in a culturally diverse community, I was to learn that not all Muslims viewed sex and intimacy as my parents had taught me—or even how Islam teaches.

"I don't agree with what you're teaching the girls," an angry mother, who also happened to be a teacher herself (albeit of a much younger group than my middle school class), said to me as she stopped me in the hall one day.

I creased my forehead in confusion. "What do you mean?"

"The books you're making them read," she said. "They're completely inappropriate."

I had to suppress laughter I was so shocked at the ridiculous of her accusation, not because I didn't agree with her, but because I wasn't "making" the students read anything. The state's education department had certain requirements for accredited schools, and the county curriculum that the Muslim school was using provided us with a list of "required reading" to choose from—and I, with the help of an administrator, had gone through the list and chose the books that, to the best of our determination, contained the least amount of inappropriate material. And the book we'd settled on for that month was the classic *Little Women* by Louisa May Alcott.

I explained this to the mother as best I could, and I told her that the way I customarily dealt with any inappropriate content in the curriculum was to include in my lesson the proper Islamic perspective on the issue— and if any discussion of physical attraction or love occurred in the books, I told her, I would simply explain to the students that though these feelings are natural and healthy, they are to be expressed fully only in marriage.

"You have no right to mention marriage to them," she said.

What? I think my confused expression said what I could not.

"In *my* country, we don't know anything about these things," she said as if in reprimand. "When I got married, I knew nothing, I mean

17

absolutely nothing." She smiled slightly. "And my husband liked that. He had to teach me everything."

I began to feel a bit uncomfortable with the conversation shift, but I tried not to show it.

"So it's not right to discuss these things," she said.

"Ever?" I said, genuinely surprised that a Muslim parent would purposefully avoid discussing the topic of physical attraction and marriage with her young adult children.

"Ever," she said with finality.

"But…" I said, hoping to keep my voice as respectful as possible. "What about what Allah says about intimacy and marriage in the Qur'an, or what the Prophet, *sallallahu'alayhi wa sallam*, said about it in hadith? Are we supposed to skip the verses and hadith on this topic?"

"We don't have to discuss these things," she said. "They can read the Qur'an, but we don't have to explain everything to them."

Is Sexual Attraction Sin?

It took repeated experiences like the ones I discussed here and in Part 1 ("Good Muslims Don't Think About Sex"), before I had this epiphany: *Many Muslims think sexual attraction itself is sinful.* Thus, these Muslims equate avoiding the topics of sex and marriage with being spiritually "pure" and "righteous." However, in practical reality, this approach translates into multitudes of Muslim youth being thrust into utter confusion, shame, and dismay when they reach puberty and have feelings and desires that they can make absolutely no sense of…
Except that their desires and stimulating dreams are eerily similar to all the "*haraam* (religiously forbidden)" videos, television shows, and movies that "good Muslims" don't watch.

Sexual Ignorance Is Not Righteousness

If we wish to raise our children as truly "good Muslims", we can start by treating them, especially our young adults, like we ask them to treat us: respectfully. And respect begins with looking at them as we should view all human beings: as individuals who are ultimately responsible for their *own* bodies and souls—and for whom our duty is primarily to convey Allah's Message—in full.

Allah says,

"O Messenger! Proclaim [the Message] which has been sent down to you from your Lord. And if you do not, then you have not conveyed His Message…"
—*Al-Maa'idah* (5:67)

If this is Allah's command to the Prophet, our example, why then do we think our responsibility is different as it relates to what the Message teaches us about physical desires, sex, and marriage? Yes, these topics can inspire discomfort and awkward questions. But we cannot allow our personal and cultural misgivings to keep us from loving and respecting our children as Allah instructed us to.

So let's give our children the opportunity to practice Islam with proper knowledge and righteousness, particularly as it relates to their natural sexual desires that make them healthy young adults being prepared for the blessing and joy of marital intimacy…

Because **good Muslims *do* think about sex**—in the way that Allah has taught them to.

This essay was first published via onislam.net

4
Muslim Girls Don't Want Sex?

~

"Then She Slapped Me"

"I remember when I was watching television as a child," my friend told me, "and there was a wedding on TV, and I got excited so I pointed to the screen and said, 'Look, Mommy! They're getting married.' Then she slapped me."

In my friend's culture, sex is such a taboo subject that even the mention of marriage is frowned upon, especially amongst women.

"So it's unthinkable to say you *want* to get married," she said, bitter sarcasm traceable in her tone. "In my country, a good girl *never* wants marriage."

My friend, the daughter of Muslim immigrants to America, shook her head, clearly perplexed by a culture she was connected to by blood but so far removed from in her heart and mind that she had difficulty reconciling that it had anything to do with her. "It's sad," she said. "It's really sad."

Asexual "Good" Muslims

Many Muslims would view my friend's culture as "backwards" and "un-Islamic" with regards to how it views women and marriage, and I can't say I disagree. But what about our own views of marriage and intimacy when it comes to our daughters and other Muslim youth?

Even in the West, many Muslim parents cringe at the thought of discussing intimacy with their children, especially their daughters—despite these same "children" sitting in front of sensual advertisements, watching sexually suggestive content on television (and in video games), and listening to music that leaves very little to the imagination. What's more is that many of these Muslim youth attend public (or non-Muslim) schools, where the subject of sex is not at all absent from male-female social interaction and where the curriculum regularly includes the topic of sex—and is not limited to heterosexuality.

Unfortunately, the message that many Muslim youth gather from this confusing existence is that in "Muslim culture," being a "good person" means being asexual, not only to the extent that you don't have physical desires, but that you pretend *no one* does—even your own parents who happen to be married with children. Thus, in the minds of many Muslim youth, marriage becomes a perfunctory "duty" that you fulfill "when you grow up," and sexual desire or pleasure plays little to no role in the union.

Double Lives of Muslim Youth

"I may as well have fun now," one Muslim girl said in defense of her sinful life with a non-Muslim boyfriend. "I won't after I get married."

When I ask Muslim youth why they assume they'll have no fun after marriage, many say that their parents don't care about compatible mates for them and that their parents will just marry them off to someone with money and status, even if they aren't even attracted to each other.

"But can't you just say no?" I ask.

"Not really," one young woman said. "Because if you do, it'll cause so many problems in the family that it's not worth it. I already accept that I won't have any say in who I marry, so I don't even think about it."

Not surprisingly, this young woman has chosen the "double life" culture that adheres to the asexual "good Muslim" culture at home, and the open intermingling outside the home (which includes having a secret boyfriend she hopes her parents never learn about).

We Don't Need Marriage Anymore?

"Today, we don't have to worry about widows and divorced women getting married," the woman told me. "They have job opportunities and a social welfare system to take care of them." The woman had been married for more than twenty years and lived a comfortable life as a homemaker to a man she loved dearly. "Polygamy was for the past, when there weren't any options for single women," she said. "Now we don't need it anymore."

When I hear statements like these, as I do often, I wonder what the woman would think if her husband announced that he would spend no more time with her (emotionally or intimately) and that he would only send her money and make sure her bills were paid. "Today, we don't have to worry about making our wives happy," he could say. "They have television and internet to entertain themselves. Marital intimacy was for the past, when there weren't any other options for married women," he could argue. "Now we don't need it anymore."

Our Needs Are Less Than Animals'?

It is quite astounding to hear arguments about why youth and divorced women should pursue fulfillment in matters other than marriage—as if satisfaction in worldly accomplishments is somehow mutually exclusive to a satisfying marital relationship. And ironically, these arguments usually come from men and women who are married themselves. This begs the question, what is *really* going on here?

Do we really imagine that by creating asexual home environments for our daughters and other youth that their natural desires will somehow disappear, and they can now focus on "more important" things? Do we really imagine that by providing only food, clothing, and shelter to widows and divorced women that all their needs in life are met, and they can live locked away from intimate interaction with the opposite sex— forever?

Amazingly, even activists for the rights of *animals* decry such thinking with regards to dogs, cats, and wild beasts. How could a human being, let alone a Muslim, suggest such a lifestyle for a fellow human being— especially when it's a lifestyle they don't accept for themselves?

Muslim Girls Don't Want Sex?

"Boys have needs," parents often say, and the underlying implication is that we should shut our eyes and turn the other way when boys fulfill them (even if they're not married). Perhaps this sort of thinking is why in some religious circles, it is viewed as an urgency to get "eligible" and divorced men married off as soon as possible—while young adult girls and divorced women need only to be "distracted" and provided for.

Not surprisingly, the idea that Muslim girls don't (or shouldn't) have sexual needs of their own is most common in misogynistic societies (and families) where a female is not viewed as a whole human being with individual needs and desires of her own, but as a commodity to be "given away" when an eligible man wants "something" to fulfill his needs. And if no eligible man requires the girl's "services," then she has no "need" to get married.

As I advise and talk to Muslim youth and divorced women struggling in cultural mindsets like these (even in America), my heart aches, and I wonder how something as beautiful as marital intimacy has been reduced to something so "unthinkable" that to merely mention the admiration of the bond can risk a girl getting slapped—by the very woman who conceived her as a result of marital intimacy itself.

This essay was first published via onislam.net

22

5
What Would You Do For Love?
Dangers of Youthful Attraction

~

The Dilemma of a Muslim Girl

Had Inaya really spent the entire day at school without hijab?

"You'll need a visitor's pass and a chaperone," Raymond had said to Inaya as she waited in the school hallway for her parents to finish registering her as a student at the American high school. At the time, Inaya was wearing hijab, and the black cloth was wrapped securely around her head, and she imagined that her abaya, the large black outer garment that she wore, looked like an oversized dress.

Inaya lifted her eyebrows. "A chaperone?"

He laughed lightly. "I know it sounds like a first date, but it's our school policy for visitors."

Inaya's cheeks grew warm, and she averted her gaze. "I'm sorry... I didn't know. I just..."

"Where are you from?"

"I'm sorry?" Inaya glanced up at the student ambassador, a confused expression on her face.

Raymond smiled, and the long dimples in his cheeks made Inaya think of the singer Usher. "I'm not good at judging ethnicities," he said.

"I'm American," Inaya said. Did her Muslim clothes make her look foreign?

"Do you want to take a look around the school?" he asked.

Inaya grinned, surprised by how comfortable she felt in the male student's presence. "I thought I needed a chaperone for that."

A smile spread on his face. "I could be your chaperone."

Inaya was silent as she rode in the back of the car after her parents finished the registration process. She sunk low into her seat until the car was far from the school. She couldn't shake the feeling of shame right then. Her mother and stepfather looked like extremists. She couldn't imagine what Raymond thought of her stepfather's obvious Arab appearance and large beard—and her mother's all black Saudi-style abaya and face veil. A wave of embarrassment passed through Inaya as she wondered what Raymond must think of her. *Ugh.* Why did he have to be standing in the hall when her parents walked out of the office?

What Will She Sacrifice for Love?

Unfortunately, the internal struggle faced by the fictional character Inaya in my novel *Muslim Girl* is not uncommon for Muslim youth, especially for those who attend co-ed, predominately non-Muslim schools. Beyond the Islamophobic sociopolitical contexts in which many of these youth are forced to live, these Muslim youth face the same struggles of any hormonal teen. Girls are attracted to boys. Boys are attracted to girls. And this physical attraction does not discriminate based on one's ethnicity, color, or even religious affiliation.

Clearly, a natural physical attraction is brewing between Inaya and Raymond, a Muslim girl and a Christian boy. But for Inaya, her struggle goes beyond mere "butterflies" fluttering within. And it even goes beyond the natural insecurity that physical attraction ignites when someone is unsure if the attraction is mutual. Rather, Inaya's struggle strikes at the very core of her identity: her spirituality and "Muslim-ness."

Will the boy even find Inaya attractive as a Muslim girl in hijab? This is the question Inaya is essentially asking herself. Regardless of the answer to this question, Inaya is in a spiritual crisis. If Raymond does in fact find her attractive in hijab, she would be compromising her religious obligations if she responds to his advances. If he does not find her attractive in hijab, she would be compromising her religious obligations if she removes her Islamic garb.

Unfortunately for Inaya, she ultimately decides to remove her hijab to "fit in" and appear more "attractive."

The Real Dilemma

For many Muslim youth who find themselves in predicaments like Inaya's, they ask themselves the same question that Inaya asked: *Will the boy (or girl) like me as a Muslim?* To the youth struggling with this situation, their dilemma appears to stem from the answer to this question. However, they do not realize that their real dilemma is the question itself.

Once a Muslim teen reaches the point that he or she is seriously asking himself or herself this question, spiritual crisis almost certainly awaits. This is because, for the Muslim, the real struggle lies in avoiding the question, not in answering it.

While it's natural to feel attracted to the opposite sex (regardless of a person's religious affiliation), Islam has placed definite limits on acting on this attraction; and marriage is the only permissible context for actively expressing this attraction, emotionally or intimately. But in the case of a Muslim woman and a non-Muslim man, not even marriage itself solves their dilemma. This is because they are not ever permitted to be married to each other—unless the man accepts Islam.

Nevertheless, in social contexts like American public school, marriage is hardly on the mind of either the boy or girl feeling physical attraction. In fact, it is often part of the "excitement" that no serious commitment is attached to acting on this "innocent" affection, hence the infamous culture of "boyfriends" and "girlfriends." In Western cultural contexts, the seemingly innocuous titles of *boyfriend* and *girlfriend* actually allude to a commitment to engage in *zina* (illicit sex) with a specific person on a regular basis.

Oblivious Muslim Parents and Dangerous "Puppy Love"

As I discuss briefly in my post "Muslims Don't Fall in Love Before Marriage," adults often make light of youth's feelings of attraction, hence the common term *puppy love*. Unfortunately, what is called "puppy love" is a lot more serious than the terminology suggests. Therefore, making fun of the very real feelings of young adult children does nothing help these youth work through these feelings and understand what they're feeling and why they're feeling it.

For Muslim parents, the scenario is often much worse because many have not reached the point where they are able to even openly acknowledge their children's feelings of physical attraction, let alone make fun of these feelings. Many Muslim parents are voluntarily oblivious to what their young adult children are going through, and these parents behave as if the mere discussion of physical attraction or sex is sinful, even in the context of marriage "one day."

Naturally, this attitude makes the discussion of working through physical attraction toward the opposite sex in the context of school or other social environments unthinkable. Thus, what results are increased spiritual crisis amongst Muslim youth (as we see in the struggle of Inaya) and increased illicit relationships between not only Muslims and non-Muslims, but between Muslim boys and girls themselves.

Ironically, many of these sinful relationships could be avoided if these Muslim youth felt comfortable talking to their parents or other trusted adults about their feelings before the attraction reached the point of physical intimacy. I myself have witnessed the almost phenomenal effect of simply letting Muslim girls and boys know that what they're feeling is completely natural and that the feeling itself is neither sinful nor something to be ashamed of. At times, the youth's ability to merely come to terms with the natural struggle of physical attraction, which in itself is not necessarily indicative of any "special connection" or fated partnership, resolves the dilemma before it even becomes a problem.

It's Not Always That Easy

As an American Muslim girl who went to public school throughout my youth, I myself often worked through the natural struggle of physical attraction to non-Muslim (and Muslim) classmates. Undoubtedly, after the mercy of Allah, my "saving grace" that protected me from falling into the sin of *zina* was my ability to be open with myself psychologically and spiritually about the completely natural feelings that I was experiencing, without feeling sinful or ashamed about what I was going through (an ability I am certainly indebted to my parents for).

However, it's not always that easy. And this is where both Muslim parents (or trusted Muslim elders) and Muslim youth need to be very honest with themselves and each other when giving and seeking advice. Every case of physical attraction is not merely "puppy love," which youth can presumably mentally work through by merely accepting the natural feelings of physical attraction that they're experiencing.

While it is true that the intensity of physical attraction outside the context of marriage is often fueled by *Shaytaan*, this knowledge alone does not necessarily solve the dilemma. Moreover, even heeding the oft-repeated religious advice to "simply" pray and read Qur'an does not remove the problem altogether though prayer and recitation of the Qur'an are certainly helpful in weathering the storm of emotions and desires.

In the most serious cases of youthful attraction, intense physical attraction is coupled with deep affection that has penetrated the hearts of both the girl and the boy, thus culminating into what is for all intents and purposes "falling in love."

When the mutual attraction reaches the level of what feels like genuine love, staying away from sin is not so easy, and the youth often find themselves seriously pondering the question, "What are you willing to sacrifice for love?"

Fortunately, for some Muslim youth, their answer is resoundingly, "Nothing, if it compromises my soul." However, as we can see in the case of Inaya's attraction to the student Raymond, in far too many cases, the concept of protecting one's soul becomes blurred until some youth decide that it is some aspects of Islam itself that must be sacrificed in answering this question.

26

This is when we begin to see manifestations of the very real spiritual dangers of youthful attraction. Thus, this is also where parents and trusted adults need to put aside their misgivings about the topics of physical attraction and "young love" and become more vigilant, understanding, and available to youth who are genuinely trying to save their souls from sinful demise.

This essay was first published via onislam.net

6
He Distracts Her From Allah
When Love and Worship Collide

~

From the Journal of Renee

I returned from the masjid to my college dormitory room late Saturday night, shaken and moved. I glanced at the clock. It was three minutes after ten. Where had the time gone? I slowly shut my eyes, hoping to digest everything better that way. I let the events of the afternoon, evening, and night wash over me. I hoped to analyze my reason for unrest as I had earlier concerning my faith.

It was Yusuf's poem, I concluded, that affected me most. As I recalled his monologue, I felt a storm of emotions that I couldn't give name to. I could think only of the lyrics to a song I'd heard Courtney playing over and over when my parents weren't home.

> I felt all flushed with fever, embarrassed by the crowd
> I felt he found my letters, and read each one aloud
> I prayed that he would finish, but he just kept right on
> Strumming my pain with his fingers
> Singing my life with his words
> Killing me softly with his song

Years later, I learned that these were the words to the song "Killing Me Softly" that I heard Lauryn Hill singing from my sister's stereo, though I have no idea who wrote these words originally. But, at that moment, it didn't matter. And I didn't care.

All I knew was that these were the only words that could give name to the emotions I had felt as the young man I'd met at the "Ask About Islam" table stood on a portable stage in the basement of a local masjid. I couldn't remember his name—they had said it when they introduced him.

Naturally, he had not been the only performer. But he was the only one I remembered so vividly.

Weeks later, when I attended another Muslim event with my friend Sumayyah, I was pleasantly surprised to learn that Yusuf was one of the performers. When the time for his performance grew near, I was taken aback by how packed the seats became all of a sudden. I was impressed.

Apparently, he was well known in the area. I was grateful to Sumayyah for reserving our seats early on.

I was speechless by the time Yusuf finally stepped onto the stage. I barely noticed the three men seated at the rear of the platform, the one in the middle holding a small drum. But after Yusuf reached the microphone, their voices resonated in a harmonizing tenor above the gentle beating on the drum, reminding me of native music from South Africa. Yusuf wore a long white thowb that lifted and clung to him slightly with the wind, revealing his athletic form beneath the thin fabric.

I was offended that Sumayyah thought I wanted to marry him. That was the furthest thing from my mind. I only wanted to talk to him on the phone and get to know him better. But I couldn't escape the stinging pain I felt in my heart upon realizing I didn't even stand a chance at attracting his attentions.

The Reality of Submitting to Allah

The reality is that, as we strive to submit to Allah, there will always be other distractions, especially from the opposite sex, as we can see in the case of Renee in the excerpt from my novel *Realities of Submission*. Clearly, Renee's trips to the masjid and Muslim events become so meaningful to her largely because she has the opportunity to see Yusuf and enjoy his presence.

However, what is dangerous about Renee's fascination with Yusuf is that she does not necessarily want to marry him, and even the suggestion of marriage offends her. She openly admits that she wishes only to talk to him on the phone and "get to know him better."

Unfortunately, Renee's mindset reflects that of many Muslim youth in today's world. For too many of them, the masjid represents less a place to draw closer to Allah and more a place to draw closer to the young man or woman who has captured their affections.

A scholar was once asked, "Why do we get so easily distracted by the life of this world when we know it is worth very little in comparison to the Hereafter?" The scholar responded, "Because the life of this world is in front of us."

And Yusuf was in front of Renee, as the opposite sex is in front of Muslim youth.

It is easy to scoff at youth like Renee, who appear to be doing something sacrilegious when they go to the masjid or a Muslim event looking forward to seeing someone they are attracted to. Some Muslims might even proclaim that it is better for them to stay home than to come to places of Allah's remembrance with impure intentions.

However, we should hesitate before passing judgment, lest we discourage Muslim youth from coming around Muslims at all. Excitement to see the opposite sex, especially in one's teens when hormones are raging, is completely normal, and this excitement doesn't "magically" disappear when we enter the house of Allah or attend an Islamic lecture. Our humanity follows us wherever we go, even in the privacy of our homes and even during overt acts of worship like prayer and supplication to Allah.

Staying away from places of worship and activities where one is likely to be reminded of Allah cannot possibly solve any problem, let alone a problem that is inherently spiritual. If anything, staying away from places of where Allah's name is mentioned will only worsen the problem. Thus, the only solution is for the young man or woman to continuously strive against impure intentions, especially when they enter the house of Allah.

We do not stand before Allah because we are already pure. We stand before Allah because we hope to be purified.

This is the lesson we need to teach Muslim youth who, like Renee, are struggling with natural raging hormones and attraction to the opposite sex. And this lesson is all the more important for the youth to inculcate into their practical lives as they enter the blessed month of Ramadan, a time for seeking Allah's forgiveness, His mercy, and salvation from the Fire.

When Worship and Love Collide

One fact of life that both Muslim youth and adults need to understand is that our worship and human weakness will constantly collide and be at odds with each other during our time on earth. We cannot remove this reality from our lives any more than we can avoid ultimately standing in front of Allah on the Day of Judgment. This is all part of Allah's *qadr*, His divine decree for us.

Our job then is to face these tests by turning to Allah and constantly striving against succumbing to our lower desires. However, when we do fall short and sin, it is crucial that we understand, in the depths of our hearts, that Allah is All-Forgiving and Most Merciful to those who continuously engage in *jihad al-nafs*, the internal battle of the self against the self.

Thus, when youth like Renee find that an attractive boy or girl distracts them from Allah, they should know that all hope is not lost, even if they at times give into human weakness. They should continue to come to the masjid. They should continue to come to Muslim events. And they should continue having hope in Allah's mercy and forgiveness.

Because, when love and worship collide, staying away from the masjid and other places of Allah's remembrance cannot protect us from facing ourselves, and more importantly, it cannot protect us from facing Allah.

This essay was first published via onislam.net

7
Righteous People Don't Have Desires?

~

I remember when I first read the story of the marriage of Prophet Muhammad, peace be upon him, to Zaynab bint Jahsh, the divorced wife of his adopted son Zaid ibn Haritha, may Allah be pleased with them. Although I was relatively young when I happened upon this story, I was deeply moved. I remember thinking how beautiful it was that the Prophet was able to put Allah before anything else, even in his inclination to marry Zaynab bint Jahsh.

It wasn't until years later that I realized that the account that I had read of Prophet Muhammad and Zaynab (which reported that the Prophet felt a personal inclination to marry Zaynab after Zaid divorced her) was disputed amongst Muslim scholars regarding its authenticity. The scholars explained that because the marriage of the Prophet to Zaynab was a command from Allah, it is incorrect to assert that the Prophet had any feelings for Zaynab whatsoever prior to marriage. Some scholars even stated that this version of the story was fabricated by non-Muslim orientalists who wished to destroy the honor and integrity of the Prophet by attributing to him any physical attraction to Zaynab.

"It is blasphemous to accuse the Prophet of desiring Zaynab!" they said. "He was just worried about what people would think if he married the divorced wife of his adopted son because that was against Arab custom."

Yes, undoubtedly, the Prophet's marriage to Zaynab was a command from Allah to clarify that adopted sons should not be viewed as blood sons regarding the impermissibility of marrying a son's former wife. Thus, naturally, due to Arab custom regarding adopted sons, the Prophet was concerned about how people would view the marriage.

But I remember being utterly confused. I couldn't fathom why it would be considered blasphemy to believe that the Prophet was attracted to Zaynab after Zaid divorced her. And why was obeying the command of Allah mutually exclusive to natural human attraction?

It appeared to me that the underlying issue was that the alleged blasphemy was in believing that prophets experienced physical attraction or desire prior to marriage, and this baffled me.
Is Desire Unbecoming of Prophets?

Allah says to Prophet Muhammad, peace be upon him:

"Not lawful to you, [O Muhammad], are [any additional] women after [this], nor [is it] for you to exchange them for [other] wives, even if their beauty were to please you…"
—Al-Ahzaab (33:52)

Furthermore, regarding the famous story of Prophet Yusuf and the plot of the women, Allah says:

"He said, 'My Lord, prison is more to my liking than that to which they invite me. And if You do not avert from me their plan, I might incline toward them and [thus] be of the ignorant.'"
*—*Yusuf (12:33)

If desire itself is unbecoming of prophets, why did Allah mention to the Prophet that the prohibition on marrying more wives remains "even if their beauty were to please you"? Furthermore, what then was the severe struggle that Prophet Yusuf is referring to that inspired him to desire prison lest he fall victim to it—and that he feared he might incline toward?

True Honor Is in Overcoming Difficulty, Not in Never Facing It

By removing even the possibility of natural human desire from prophets' existence, we have inadvertently lowered their status while raising ours to a level higher than theirs. After all, it is well known that the one who must overcome difficulty is of a much higher status than the one who does not experience it in the first place. This is one explanation for why believers will ultimately enjoy a status even higher than angels. We as humans have the option to fall short in obeying Allah; angels don't. Thus, our obedience is more remarkable and praiseworthy in the sight of Allah.

Why then do we remove from prophets the human honor borne of struggle?

The Prophet was once asked, "O Messenger of Allah, which people are tested most severely?" The Messenger of Allah, peace and blessings be upon him, said, "They are the prophets, then the next best, then the next best. A man is tried according to his religion. If he is firm in his religion, then his trials will be more severe, and if he is weak in religion, then he is tried according to his strength in religion. The servant will continue to be tried until he is left walking upon the earth without any sin" (Sunan At-Tirmidhi 2398, graded *sahih* by At-Tirmidhi).

Why then do we view it as "unbecoming" or "blasphemous" for the severe trials of a prophet to include the trial that nearly every man and woman faces on earth, that of being attracted to the opposite sex?

Although it is undeniable that the Prophet, peace be upon him, married Zaynab only in obedience to Allah's command, why is the mere *possibility* of his being attracted to her after the divorce viewed as slanderous or blasphemous? Rather, what would be slanderous or blasphemous is to suggest that a prophet crossed any moral boundaries, married for selfish reasons, or acted *purely* on attraction alone.

Are We Imitating Christians When Defining Righteousness?

Today, many Muslims view physical desire as "sick", filthy, and unbecoming of those who "truly" love Allah. This is possibly why we cannot imagine any righteous person, let alone a prophet, having desires at all.

In a hadith narrated by Bukhari and Muslim, the Prophet, peace be upon him, said, "Surely, you will follow the ways of those nations who came before you, in everything as one arrow resembles another (i.e. just like them), so much so that even if they entered a hole of a sand-lizard, you would enter it." The Companions said, "O Messenger of Allah! Do you mean to say that we will follow the Jews and the Christians?" He replied, "Who else?"

And today, it seems that this lizard hole is our view of physical attraction between men and women.

In the Catholic church, the highest post for a man (that of Pope) is given to one who neither marries nor engages in any sexual intimacy; and the holy women (the nuns) are those who vow celibacy for life, thus shunning any desires, even in the sanctity of marriage.

Yet no such "honor" exists in Islam. In fact, in the Sunnah, this is considered a form of extremism. Why then are we allowing similar beliefs to enter our minds and hearts?

Yes, most Muslims acknowledge that the Prophet had desires *after* marriage, but many view it as slanderous to believe he had attraction *before* marriage—even toward women he proposed to and wanted to marry.

Yet, in the famous account of Juwayriah bint al-Harith first meeting the Prophet, Ayesha is reported to have immediately disliked seeing Juwayriah because she was extremely beautiful, and Ayesha spoke of the Prophet also seeing her: "I knew he would see what I saw [i.e. her beauty]" (Abu Dawud).

Unfortunately, in our zeal to defend the character of the Prophet, we deny his humanity. So many of us wish to believe that his marriages were inspired "purely" by higher goals of freeing slaves, making peace between warring tribes, and eradicating tribalism and racism. And although these higher goals certainly existed, it is odd to view them as mutually exclusive to physical attraction or desire.

When I hear claims like these, I often wonder, "What woman of today would view it as praiseworthy if her husband was not the least bit attracted to her prior to marriage?"

Why then do we find this preferable or "honorable" for the Mothers of Believers?

Our Self-Serving Definitions of Righteousness

In truth, many of our assertions about "righteousness" and the Prophet's alleged lack of physical desire are made for selfish reasons: Often, Muslims today simply wish to deny obvious parts of their faith, namely the permissibility—and possible praiseworthiness—of a man marrying more than one wife. And given that the life of the Prophet, peace be upon him, is in obvious contradiction to this view, we wriggle out of blameworthiness by claiming that the Prophet didn't marry for the reasons other men marry (i.e. due to physical attraction). Thus, any man who is attracted to a woman (especially if he is already married) has committed a "crime," even if it culminates in the honorable institution of marriage as sanctioned by Allah.

Honesty Is True Righteousness

Speaking the truth is something that is an important virtue in all faiths, so it is undeniable that true Islamic righteousness is in being honest—with ourselves and with the world. And a good place to start is concerning the remarkable beauty and mercy in Allah allowing men and women to be physically attracted to each other such that we find immense joy and pleasure in each other after marriage.

And what better reflection of righteousness is there than being grateful for these favors?

This essay was first published via onislam.net

35

8
"But She Looks So Good!"
When Men's Desires Rule

~

Heart racing, Salihah lifted her nine-year-old daughter from the bed and clumsily carried her to the living room. Salihah's legs nearly collapsed under the weight of the sleeping girl, but Salihah didn't have time to wake Noor. They needed to leave—now. Malik would be home any minute, and Salihah wanted to leave before her husband returned.

Outside in the car, Salihah's hand trembled as she buckled Noor's seatbelt. Salihah stepped back to close the door, but the sound of Noor moaning and stirring in her sleep halted Salihah's movements. For a moment, Salihah studied the soft, innocent features of her daughter's face, and tears filled her eyes. *What kind of mother am I? How could I have been so blind to what was happening?*

Salihah sighed as she shut the back door and slid into the driver's seat. Her heart was heavy as she pulled out of the driveway to her home and steered the car into the quiet street. She had no idea where she was going, but she knew she had to get away. She felt terrible that she hadn't left the day Noor told her what Malik had been doing—for more than a year.

"Tell her to wear hijab at home," the imam had advised a distraught and shaken Salihah three weeks after Noor had broken down and told her mother what had happened. "And it's probably best if she doesn't sing or dance in the home anymore."

"Mommy, mommy, watch this!" In the car, tears slipped down Salihah's cheeks as she recalled her daughter's bursting energy two years before. At seven years old Noor was all laughs and giggles as she showed her mother a silly dance routine that she and her friends had thought of. If Noor and her "girl crew" (as Noor called them) were feeling particularly energetic, they'd think of some silly lyrics to sing along to their routine as they showed it off to their mothers.

Salihah clinched her jaw as she recalled how stupid she'd been to think a childhood friend of Malik's could give her "Islamic" advice.

"She's an attractive little girl," the imam had said, an apologetic grin on his face. "That's not an easy situation for men, especially stepfathers."

"Oh Allah, Muslims Too?"

Growing up, I often heard stories about sexual abuse and oppression of women, and I always found them bizarre. Their horrific reality was so far removed from my sheltered existence that I couldn't fathom them beyond the plot of a chilling, fictional drama. But as I got older, I began to see the world around me for what it was: fragile, dangerous, and often terrifying. And I began to realize that the loving, spiritually-rich home that defined my childhood was not what defined that of thousands of other people.

As naïve as it sounds to me today, as a youth, the most incomprehensible reality for me to face was that Muslims were amongst the thousands of sufferers—and oppressors. I know now that this naiveté was born from a deeply rooted concept of Islam that I held in my heart and mind. When I was a child, my parents—through word and deed—instilled in me and my siblings what it meant to be Muslim, and I innocently imagined that all Muslim parents had done the same.

"But You're a *Fitnah* to Men"

Years ago when my family moved from America to Saudi Arabia, I was in the new country only a short time before I experienced one of my first "spiritual culture shocks." Though I was wearing the full, all black, Saudi-style abaya and face veil, I was told I should also cover my eyes.

"If a camel were to wear a face veil, it would be attractive," someone told me, repeating what her husband had told her that a prominent sheikh had said (and apparently what he had told her to tell me so that I would be inspired to be a "better Muslim").

Maybe it was the "American" in me, but when I first heard this, I had to suppress laughter. But I maintained my composure and told her that, as a Muslim, I cover based on the words of Allah and His Messenger, peace be upon him, not based on the words of a man—no matter how "knowledgeable" he was known to be.

"But it's a *fitnah* [a tremendous trial and difficulty] for men," she said. "What if a man sees your eyes and gets attracted to you?"

"The only person I have to protect from *fitnah* is me," I said, hoping she could hear with her heart more than her ears. "And it's a *fitnah* for *me* to carry on my shoulders the burden of men's desires. I fear for my soul if I were to believe that it's my responsibility to make sure men never desire me. My Lord didn't put that burden on me, and I refuse to put it on myself."

They Don't Know Islam

It was after repeated encounters with Muslims who believed that I needed to cover my eyes (and went through great lengths to convince me of my "crime") that I had the epiphany.

For years I had been confounded by incidents of oppression of girls and women (which many predominately Muslim cultures were guilty of). And for the life of me, I couldn't muster even a partial understanding of what led to such madness in people who professed to be Muslims.

They don't have Islam in their lives.

It was something my parents had said repeatedly while I was growing up: *Islam is a way of life, and any Muslim who doesn't understand this—in word and deed—doesn't have Islam in their lives.* "No, I'm not saying they are not Muslim," my father would say. "I'm saying they don't know Islam."

It's Not Your Burden To Bear

Allah says,

"On no soul does Allah place a burden greater than it can bear…"
—Al-Baqarah, 2:286

Yet it is unfortunate that humans place on one another burdens greater than they can bear.

Amongst Muslims, some go as far as to teach something similar to that of the ancient Christian church: that females' very existence is a perpetual curse—and that even Allah's guidelines are not sufficient in protecting them from harming themselves and others.

A girl is sexually abused and is told to wear hijab at home…
A woman obeys Allah and is told she's still in sin….

Why?

"Because she looks so good."

But this twisted thinking comes only from those whose lives have not been graced with the full beauty of Islam. So it is our obligation to share with them Allah's message—and to let them know that it is not men's desires that rule human life in this world. It is the desires of Allah. And the only *fitnah* that should inspire anyone—man or woman—to make changes in life is the *fitnah* of ignoring His desires.

This essay was first published via onislam.net

38

9
Are You in Love?
Understanding Young Love

~

"Muslims don't fall in love before marriage," the woman said proudly. "That's something only non-Muslims do."

When I first heard this statement, I was confused. But maybe I was misunderstanding what the woman meant. Perhaps the woman was just saying that Muslims don't have sex before marriage (or at least that they're not supposed to). Muslims don't live together and "play house" before deciding whether or not to take the "big step" and get married. Perhaps in the mind of this woman, and that of Muslims who shared her sentiment, this was "falling in love" and thus something Muslims simply did not do.

"I love a boy. Can you help me?"

I had just finished teaching a class at a Muslim weekend school when I was approached by a girl who appeared to be about thirteen years old. "Can I talk to you?" she said to me. "I need some advice."

"Sure," I told her, "no problem."

"At school, there's a boy I love," she said, "and I don't know what to do about it." She glanced sideways to make sure none of her peers or elders could hear her talking to me. "Can you help me?"

"How did you meet him?" I asked.

"He goes to my school."

"But how did you meet?"

"He just goes to my school," she said again, slight confusion on her face.

"Yes, I know," I said. "But how do you know him? Do you talk on the phone? Do you meet up at school?"

"No," she said. "I barely know him."

Now it was my turn to be confused. "Are you *trying* to get to know him?"

"No." She appeared taken aback by the question. "I'm Muslim."

"Then what's the problem?" I said.

"I love him, and I know it's wrong," she said. "I tried to stop it, but I can't." She looked desperate as she looked at me. "What should I do?"

39

"Listen," I told her. "It's not a sin to be attracted to boys."

What Love Means

Merriam-Webster Dictionary defines love as "a feeling of strong or constant affection for a person." It also defines love as "attraction that includes sexual desire" and "the strong affection felt by people who have a romantic relationship."

Based on the definition of love, loving a person or "falling in love" can include an intimate relationship (and thus can involve sin if the man and woman are not married), but love itself is not contingent upon any conscious actions on a person's part. In fact, love can be confined to a person's heart without the other person ever knowing anything about it.

Therefore, love outside the bounds of marriage is not necessarily sinful, and it's certainly not sinful to "fall in love" before marriage.

So I'm Not in Sin?

After I told the girl that it isn't sinful to be attracted to boys, the girl's eyes widened. "It's not?"

"No," I said. "It's just the way Allah created us. We can't help it. Girls will be attracted to boys. Boys will be attracted to girls. And after lowering our gazes and staying away from what's wrong, there's nothing we can do about that."

"But I thought…"

"It's what you say or do about this feeling that can make it sinful," I said. "If you just have this feeling in your heart and you don't do anything about it, that's not wrong. But you can pray to Allah to make the feeling go away," I suggested, "especially if it's distracting you from other things."

She looked positively relieved. "Thanks," she said, smiling broadly as she walked away.

Puppy Love

When I was growing up in America, I'd often hear adults laugh whenever an adolescent or teenager was attracted to someone. Their tone was often playfully condescending when they waved their hands dismissively saying, "Oh, that's just puppy love. These kids have no idea what love means."

And perhaps the adults were right. Maybe "kids" really don't have a clue what love means. Maybe what these youth are feeling is just "puppy love," a strong feeling of attraction that would pass with time and about which they would laugh about later.

But even so, this doesn't invalidate the authenticity of the young person's feelings. In fact, they may very well may fit into the definition of "love," even if the love is short-lived and won't amount to much more than an overwhelming sense of desire for someone.

When Young Love Is Real

Often when we think of real stories of young love, we turn to the pages of ancient history or folklore. In the famous Shakespearean drama *Romeo and Juliet*, the character Juliet is reportedly only thirteen years old while Romeo isn't much older. However, in the Shakespearean era, the concept of young lovers was not limited to fiction or drama.

In earlier times, particularly in European (or "Western") history, it was not uncommon for young men and women to fall in love and marry quite young. In fact, if a person was unmarried by the age of twenty, this was frowned upon and the person was feared to be "too old" for any hope for marriage. In Islamic history, the love of young Ayesha toward Prophet Muhammad, peace be upon him, is often cited.

However, it is not only in fictional tales and "days of old" that young love has proven real. In the modern world, there are many true stories of young love, and they continue to happen each day.

Famous Young Love

When I was in high school, one of my favorite songs was "Everybody Plays the Fool" by Aaron Neville, and I often think of this song when I think of young people falling in love. This is not only because the song itself alludes to the foolishness young people often fall into in the name of love, but also because the singer himself experienced young love.

Aaron Neville is reported to have met his beloved while they were both around fifteen or sixteen years old. The young couple got married when they were only eighteen, and they were married for almost fifty years when his wife died from cancer in 2007.

The famous singer Celine Dion also experienced young love. She is reported to have met her future husband René Angélil when she was only twelve years old and he was thirty-eight. They began a relationship when she was only nineteen years old, and they remain married today.[2]

Are You in Love?

This is a question that young people often ask themselves. Unfortunately, it is also a question they are often left alone to answer. Perhaps, what they are experiencing is just "puppy love" that amounts to a passing "crush." Or maybe what they're experiencing is genuine young love the like of which fascinates us from fiction stories, ancient history, and modern day love stories.

But perhaps what they are experiencing is something in between—a feeling that will one day pass but consumes them so much today that it drives them to act on it in the most reckless ways, especially if they are unable or unwilling to marry the person they love.

Such is the affair of many youth today, Muslims among them.

This essay was first published via onislam.net

---

[2] René Angélil died January 14, 2016 at the age of 73.

10
Why Can't I Marry Who I Want?
When Parents Say No To Marriage

~

Aminah's Dilemma

What was so wrong with Aminah marrying Zaid? What was she supposed to do? Live with her parents for the rest of her life? It frustrated Aminah that her mother wouldn't give up her obsession with Aminah marrying Abdur-Rahman, the son of a family friend.

On the phone, Aminah listened to Zaid talk about her beauty, and she was undoubtedly pleased... But as Zaid talked on and on about her white skin, Aminah became uncomfortable.

"Zaid, I'm Black," she said, realizing for the first time that he might not know she was African-American. Her race was often a source of confusion for others because of her white skin.

Zaid laughed. "You're not black," he said.

Aminah could hardly believe her ears. Why was he laughing at her? "Yes, I am," she said. "I thought you knew that."

"You'll never be black to me."

Aminah hung up the phone and hesitated before walking out the door. She really wanted to marry Zaid, but now she didn't know what to think.

Was Zaid like the prejudiced person who saw it as a blessing to *not* have brown skin? If Aminah married him, would he expect her to rejoice in being spared her father's genes? Aminah abhorred the very thought. She was just as much a child of her father as she was of her mother. But her mother was white American, with blond hair and white skin, a personification of "American beauty."

Was it coincidence or corruption that made Zaid, a Pakistani, desire that very thing?

We Shouldn't Care What Color He Is?

In the excerpt from my novel *Footsteps*, the character Aminah finds herself in a dilemma. She wants to marry Zaid, the young man she's attracted to, as opposed to the young man her mother wants for her. Then Aminah discovers underlying cultural differences between her and Zaid related to her ethnic background, and she becomes confused. As a young woman descendent of African slaves brought forcefully to America centuries ago, Aminah is particularly sensitive to issues of skin color and believes that viewing white skin as superior to dark skin is indicative of racial prejudice and bigotry. However, Zaid does not have the same outlook or sensitivity. He believes that dark skin is unattractive, and it doesn't occur to him that his open admiration for Aminah's white skin and his telling Aminah that she'll never be black to him are not only deeply offensive but also incite difficult identity questions that cut at the very core of Aminah's existence.

When Muslim youth of different cultural backgrounds become attracted to each other, there are typically at least two reactions from others. One is outright dismay, often on the part of family members and fellow cultural members who cannot fathom that one of "their own" would marry outside their ethnic group. The other reaction is one of genuine happiness, as people see the intercultural relationship as a sign that racism and bigotry are being dismantled, as they were at the time of the Prophet, peace be upon him.

On the surface, the first reaction might seem unethical and the latter ideal. After all, the Prophet, peace be upon him, taught us that Muslims should marry for the sake of Allah and that a woman's guardian should accept the proposal of any man whose character and religious commitment please him. Today, in many religious circles many Muslims understand this to mean that parents should completely ignore "superficial" traits like someone's skin color, nationality, or ethnic background when deciding on the best marriage partner for their daughter (or son).

However, while skin color, nationality, or ethnicity alone cannot be the sole reason that someone is rejected for marriage, a person's religious commitment and character alone are not sufficient reasons to agree to marriage. Personal and cultural compatibility also must be considered, especially since the marital relationship goes far beyond mere friendship and involves intimacy, raising children together, and building one's entire life (and possibly the foundations of a community) with another person.

It is in this realm of compatibility that seemingly superficial traits like race, nationality, and ethnic heritage must be considered in the decision-making process even if these traits do not ultimately prove to be "deal breakers" for the man and woman. In fact, it would be remarkably naïve and irresponsible for anyone involved in the decision-making process, whether the parents or the potential mates, to completely disregard the significance of these traits when discussing potential marriage partners.

Naturally, the impetus of the marriage decision must be based on what Allah and His Messenger told us to focus on: the person's religious commitment and character. However, by no means does this mean that Allah or the Prophet is asking us to enter ourselves or those under our guardianship into marriages that completely ignore our or their individual and cultural needs. Therefore, it is our responsibility to carefully consider every possible personal trait or cultural circumstance that could significantly affect the man and woman's future together.

Marry for the Sake of Allah?

Like the character Aminah from the story *Footsteps* who is frustrated that her mother doesn't want her to marry Zaid, many Muslim youth are frustrated that their parents won't agree to let them marry whom they want. Oftentimes when these youth complain about their dilemmas, they openly accuse their parents of being closed-minded and racist. And unfortunately, many Muslim parents are indeed more committed to superficial traits like skin color and identical ethnicities than they are to their children's personal happiness, compatibility, and spiritual contentment in marriage. In fact, many Muslim parents are more willing to marry their daughters and sons to men or women who do not even identify with Islam than they are to marry their children to righteous men and women of different racial or cultural backgrounds.

However, the sins of these parents cannot justify the other extreme: completely ignoring significant personal and cultural differences simply because we're "in love" or find someone of a different race or background extremely attractive. Yes, we should marry "for the sake of Allah." But let's not forget that part of marrying for the sake of Allah is honestly considering whether or not we can live with all that Allah has made apparent to us, and that includes everything from a person's skin color to their personal and cultural patterns that are as much a part of them as our own are a part of us.

This essay was first published via onislam.net

11
"But She Must Be a Virgin!"

~

What Will He Think of Her?

Tamika's heart pounded, and sadness overwhelmed her. Part of her wanted to marry him, but she couldn't. There was so much he didn't know about her, and she doubted he would want to marry her after he found out. Tamika hung up the phone feeling as if she had given up a piece of her heart. A lump developed in her throat, and she wondered if she had made a mistake telling him no.

There was a part of Tamika that resented this Muslim man who wanted to marry her. Tamika knew her feelings were unjustly critical. But he'd spoken against college students having boyfriends and girlfriends, and his words opened up wounds that she had hoped to heal.

Tamika had made many mistakes before becoming Muslim. Caught up in the social life of high school, she hadn't seen herself drowning. Parties and clubs were regular scenes for her, and they were always filled with alcohol, marijuana, and good-looking men. She dressed the part, played the part, and eventually became the part. She partied, drank, and did whatever everyone else did. And finally, as a cruel climax to her degenerate life, she became involved with a young man who was known for crushing hearts. It was a harsh introduction to the world of men. He would be the first and last boyfriend she had. Scarred by the experience, she had turned to the church and vowed to give her life to God. Now, as a Muslim, she wanted to forget about her past sins.

Later, when Tamika saw the Muslim man again, she let him know she changed her mind. She would marry him after all.

"What were you afraid of?" he asked.

Tamika grew silent, unsure how to respond. She had pushed her insecurity about her past to the back of her mind, and her healing was in choosing to forget. It was easier to pretend it had never happened than to risk that her confession would sour what they had found in each other. But now she felt cornered, and as her mind raced in search of a safe response, she realized honesty was her only option.

She tried to gather her thoughts. "You," she said finally.

He wrinkled his forehead in confusion. "What do you mean?"

"I wasn't always Muslim," she said, letting the implications of her words sink in.

With an empathetic sigh, he shook his head in self-reproach. "I'm no angel, Tamika," he said, "and I didn't expect you to be one."

"I was afraid you'd judge me for it," she said.

"Tamika." He drew in a deep breath and exhaled slowly. He couldn't look at her. He bit his lower lip and stared distantly in deep thought. "I *was* always Muslim," he said finally, confessing his sins as their eyes met, "so I have no excuse."

Is Being a Virgin Really That Important?

In the excerpt from my novel *A Voice*, Tamika is reluctant to agree to marry a Muslim who proposed to her because she's afraid that he will judge her for a past sin. She is no longer a virgin, and she thinks this will be a "deal breaker" for him. However, to her surprise she learns that although he himself grew up in a Muslim family, he is not a virgin himself. It makes no difference to him whether or not Tamika fell into sin in her past life. In fact, when he asked to marry her, he had never assumed she was a virgin in the first place. In any case, it is apparent that Tamika's regret for her past sin is affecting her sense of self-worth as a Muslim even though her sin occurred before she even accepted Islam.

And Tamika is not alone. Many Muslim women, including those who grew up in Muslim families, are facing a similar struggle. They fell into sin and lost their virginity. But later they felt bad, gave up the sin, and repented to Allah. Yet they still despair over their wrongs.

Allah says,

> *"Say, O My slaves who have wronged their souls!*
> *Despair not of the mercy of Allah.*
> *Verily, Allah forgives all sins.*
> *Truly, He is Oft-Forgiving, Most Merciful."*
> —Al-Zumar, 39:53

However, humans are not so merciful.

Hypocrisy and Double Standards of Muslims

It's a scenario that can make any Muslim woman upset. A Muslim man lives a life of sin in youth, and he might even have a girlfriend that even his parents and other Muslims know about. But they look the other way.

He is a boy after all, they might say. Then when it's time to get married, this man demands to marry only a virgin. If he finds out that the woman he wants to marry had a single "inappropriate relationship" with a man, he refuses to even *consider* her for marriage.

Furthermore, even if the woman never committed *zina* (fornication or adultery), the man will likely refuse to marry her if she is divorced. His refusal will likely be even more adamant if he learns that she had children from her previous husband. This hypocritical attitude is sometimes prevalent amongst men who are themselves divorced with children.

Most Muslim Men Will Judge You

Though Allah is All-Forgiving of our sins, the harsh reality is that human beings are not so forgiving. It is an unfortunate fact that humans are overly judgmental of others, especially regarding matters that they have not experienced firsthand. "Don't judge someone just because they sin differently than you," a popular saying goes. But regarding the non-virgin bride, many Muslim men are judgmental of women whose sins mirror their very own sexual transgressions. And if a potential bride was previously married, the divorce stigma alone carries a stain amongst many Muslims that, socially and culturally, makes divorce as shameful as (if not more shameful than) having fallen into *zina*.

Not only are these double standards unjust, they are also un-Islamic, as the Qur'an and Sunnah of the Prophet (peace be upon him) do not support these views. Moreover, they are generally rooted in cultures and mindsets that are based on misogyny (hatred of women).

Often when a woman is expected to be "pure" before marriage while a man is not, this expectation is rooted in the idea that only men are fully human whereas women are objects that exist only for a man's pleasure and social image. In this misogynistic view, there are only two categories of females: those who fulfill a man's sexual needs before marriage, and those who fulfill a man's sexual and cultural needs after marriage. The former are viewed as "impure" and that latter as "pure."

Thus, if a man comes from this cultural mindset, most likely he will judge a woman harshly for any past mistakes.

He Doesn't Have To Marry You Though

Undoubtedly, it is extremely hypocritical for men to require "pure" brides while they don't hold themselves to the same standards of purity. However, it's important to remember that while the culture of misogyny is indeed un-Islamic and sinful, it is not sinful for an individual man to prefer a virgin for marriage, even if he is not a virgin himself. Likewise, a woman who is not a virgin has the right to prefer a virgin man.

However, if men (or women) are living a lifestyle of *zina* and have not repented, it is sinful for them to marry a chaste spouse, regardless of whether or not the woman or man is a virgin.

Allah says,

> *"The [male] fornicator does not marry except a [female] fornicator or*
> *polytheist, and none marries her [a female fornicator]*
> *except a [male] fornicator or a polytheist.*
> *That has been made unlawful to the believers."*
> —*Al-Noor*, 24:3

So What's the Solution?

Prophet Muhammad (peace be upon him) said, "A woman is sought as a wife for her wealth, her beauty, her nobility, or her religiousness, so choose a religious woman and you will prosper" (Muslim). The Prophet also said, "The whole world is a provision, and the best benefit of this world is the righteous woman" (Muslim).

Thus, when looking to solutions, Muslim men must ask themselves at least two questions: "What do I want from life?" and "Who will best help me achieve this?" Those men who want prosperity and success in this world (and the Hereafter) while enjoying the greatest benefit and pleasure on earth will look at potential wives and say, "But she must be a righteous believer" and view this as a foundational requirement for marriage.

Yes, other men will say, "But she must be a virgin" or "She must be extremely wealthy, beautiful, or noble" as foundational requirements for marriage. In that case, Allah will likely give those men what they desire. And in the process, He will protect the truly worthy, righteous women (virgins, non-virgins, and divorced) from falling into the unfortunate situation of having such men as husbands.

This essay was first published via onislam.net

12
I Want a Muslim Girl, But…

~

Why He Can't Marry Her: Sulayman's Story

Sulayman met Aidah during a medical internship. They worked in the same lab and had the opportunity to talk a lot during the eight-week assignment. She had graduated as a pre-med major, as had he, and she would attend a medical school near his. Aidah was attractive, easy-going, and intelligent. She had a sense of humor and was confident in herself. But what Sulayman liked most about her was her commitment to Islam.

Aidah covered in Islamic garb, even at work and school, and wasn't afraid to tell the world she was Muslim. She had been the president of the Muslim Students Association on her campus and had spearheaded many Islamic functions at her school.

Sulayman communicated with Aidah mostly through e-mail and telephone, but he tried to keep the correspondence to a minimum. Although her parents liked him from the start, he didn't feel comfortable taking advantage of that. He wanted to limit their e-mail and phone interaction to only that which was necessary to find out if they were compatible for marriage.

At times, Sulayman was so convinced that he should marry Aidah that he was ready to call her father and make a formal proposal. But there was always something holding him back, something he couldn't put his finger on.

When Sulayman finally decided to propose marriage, Aidah and her father agreed, and Sulayman suggested that his and Aidah's mother coordinate the details for the wedding. But Aidah reminded him that her mother was skeptical about them marrying so soon. But Sulayman soon learned that "skeptical" was an understatement.

Although Aidah's mother approved of her daughter marrying Sulayman, she felt that he and Aidah should wait until they both finished medical school. Even Aidah felt that it was a good idea to wait at least a year. She had just begun medical school and her family was concerned about the feasibility of her marrying before she finished. Aidah's mother was firm in her belief that they should wait, but Aidah's father was unsure if waiting was a good idea. Aidah's father wanted his daughter to finish school, but he feared that, if they made her wait to marry until then, they would be pushing her in the same direction they had pushed her older sister, Jauhara.

The signs that Jauhara should have married in college were clear to both her father and mother, but they pushed her to finish school and worry about marriage later. When a respected Muslim brother from their local community proposed, they refused the proposal on the grounds that their daughter was still in school.

The refusal upset Jauhara, who was completing her second year of undergraduate studies at the time, and she began to slowly drift away from her family, first emotionally and then spiritually. She talked to her parents less and stayed in her dormitory room for school vacations although her campus was less than two hours from home. She even discontinued her involvement with the MSA, apparently, to focus on her studies.

Jauhara, Sulayman learned, was both Aidah's rival and mentor in life, though Aidah wouldn't describe it quite like that. Jauhara had seen the side of life no Muslim woman should have, and it showed on her face when Sulayman first saw her, despite her bubbly personality and reassuring smile. When Aidah told him that Jauhara had stopped practicing Islam for several years before she returned to the religion, he wasn't surprised…

In the end, Sulayman and Aidah couldn't get married because, even after what happened to Jauhara, to Aidah and her mother, the pursuit of a college degree was more important than, and mutually exclusive to, her marriage to Sulayman.

College or Marriage?

In the above excerpt from my novel *A Voice*, we learn of the story of Sulayman and Aidah, two people who seem perfect for each other. But there is only one problem: Aidah is still completing her university studies when Sulayman proposes marriage.

Like Aidah, many Muslim women face this same dilemma each day, and there are generally two responses amongst Muslims: "Marriage is most important!" or "Your education is most important!" But what is *truly* most important? Or the two even mutually exclusive at all?

The circumstance of each Muslim woman is different, so it's difficult to say for certain how any individual woman should approach the possibility of marriage if she is still studying. However, regardless of the very real life circumstances of Muslim women who may or may not choose to delay marriage until they finish university, there remains one group directly affected by the ultimate decision: Muslim men.

Muslim Men Struggle To Find Mates

"People tell me there are plenty of Muslim women looking to get married," one Muslim man said. "But where are they?"

"I can't tell you how many times I've been interested in a Muslim woman only to have her parents say no because they want her to finish school," another man said. "And now people criticize me for talking to non-Muslim women!"

Today, many Muslim men, especially those who reside in the West or study in Western universities, are choosing to marry non-Muslim women. Though Islam allows Muslim men to marry Jewish and Christian women, many Muslims raise objections to this growing phenomenon. "Then who are Muslim women supposed to marry?" some Muslims ask. "*They* aren't allowed to marry non-Muslim men."

However, as can be seen in the situation between Aidah and Sulayman, addressing this issue isn't as simple as a Muslim man choosing a Muslim woman over a non-Muslim. The marital process of most Muslim families, especially those from predominately Muslim countries, tend to be much stricter than that of non-Muslim families from the West. Whereas Muslim homes tend to have parents (and sometimes even extended family) heavily involved in the choice of a mate, non-Muslim homes tend to view the decision as resting entirely with the individuals involved.

Furthermore, in many Muslim communities in the West, opportunities for social interaction between unmarried Muslim men and women are rare. Masjids and Muslim student events are often dictated by such strict cultural codes that often Muslims themselves are unsure what, if any, socialization would be approved of. Though Muslim parents often try to find mates for their children, Muslim youth raised in the West often refuse these prospects, especially when the potential mate is from "back home" (i.e. from their home country).

However, even for indigenous Western Muslims, the search for a marital partner can be very daunting since there are no clear "rules" about how to go about this. Some Muslim communities are lax in the interaction between young men and women, and other communities are very strict. "I don't feel comfortable talking to Muslim women," one young Muslim man said. "I just don't know what's okay to say and what would offend them."

Thus, often the only environments in which many Muslim men (and women, incidentally) feel comfortable interacting with the opposite sex are those disconnected from the Muslim community entirely. Naturally, this means that for many Muslim men, the women who are most likely to be potential wives are non-Muslim women.

"Muslim parents make you feel like marrying their daughter is this impossible process," one Muslim man said. "Who wants to go through all that stress to get married?"

Of course, the circumstances are often different for those women who converted to Islam. However, even converts to Islam are not always actively involved in Muslim communities.

But How?

In this environment, it's not surprising that many Muslim men marry non-Muslim women, especially when these are often the only women they have the opportunity to talk to without cultural restrictions. Of course, Islam itself puts limits on male-female interaction, but many Muslim cultural practices go far beyond what even Allah requires.

Thus, if Muslim parents and communities would like to facilitate more opportunities between Muslim men and women for marriage, we have to be honest with ourselves about what is really making Muslim men say to themselves, "I want to marry a Muslim girl, but...how?"

This essay was first published via onislam.net

PART II
The Difficult Reality

"Of all the questions I receive from non-Muslims—and occasionally Muslims—when I'm speaking about my faith, amongst the oddest is, 'And you don't have a problem with that?' regarding something they couldn't imagine accepting for themselves.
As if life is a multiple choice personality survey wherein we select the realities that we like best.
I can't say I have a single response to this quizzical inquiry.
But I remember once telling a woman, 'Life is life, and no matter what path you choose, you're going to face all the trials and difficulties that this life entails. I've just selected the path that offers me hope that my struggles and suffering will end at death.'"
—from the journal of Umm Zakiyyah

13
Marrying at the "Right Time"
Our Dilemma: Placing Our Trust in Allah

~

It's one of the most difficult questions faced by adult Muslims, especially women: *When should I get married? After I finish my studies, or now?*

When I think of this dilemma, I often remember the advice of my parents: **When it comes to marriage, the most important question is not *when* to get married but *to whom*?** And it is only Allah who knows the companion He created for us in this world and in the Hereafter. Therefore, when seeking to answer the question of when (and whom) to marry, we should turn to Allah and ask His guidance.

Allah says,

> *"And when My servants ask you concerning Me,*
> *then [tell them], I am indeed near.*
> *I respond to the prayer of every suppliant*
> *when he calls on Me...."*
> —*Al-Baqarah* (2:186)

It is of the immeasurable blessings of Allah that the believer is promised correct guidance when he or she turns sincerely to the Creator for direction. However, we often miss out on this tremendous blessing when we live our lives guided not by what Allah has shown us as a result of our supplications, but what humans and society (and our *nafs*) have suggested due to human desire and experience.

We Think We Can Plan Life

So many of us imagine that we can plan life and cover each important milestone at the "right time." Thus, when we think of getting married, having children, or even taking practical steps toward crucial spiritual improvement, we mentally write for ourselves schedules, which we follow religiously, often without ever raising our hands in supplication to ask Allah if these approaches are best for us.

Fortunately, growing up, I was taught this profound lesson by my parents: **There is no such thing as the "right time" for anything in life.**

There is only "the right time for *you*." And *your* "right time" is something of which only Allah has full knowledge.

Make Wise Choices

No, this doesn't mean we should avoid making judicious decisions based on our experience and wisdom—or even based on those personal desires and dreams we have. It just means that as we plan, we should also remember that Allah plans—and His plan is always best.

And it is often the case that submitting to Allah's plan results in no major changes to the schedules we've set for ourselves: Certainly, sometimes our schedule and Allah's schedule are in harmony with each other.

Nevertheless, even when we must alter our plans after consulting Allah, our *du'aa* and *Istikhaarah* guarantee that we are protected from harm and that we reap the best in this world and in the Hereafter as a result of our *tawakkul*. It is often only much later in life that we realize the immense blessings we've reaped from Allah guiding us to change our previously much-coveted plans.

Lessons from Qur'an: Story of Mary

If we look in the Qur'an at the story of Mary, the mother of Jesus (peace be upon them) we learn a powerful lesson about the wisdom of Allah as it relates to *qadr* (divine decree) regarding our respective "right times" for major milestones in life.

Allah says:

> *[The angel] said: "I am only a Messenger from your Lord [to announce] to you the gift of a righteous son." She said, "How can I have a son, when no man has touched me, nor am I unchaste?" He said, "So [it will be], your Lord said: 'That is easy for Me.'*
> *...*
> *'And it is a matter (already) decreed.'"*
> —*Maryam* (19:19-21)

Perhaps, it is our human weakness and modern thinking that allow us to read over and over again about the knowledge and wisdom of Allah while we continue to rely primarily on the knowledge and wisdom of ourselves. For certainly, if we apply to the story above *our* perception of the "right time" to have children, the life of even the greatest woman would fall short.

We fret: *But what will I do about children, finishing my degree, and all the others things I want in life? How will I achieve all of these if I marry now?* Yet Allah says, "That is easy for Me."

Challenges: Obstacles Placed By Parents

Unfortunately, in today's world, it is often the parents—not the adult children themselves—who are most concerned with worldly goals (in the absence of *du'aa* and *Istikhaarah*) when deciding whether or not to marry "early." And with today's ever rising standards for "education," this concern requires Muslims to wait later and later to get married.

In many such cases, it is the Western model of *Live your life first* that is coveted in the hearts and minds of these Muslim parents, even if only subconsciously. However, a point that Muslims often overlook when seeking to emulate the Western model of delaying marriage is this: **In the West, the "live your life" motto often includes intimate relationships between men and women until it's the "right time" to get married**. In this model, the only "sin" involved is in making the intimate relationship legitimate "too soon."

It is indeed heartbreaking that many of the adult sons and daughters of ambitious Muslim parents understand this model quite well—even if their parents don't—and they *live* the Western model (in secret) rather than risk scorn and ridicule from their family and culture for "marrying young"— even when they are spiritually, psychologically, and financially (in the case of men) ready to marry.

Nevertheless, we cannot deny that it is definitely commendable that sincere parents wish to secure for their adult children the best scenario in which to enter marriage. However, as parents, we often forget a profound fact when making such unilateral decisions that encourage our children to delay marriage later and later into adulthood: **Our children do not belong to us. They belong to Allah.**

Our guardianship over our sons and daughters is merely an *amaanah*, a serious trust and tremendous responsibility—not a dictatorship giving us full reign to force on them our personal desires and goals (even if well-intentioned).

If we betray even one aspect of this *amaanah* (especially if this betrayal harms our children in any way), we will certainly answer to Allah for this on the Day of Judgment.

Heartbreaking: Story from Riyadh

One of the most heartbreaking stories that illustrate quite lucidly the seriousness of this *amaanah* is a true story regarding a father and his sickly daughter:

One of the scholars from Riyadh narrated that they visited a hospital and found a man with his daughter, who was very ill. The daughter was forty years old and had never married, for every man who had come for her, her father rejected.

The scholar said that the woman's father was from the greediest of people. The father was a person of the dunya, *but his* dunya *did not benefit him. He had many offices: real-estate, cars and clinics; however, it was known amongst the people that if his daughter were to be married, a suitor cannot marry her except with hundreds of thousands [in wealth]. Thus, all of the young men who came to propose were rejected because they were youth lacking wealth. And due to the circumstances of the people, the men wishing to marry her could not afford to pay the high* mahr *[stipulated by the father, not the daughter herself]. So every righteous man who came, he was asked about his employment and his cars and his salary and if the suitor informed the father that he did not have the precise qualifications he stipulated, then he was turned away. This continued until the daughter reached forty years of age. Then she suffered an acute illness and was admitted to the hospital.*

Then, due to the severity of her illness, death became imminent.

And, certainly, death is the time to meet the One who judges between parties, and there is no Judge except Him, the One who implements justice between the oppressed and the oppressor.

When it was clear to the daughter that her death was but moments away, she said to her father, who sat at her bedside:

"O Father, come close!"

So he came close to her.

She said to him, "Say Ameen."

So he said, "Ameen."

She said again, "Say Ameen!"

So he said, "Ameen."

Then she said a third time, "[O Father!] Say Ameen."

And he said, "Ameen."

Then she said to him these final words before passing away: **"May Allah prohibit for you Paradise as you have prohibited for me the delicacy of marriage."**[1]

Final Note: A Prayer for Our Souls

O Allah! Protect us from going astray or leading others astray!
Protect us from being oppressed or oppressing others!
And O Allah! In any decision we make in life—whether regarding our own
lives or the lives of our children—make us turn to You for Guidance,
seeking Your pleasure and Your pleasure alone.

This essay was first published via saudilife.net

[1] Original story taken from http://www.islamic-life.com/forums/heart-softeners/aameen-900

14
Is the No-Polygamy Contract Wise?

~

From the Journal of Renee

"I hope you don't plan on doing something like that," I said.

His smile faded. "Doing something like what?"

"Marrying another wife."

He was quiet for some time. "Of course not."

"Good." I folded my arms across my chest. "Anyway, I read that I can put a no-polygamy clause in my contract."

He nodded slowly. "I read that too."

"I hope you know I'm putting it in there."

"Really?"

"Yes."

We didn't speak for some time.

"What if I don't want to sign it?" he said.

I shrugged. "It doesn't matter to me. I just won't marry you."

"You would turn down a good brother for something like that?"

"If he's a good brother, he wouldn't mind signing it."

"Now, that's not true."

I shrugged again. "Whatever. It's what I think."

"Some brothers I know think it's *haraam* [forbidden] to sign it," he said. I could tell he was trying to use my religious sensitivities to make me back down from the no-polygamy clause.

"So?" I said.

"So I'm not sure if it's okay."

"Honestly, I don't care what you think," I said. "All I know is that whoever I marry is going to sign that. Otherwise, we won't be getting married."

"And if no one signs it?"

"I just won't get married. It doesn't matter to me."

There was an awkward silence.

"You're really serious, huh?" he said, looking at me with concern, but I wouldn't meet his gaze.

"Yes."

"Does it really mean that much to you?"

"Yes."

"But why?"

I looked at him. "Would you want your wife with someone else?"

"But that's different—"

"How is it different?" I challenged.

"Polygamy is *halaal* [permissible]," he said.

"I didn't say adultery. I said someone else. She could divorce you and marry your friend," I said. "That's *halaal.* But would you like it?"

His eyebrows rose as he thought about what I said. "No, I wouldn't."

"Then why are you surprised when I feel the same way?"

"But it's in the Qur'an. That means it's not the same for you. Obviously, women can handle it."

"Just because it's in the Qur'an doesn't mean everyone should do it."

"Then who should?"

"Honestly, I don't care. I just know it's not me."

"But how do you know?"

At that I grew impatient. "How do you know you can handle another woman?" Before he could answer, I went on. "You don't. So why do it? Or, better yet, why not just be patient and see how you can handle just one?"

He shrugged. "You have a point."

"I know I do. And you don't."

A grin formed on his face, and he shook his head. "Okay, you win."

Because I didn't know what to say and was too upset to smile with him (though I did feel the urge to laugh at myself), I got up. "I should get home," I said. "I told my mother I'm going for a walk. I don't want her to think I'm kidnapped or something."

"Or to know the truth," he said.

Unwilling to display amusement, I nodded. "*As-salaamu'alaikum,*" I said, giving him the standard Muslim greeting of peace in an effort to end the conversation. I didn't wait for his reply.

Later in my room, I reflected on what I'd said and wondered if it was the full truth. I certainly was not willing to live in polygamy, but I doubted I'd turn down the opportunity to marry someone I really cared about just because he didn't sign the no-polygamy contract.

Still, I refused to get married without the clause in there.

Realities of Submitting to Marriage

In the above excerpt from my novel *Realities of Submission*, the narrator Renee is discussing marriage with a man who is interested in marrying her, and like many women, she does not want to deal with the possibility of her husband taking another wife. In order to ensure that this does not happen, she is stipulating a no-polygamy clause in her contract. However, will this stipulation protect her from the endless "unknowns" that are inevitable after agreeing to marriage?

Frustration After Marriage

"I dropped out of school and gave up my career for him. I even abandoned my dreams and became a stay-at-home mom. Now he wants to tell me how to dress and practice my faith! I feel like a sex slave with no rights except picking nice meals and pretty clothes. I can't take this anymore."

Many women gush at the thought of finding the "perfect man," and often this sense of excitement continues after marriage for women (and men). However, after years of living together, it is not uncommon for men and women to face difficulties and trials. The man and woman knew that marriage would mean sacrifice, but in the beginning stages, it's impossible to know exactly what that means.

For women who marry while they are completing their studies or before they obtain a university degree, marriage often means letting go of this educational pursuit, at least for a time. If they become pregnant after marriage, many women give up on their education and career altogether. Though this sacrifice is often voluntary, many women complain that their husbands, who were very supportive of their education and career prior to marriage, insist that they drop out of school and give up their career and dreams completely after they are married, especially once children are in the picture.

However, their frustrations do not stop there. Many women complain that their husbands, particularly those men who consider themselves religious, go as far as to micromanage their dress and religious practices. And because these women wish to be good, righteous wives, they feel obligated to listen to their husband's demands, even as they see no Islamic need to adjust their hijabs and religious opinions.

Unfortunately, though "swallowing your pride" and obeying the husband seems like the right thing to do, if the woman's concerns are left unaddressed for an extended period of time, she may become extremely frustrated such that she ultimately wants out of the marriage, or even out of Islam itself.

Can a Marriage Contract Help?

Too often when women are negotiating the marriage contract, they focus on what they want from the man or the relationship (such as "no polygamy") as opposed to what they want and need for themselves. In the case of Renee above, though her insistence on a no-polygamy contract is well within her rights (as it is for any woman), perhaps it would be best for her (and other women) to shift her focus to matters that would benefit her life, mental health, and spirituality regardless of the choices her husband might make down the road.

What if, when writing the terms of her marriage contract, Renee focused on her desire to live as a mentally and spiritually independent, successful woman, as opposed to her desire to never share her husband?

In other words, what if women used the marriage contract to think long-term regarding their own actions and choices as opposed to those of their husband?

A Suggested Marriage Contract

Here are some suggested marriage contract stipulations that women might want to consider, even if they do not foresee any serious obstacles or disagreements with their future husband:

- *I have the right to continue my education, and I will have my husband's full support, such that he will not seek to deter or prevent me from this. If there are any concerns regarding the care of the children, we will come to a mutually agreeable arrangement that respects the rights of both the children and myself.*
- *I have the right to own my own business or to pursue a career path of my choice, and I will have my husband's full support, such that he will not seek to deter or prevent me from this. If there are any concerns regarding the care of the children, we will come to a mutually agreeable arrangement that respects the rights of both the children and myself.*
- *I have the right to practice Islam in a manner that I believe is most correct in front of Allah. Under no circumstances will my husband compel me to understand or practice Islam differently from what I believe or understand to be right.*
- *In religious matters in which there is a legitimate disagreement amongst scholars, my husband will not compel me to follow the opinion that he favors, as I have full right to follow the point of view that I believe is most correct, even if it differs from his.*

- *Regarding any personal or religious matter in which my husband and I disagree, we agree to first seek a mutually agreeable conclusion between ourselves. If this is not possible, we agree to seek the counsel and input of an arbiter whom we both respect.*
- *Above all, we agree to put Allah first and last in everything and let the ultimate decision rest in His hands through seeking righteous advice from others and making* du'aa *(sincere supplication) and* Istikhaarah *(the prayer for making a decision) before coming to any final conclusion.*

If women wish to add the stipulation of no-polygamy, they can feel free; but it is perhaps best long-term to make the primary focus of the marriage contract on the their own needs and goals, as opposed to the men's desires and choices.

This essay was first published via onislam.net

15
What Problem Do You Have with the Sunnah of Polygamy?
An Excerpt from *Realities of Submission* by Umm Zakiyyah

~

From the Journal of Renee

"What problem do you have with the Sunnah of polygamy?" my husband asked me, as if in rebuke.

I glared at him. "What problem do *you* have with the Sunnah of monogamy?"

If there was one advantage I had over my husband during this time, it was that he simply could not win an argument with me. I almost always had the last word, and this wasn't because I insisted on it but because we would get to a point where he couldn't think of anything logical to say in response to my words. So the argument would end.

Although I was most often victorious in our war of words, I cannot say I was victorious in the battle most significant to me—that to win my husband's heart. Rationally, someone might point out that I already had. But that's not what I wanted. I wanted his heart inclined *only* to me.

Another battle I wasn't sure I was winning was the one being waged in my heart and mind. I had begun to wonder, *What if my husband's right? What if I should remove the no-polygamy clause?*

Today I wouldn't entertain thoughts like these. I know a woman has full rights to lay down some ground rules before entering a marriage. And once she does, she's under no obligation to revisit them, and most certainly not for the man who signed them off and whom she wouldn't have married without them.

But I was still young, still learning, and was thus easy prey in falling victim to the one thing the fraternity had perfected to a science—casting doubt.

Even after leaving the sorority and moving beyond this period of my life, I met sisters who had been taught something similar to what my husband and I were being taught back then—that a woman's not wanting to live in polygamy was indicative of weakness of faith and an unwillingness to embrace her religion in full.

Today I see it as the other way around. Those men, and women, who have difficulty believing that a woman doesn't have to live in polygamy and nor is she compelled to like the idea for herself—even if it's her reality—are in actuality the ones suffering from weakness of faith, because they haven't yet embraced fully a proper belief in Islam.

Belief in Islam means having full faith in the Wisdom of Allah—in His obligating and forbidding, in His encouraging and discouraging, and in His giving humans no choice in certain matters while giving humans full choice in others. Clearly, one of the matters in which human choice is most extensive in our religion is that of marriage—from the very choice of a spouse, to the conditions under which one will live with that spouse.

Yet even after choosing a mate and laying down conditions, I know there are matters that we cannot choose—like the inevitable tests that will enter our marriages.

Even so, of the unexpected—and expected—marital trials, Allah does not once ask a believer to "love" or "prefer" these trials.

Polygamy is a trial.

If I'm a "weak Muslim" because I don't wish a trial on myself, I say this weakness is closer to Islamic faith than the claim of loving to be tried. It is nearer to righteousness to be ever aware of human weakness in yourself than to suffer from the façade of strength and be unable to live up to your claim.

I choose to be wise.

I do not want polygamy in my life, not because I don't believe in what Allah revealed, but because I do. He promises that He'll test the believers and purge from them those who are not true to their claim.

And I don't know if I'll pass.

I have lived a little, so I know there are women for whom the trial has brought much good, and who wouldn't change their lives for the world. But even these women—with only rare exceptions—are like the believer relieved from excruciating pain who wouldn't take back those years of suffering because of all the good it has brought to her life, and continues to bring.

Certainly, with trial comes recognition of one's purpose on earth, the realization of the crucial affair of the soul, and the increased certainty that we will one day meet our Creator and stand before Him in final Judgment.

Yet no person who believes in Allah and the Last Day will say, "I want Allah to put me to trial." This is what I'd be saying if I claim a love or preference for something in which Allah has placed a different reality in my heart.

If Fatimah bint Muhammad and Ayesha bint Abu Bakr were not excited about this prospect in their lives, how amazing would it be for me, Renee Morris who does not even know her position before the One who lauded their station in Islam, to claim I have something in my heart that even they never claimed.

My heart goes out to those men whose ignorance and weakness of faith inspire the remarkable imagination that their wives, and believing women, will be closer to Islam by claiming to be better than the torchbearers of Allah's religion, expressing a love and preference that not a single Sunnah can be brought, except in opposition to what they claim.

To read the full novel, visit uzauthor.com

16
Polygamy, Not My Problem

~

"If you don't want your husband to marry another woman," the imam said, "then reflect on the hadith of the Prophet, *sallallaahu 'alayhi wa sallam*. You should love for your sister what you love for yourself."

I turned off the video and sipped my tea in the silence of the room. I had planned to watch the prominent imam's entire lecture on the subject of plural marriage in Islam, but I couldn't get past the first few minutes.

It wasn't that I disagreed with his point. After all, it is true. If Muslim women who are already married think of a potential co-wife as a sister in Islam instead of a potential rival, then sharing a husband wouldn't be so difficult.

But is this mental shift really as simple as people make it sound?

Is it even realistic?

Women's Role in Polygyny

"What role do you think women play in polygamy?"

I had just arrived for a meeting at the home of a community leader and his wife when he asked me this question. The inquiry took me off guard because it was unrelated to the subject of the meeting. He wasn't asking about the details of women's role in a Muslim marriage (He already knew that). He was asking what role they play in ensuring that a husband's pursuit of and subsequent life in plural marriage is successful and relatively uncomplicated.

"They don't have one," I said.

I could tell he hadn't expected this response. Then again, I hadn't either. But it was what I honestly felt.

Brows furrowed, he asked, "What do you mean?"

"She's not the one taking another wife—he is," I said. "So the burden is on his shoulders, not hers." □

"But don't you think women have some responsibility in making it work?"

"No, I don't."

The shocked silence in the room made me realize I should clarify.

"I'm not saying she has no accountability to her co-wife," I explained. "The co-wife is her sister in Islam, and she can't violate her sister's rights."

I went on, "But what I mean is, beyond her normal duties when her husband is married to only her, her role doesn't change when he marries someone else. But the husband's role *does* change because he chose polygamy."

He nodded, beginning to see my point.

"And when a man marries another woman," I told him, "he must understand that his first wife will naturally be hurt and upset. But this comes with the package. And if he can't handle this natural hurt and upset without blaming his wife or asking *her* to change, then he's the one at fault. Women will be women," I said with a shrug. "And if a man doesn't fully accept what that means in reality, then he's not ready for polygamy."

Stop Addressing Women, and Talk To Men

Though it has been many years since I had this conversation with the community leader, my views have not changed. If anything, they have become more resolute. And if there were any advice I would give to Muslim leaders who wish to tackle this topic with any success, it would be this: "Stop addressing women, and start addressing men."

Allah says,

"And if you fear that you will not deal justly with the orphan girls, then marry those that please you of [other] women, two or three or four. But if you fear that you will not be just, then [marry only] one or those your right hand possesses. That is more suitable that you may not incline [to injustice]."
—*Al-Nisaa'* (4:3)

The more I reflect on this *ayah*, the more I get a small glimpse into the infinite wisdom in these words. Specifically, five points stand out to me:
* Allah is addressing only men in this *ayah*.
* No advice or instructions are given to women regarding plural marriage.
* Allah is asking men to engage in careful introspection when determining whether or not to pursue polygamy.

69

- The last part of the *ayah* clearly implies that marrying more than one woman results in increased responsibility (and thus accountability) as opposed to marrying only one woman.
- The last part also suggests that polygamy itself will be a challenge—so much so that Allah tells men outright that being married to only one increases the likelihood of the man being just to his wife.

One Is Best For You?

No, I'm not suggesting under the guise of *naseehah* that "one is best for you" while secretly hoping that no man engages in this Sunnah. Actually, in my heart of hearts, I do hope that men (at least the ones responsible and financially capable) find a way to make plural marriage work—with wives by their side who are both fulfilled and pleased. Otherwise, there will be an ever-growing list of single—never-been-married, widowed, and divorced—women denied the joys and blessings of an Islamic marriage.

But what I am saying is that whatever responsibility exists in making the Sunnah of polygamy work rests almost entirely with the man, who must engage in careful introspection, seeking advice, and making *du'aa* and *Istikhaarah* when making this difficult decision and subsequently living with its naturally challenging consequences.

It goes without saying (or at least it *should* go without saying) that if a man's current wife doesn't wish to be in polygamy, it is illogical to ask her to shoulder the responsibility of making successful something that she neither desires nor chose.

Real Men

The real man is the one whose good treatment, patience, and understanding will inspire even the most reluctant and upset wife to stay with him—even as she may never like that polygamy is part of her life.

In other words, real men implement the Sunnah of being men.

Time and time again I speak to women who have helped their husbands find another wife, supported their husband's decision, or even made a habit of speaking or writing about the beauty of this Sunnah. Some have even gone as far as to share their home with a co-wife (something even I would not suggest or recommend). Yet, despite Muslim women having gone over and beyond the call of duty in trying to overcome their natural dislike for sharing their husband (as a simple Google search on polygamy will reveal), advice, lectures, and complaints by Muslim men on the subject of polygamy continue to focus on the actions and thoughts of women—with the apparent goal of inspiring women to *love* the arrangement and relish in its blessings by giving their husbands "no problems" with the pursuit.

Ah… If only…

But the fact of the matter is that Allah created women with a natural reluctance and dislike for sharing their husbands.

You Don't Have To Love Polygamy

When I speak to women struggling in polygamy, one of my first pieces of advice is to accept that polygamy is inherently difficult and painful for women. It's not "supposed to" be enjoyable or desired, I tell them—even though this natural difficulty and pain does not preclude having a loving, fulfilling relationship with your husband though he's married to someone else.

Those women who seek to "love polygamy" often live in psychological and emotional turmoil as they deny themselves the right to hurt or even cry. They feel guilty for any resentment or emotional outbursts, and their husbands, unfortunately, often berate them for their struggles. "This is the Sunnah," their husbands may say, "so if you don't love it, you have weak *emaan*,"—and, tragically, the wives believe them. Ultimately, many of these women simply "break" and become so embittered and spiritually traumatized that they blame Allah or Islam for their misery—when neither Allah nor Islam asked them to "love polygamy" in the first place.

The Only Advice Men Need

Be a man.

In my view, this summarizes the essence of the *only* advice men should give (and receive) regarding polygamy.

And, no, being a man doesn't mean diving into polygamy while completely disregarding the first wife's feelings. Sometimes, as we know from the famous story of Ali and Fatimah (may Allah be pleased with them), it may actually mean not pursuing polygamy at all.

The Reminder Benefits the Believer

"None of you truly believes until he loves for his brother what he loves for himself."
—Prophet Muhammad, *sallallaahu 'alayhi wa sallam*
(Bukhari and Muslim)

Yes, women, like all believers, can benefit from reminders for their souls, and these reminders may or may not inspire them to accept polygamy in their lives. Either way, women *should* love for their sisters what they love for themselves—as should men with their brothers.

But suggesting that this means a woman should accept polygamy and love for another woman to marry her husband is little different than suggesting that a man should accept divorce and love for his unmarried friend to marry and enjoy his beloved wife.

So, dear imams and *du'aat*, let us ask men and women to focus on their own responsibilities and roles, not someone else's.

And by the mercy of Allah, as a woman, polygamy is not one of mine.

This essay was first published via onislam.net

17
Thank God I'm a Woman

~

"Fear Allah," the woman was advised by the local imam upon seeking a *khula'* from her husband. "Marriage is serious. Don't you know that a woman who divorces her husband for no reason will not even smell Paradise?"

The words fell upon the woman like a prison sentence. She had been married for almost ten years, but she didn't know if she could take it anymore. She couldn't remember the last time she even opened the Qur'an. She barely paid attention in prayer. She was no longer motivated to even raise her hands in supplication to Allah...because she believed that what she truly desired—peace of mind, some semblance of marital security, and a home where her husband's *other* wife didn't live down the hall—made her a bad Muslim. So she "feared Allah," telling herself to be patient with what Allah decreed...

I Thank Allah That I'm a Woman

In reflecting on the fact that all humans—men and women—must stand before Allah on the Day of Judgment and answer for their conduct in this world, I thank Allah that I am a woman. It's not that I imagine that women on a whole exhibit better behavior than men. It's just that if a woman were to pick up an Islamic book on marriage, listen to an Islamic lecture about the roles of spouses, or seek the advice of a local imam for her marital struggles, she often is not left guessing: Her primary responsibility lies in serving her family and pleasing her husband. The message may rarely come packaged in the way the Sunnah requires (i.e. with kindness and empathy), but it is unambiguous nonetheless. Thus, even from worldly sources, a woman's code of conduct is laid out quite clearly, with little to no "wiggle room."

Unfortunately, however, this sometimes translates into women being denied their rights, as in the tragic example above, and this is something that troubles me deeply and for which I cannot even pretend to see the silver lining. Yet, for the man, the situation is quite different...

*No, it's not correct to casually chat with non-*mahram *women, but if you hope to guide her to Islam...*

No, you shouldn't look at pictures of uncovered women, but if you would like to marry her...
Yes, you should allow your wife to go to the masjid if she likes, but if you fear a greater harm...

Don't get me wrong. I realize that there are definitely times when something that is generally permissible may become forbidden, and when something that is generally forbidden may become permissible. I'm only saying that the "justified advice" that is popular today—which usually comes from well-meaning laymen to women under their care—very often leans in one direction: that which favors the desires and circumstances of men.

Although this privilege may seem to work in a man's favor, ultimately, it may do the exact opposite for his soul...

Men of Paradise

The Prophet, *sallallaahu 'alayhi wa sallam*, once said, **"The best of you are the best to your families..."** (Tirmidhi, *sahih*).

And it is the best of us who will earn Paradise when we die.

So if you want to see a man of Paradise, you may not find him in the first row of prayer in the masjid. You may not even find him amongst those who've memorized the most Qur'an. And no, you might never find him amongst the hundreds of "callers to Islam" invited to give Islamic talks.

But if you were to ask Allah to give you just a glimpse of what earned this man such a lofty station in His eyes, perhaps this is what you'd see...

A mother quietly smiling to herself after her son has come to visit to make sure she is all right.
A son looking up to his father proudly as they walk together to the masjid.
A woman who is unwell waking to find the house clean and dinner cooked.
A daughter or son rushing to greet Daddy at the door because they know he'll give them a warm smile and a hug.
A wife throwing her head back in laughter after her husband whispers a joke in her ear.
A man racing his wife and playfully competing with his children...
And an entire family—a mother, father, wife, sons, and daughters— blinking back tears at the mere thought of living in this world without such a man as the one Allah has given them as a son, husband, or father...

In other words, if you want to see a man of Paradise, he is the one who has, *bi'idhnillaah*, created for his family a paradise on earth.

This simple truth is one that nearly all married women striving for Paradise understand with respect to their roles on earth. In fact, it is one that women are not allowed to forget. Islamic books, lectures, and imams giving women advice do not give them this opportunity.

That these same books, lectures, and imams (even if unintentionally) allow many such missed opportunities to men is why I thank Allah I am a woman.

"And remind, for verily, the reminder benefits the believers."
—Al-Dhaariyaat (51:55)

As a believer who is full of faults, I myself can testify to the benefit that constant reminders about my soul have done for me on earth. It's terrifying to imagine how my life would be without them.

That so many of my brothers are often denied these life-altering reminders for their souls—lessons that they will certainly be held accountable for when they meet Allah—is why, truly, from the bottom of my heart, I thank God that I'm a woman.

Original version published via SISTERS Magazine (September 2012)

18
Maybe It's Divorce We're Taking Lightly

~

"This is really a shame," the woman said. "The divorce rate of Muslims is so high. Why are Muslims taking marriage so lightly?"

It's a question we've likely all heard or uttered by our own tongues. But the more I live, the more I'm developing a different perspective…

Anisa's Story

Anisa was twenty-two when she got married, but she was sixteen when she met eighteen-year-old Samir. They met in Honor Society and were drawn to each other, the only practicing Muslims at school. Anisa wore hijab, and Samir spoke openly about Islam. Though they shared no classes, they saw each other during the club's weekly meetings after school.

Neither Anisa nor Samir thought much of their frequent talking. But there was so much to discuss and so much that drew them together. They shared the same goals in life, and they both dreamed of teaching Islam on a large scale.

When Samir graduated, Anisa couldn't escape the sense of sadness that overwhelmed her, but she tried to focus on school. She kept telling herself it was just loneliness. But something deep inside said it was something more…

It was a year before Anisa and Samir got back in touch. Anisa was browsing a friend's Facebook page when she saw Samir's profile. Her heart pounded in excitement, and her hand trembled nervously as she sent him a friend request. Less than an hour later, he accepted, and it was clear that Samir was excited to hear from her.

They talked online almost every day after that. But they still didn't admit to themselves what was happening. But when Anisa gave Samir her phone number and told him the times to call (when her parents weren't home), she started to feel a little guilty. But they talked mostly about Islam and what they envisioned for themselves in the future…and in marriage.

Anisa was eighteen and months away from graduation when Samir surprised her by visiting the school. It was time for Honor Society, but when she saw Samir, she couldn't bring herself to go inside.

"I had to see you," he said as they walked down the hall. They both kept their hands tucked deep into their pockets, but they couldn't avoid the furtive glance. "I miss you, Anisa."

The words sent Anisa's heart fluttering, and she barely found her voice. "Me too." When she realized that her response made no sense, they both laughed awkwardly.

They were sitting on the bleachers outside when Samir said, "I know it's wrong to have these feelings…" Anisa averted her gaze, her face growing warm in embarrassment. "But I can't take this anymore. I need to be with you…properly, you know?"

"No," Anisa's mother said later that night when Anisa confided in her about Samir. "You are too young. Besides, he's not from our country. It can never work. I'll mention none of this nonsense to your father. Stupid girl, don't go and ruin your life for some boy."

"I'm not giving up," Samir said on the phone the next day, but his voice betrayed how heartbroken he was. "I'm talking to your father."

"Stay away from my daughter!" A week later, Anisa shuddered as her father's voice carried to the solitude of her room. She heard the front door slam, and she rushed to the window, her heart dropping as she saw Samir walking to his car, shoulders slouched.

"I'm not giving up," Anisa told Samir on the phone the next day.

"I wish we could run away together," Samir said, a hint of humor in his sad tone. They both laughed, but when Anisa hung up the phone, tears stung her eyes.

When Anisa was twenty-one years old and in her third year in university, her parents said they had found a "good boy" for her.

"You will not refuse Abdullah," her mother said the night before Anisa was to meet him. "Your father worked very hard to find the right match for you. Abdullah finished medical school and comes from a good family. Do not disappoint us."

Samir met Anisa on campus after she told him the news. Anisa cried unabashedly as Samir fought back tears, but he couldn't keep himself from pulling Anisa close to him. Islamic limits blurred at that moment, and neither cared. They just wanted this moment, which they would never have again.

Naturally, Anisa's marriage to Abdullah was strained from the start. Her heart was attached to Samir, and no matter how hard she tried, she could not loosen the hold Samir had on her heart. But she convinced herself that her mother was right. A good Muslim girl did what her parents wanted, even if it wasn't what she wanted for herself.

"We are good Muslims, Anisa," her mother had said after Anisa and Abdullah met. "We are not forcing you. Allah forbids this. But if you do not marry Abdullah, know you are breaking your parents' hearts, and I will never forgive you for that."

Abdullah was a good man, Anisa could not deny. He provided for her and spent quality time, but he did not share Anisa's love for Islam or her outlook on life. Even though they didn't have children, Abdullah asked her to drop out of graduate school and focus on her "Islamic duties." He said a good Muslim woman doesn't mix with men—even though his job at the hospital required just that, as did his casual friendships with female coworkers.

When Abdullah suggested Anisa remove her hijab, she was aghast. She cried to her mother, and to Anisa's shock, her mother told her to obey her husband. "We are living in difficult times," her mother said. "There's no point in putting hardship on yourself."

Anisa felt uncomfortable when she walked outside uncovered for the first time, and she could never bring herself to accept this new life. She became so ashamed of herself that she stopped reading Qur'an and she barely prayed. Ultimately, Anisa fell into deep depression and fought thoughts of suicide.

On one particularly distressful day, Anisa took a walk. As the sun warmed her hair and bare arms, Anisa reflected on her life, and she found that she didn't even know herself anymore.

"Anisa?"

Anisa's private thoughts were disrupted, and she looked up to find Samir opposite her…and a beautiful woman in hijab with a baby stroller.

Shocked and ashamed, everything came back to her in that moment. She felt angry with herself, her parents, and even Abdullah. But she would get her life back, she told herself, even if it meant divorce…

The Reality of Divorce

Like the fictional character Anisa, most people who reach the point of divorce have a long history of practical and psychological struggles that led them to that point. These men and women do not fantasize about divorce, and they do not take marriage lightly.

"The decision to divorce is never easy, and as anyone who has been through it will tell you, this wrenching, painful experience can leave scars on adults as well as children for years."[3] For Muslims this decision is all the more difficult because they have to consider the repercussions in this world and in the Hereafter.

Is Divorce As Bad As We Think?

Though it is unquestionable that preserving a marriage is of great importance in Islam, the stigma attached to divorce and the vow "till death do us part" are not Islamic concepts.

Allah says,

> **"…No person shall have a burden laid on him greater than he can bear."**
> —*Al-Baqarah* (2:233)

In the chapter *Al-Talaaq* (Divorce), Allah says,

> **"…And whoever fears Allah and keeps his duty to Him, He will make a way out for him [from every difficulty]. And He will provide him from [sources] he never could imagine. And whosoever puts his trust in Allah, then He will suffice him."**
> —65:2-3

Therefore, it is imperative that we not place impossible restrictions on ourselves. Whether a believer is married or divorced, Allah's mercy, love, and provision are always near.

Another Point of View

When we look at divorce honestly, we often find that amongst Muslims, it is not always the one seeking divorce who is taking marriage lightly. It is sometimes the parents and families who compel the Anisas and Abdullahs of the world into marrying for the sake of tradition or image—or parents and families whose complete lack of involvement leave youth without guidance when embarking on this life-altering milestone.

Naturally, whether the marriage is "forced" or decided without proper guidance, it is likely only a matter of time before divorce is sought as a last resort to restore psychological or spiritual peace. And when these men

---

[3] "Divorce: The Most Difficult Decision You Will Ever Make." Excerpted from *The Complete Idiot's Guide to Surviving Divorce*. BookEnds, LLC. Cited October 23, 2012 on http://life.familyeducation.com/divorce/divorce-counseling/45515.html

and women raise their hands to Allah and ask for relief, who are we to say they're discounting the heavy responsibility of marriage? Divorce at such times may be a tremendous blessing for them.

And we should not take this lightly.

This essay was first published via onislam.net

19
No Woman Should Have To Choose
Reflections on Abortion

~

I met Layla a few years before I graduated from high school and went to college. She was one of those girls who made your heart swell in pride when you saw her. "Yeah, that's right," I'd think when her name appeared in yet another newspaper article or was mentioned in the local news for winning yet another scholarship, award, or competition. "I'm Muslim just like her." And it didn't hurt that she always looked good—in person and in pictures—with how she wrapped her hijab and coordinated her clothes, which were amazingly always in style.

Her university was not too far from my home, and despite her busy schedule, she found time to meet up with me and some of my friends to teach us "the ropes." She gave us tips on writing college essays, giving public speeches, succeeding in college despite anti-Muslim sentiments, and even staying fit.

So yeah, we loved her. Or perhaps that's an understatement. We *adored* her.

Rumors About Layla

The rumors started as whispers, and to be honest, I didn't pay much attention to them. "Did you hear Layla has a non-Muslim boyfriend?" "I hear he's really popular on campus." "Do you think her parents know?"

"Why are Muslim girls the only ones who have to watch their reputation?" Layla blurted one day before she showed us an aerobics routine. I was almost tempted to ask her what she meant, but seconds later, the workout music was playing and the opportunity passed.

Months later, I sat on the carpet in the city masjid when the imam stood to make an announcement. We had just finished the Friday prayer, and many of us were preparing to go home. "Pray for Layla," the imam said. My head jerked up in surprise, and my heart pounded as I waited for an explanation. It wasn't the norm to mention someone's name like that, unless they were in bad health or dying. "She's been admitted to the hospital for internal bleeding," he said, "and the doctors can't control it…"

"No Woman Should Have To Make That Choice"

Thankfully, Layla survived, but it wasn't long before we learned that Layla didn't appreciate the imam's public plea for prayers. She had gotten pregnant and had decided to get an abortion, but she ended up fighting for her own life after the procedure.

"I prayed for Allah to seal my heart," Layla told me. It was years after the ordeal, and I sat across from Layla on a couch in her apartment. She had moved on and was now engaged to be married, and she had just finished telling me about her fiancé and wedding plans.

I wasn't even sure I'd heard Layla correctly, but I saw tears shining in her eyes before she wiped them away. "I figured, that way," she said, "the regret wouldn't hurt so much."

I didn't know what to say. I wasn't a close friend of Layla's, at least I didn't consider myself to be, so I was unsure if the words were really meant for my ears or if she was just speaking her thoughts aloud. But either way, her words made me shudder.

"Abortion isn't about women's rights," she said, and this time, I knew she wanted me to hear. It was like old times, and she was teaching me "the ropes," this time in hopes that I *wouldn't* follow her example. "It's one of the most oppressive things you can do to a woman during her weakest moments. When you're young and confused, the last thing you should be asked to decide is whether or not to kill your own child. No woman should have to make that choice."

Life or Death

In both secular and religious circles, the discussion of abortion generally focuses on whether an unborn child should be granted life or death, and whether or not the choice itself can be justified on moral or religious grounds. In Islamic circles, the discussion focuses on the definition of "life." Is the fetus a full human being before the soul enters its body? If not, then is undergoing an early abortion taking an innocent life? Islamic scholars continue to be divided on this issue.

But for the Muslim woman with an unwanted pregnancy, the dilemma goes far beyond religious and political disagreements related to pro-life or pro-choice. When the seriousness of the decision weighs heavily on her, the personal and social pressures can feel like "life or death" for the woman herself.

The Pregnant Woman's Dilemma

Like Layla's experience, the problems that unmarried pregnant women face can be so overwhelming that they are willing to risk their own well-being in undergoing an abortion. Fear of ruining one's reputation, dishonoring the family, and irrevocably disrupting one's life, education, or career are just a few of the pressures that push women to consider abortion—even as they might want to keep the child. For women who come from cultures that put heavy emphasis on "family honor," not getting an abortion can mean subjecting themselves to possible death in the form of an "honor killing" should the family discover the illegitimate pregnancy.

However, unmarried women are not the only ones who face the "abortion dilemma." Married women with "high risk" pregnancies are often given medical advice favoring terminating the pregnancy. This is particularly the case for women who could lose their own lives if they carry the child full term. When pregnant women are faced with such dangerous circumstances, many begin to consider abortion as a justifiable option, even if they are practicing Muslims who generally consider abortion to be a grave sin.

Aftermath of an Abortion

"After I had the abortion," Layla told me, "I had so many dreams of my baby. I was scared to sleep sometimes. I was haunted by that terrible mistake for years." She looked away from me. "Even now, I regret what I did, and the dreams won't go away."

Many abortion discussions focus on the moral questions of pro-life and pro-choice, but for women who follow through with an abortion, the "pro-choice" decision is only the beginning of the struggle. In addition to medical and physiological risks connected to the procedure, there are emotional and psychological side effects as well.

Many mental health experts teach that guilt, regret, depression, and even suicidal thoughts are quite common in women who undergo abortion, and the intensity of these feelings is directly related to the woman's belief system about her body, the unborn child, and life in general. Thus, women who adhere to an ideology that frowns upon or outright forbids abortion will likely have a more difficult time emotionally or psychologically than women who feel justified morally, whether because they were unmarried and genuinely felt that abortion was the wisest or safest choice, or because they were married and feared for their life or the life of their child.

However, some mental health experts argue that regardless of what a woman believes about the morality or justification of an abortion, she is likely to suffer emotionally and psychologically as a result of the procedure. This is primarily because by psychological standards, abortion is considered a form of "trauma," hence the frequently used term *post-abortion syndrome* (PAS).

Impact of Abortion on Family and Society

When Layla shared her view that merely giving a young woman the option to abort her unborn child is a form of oppression, she was unwittingly speaking about the impact of abortion beyond a person's physical or psychological experience. Naturally, any serious personal decision that affects family life and has social and political implications cannot be discussed only in the context of someone's personal choice, even if this personal choice is granted and preserved.

In the context of a family, one woman's decision to abort can affect how other family members process and handle a future decision of that nature. In the case of Layla, her life-threatening experience, which was arguably the direct result of her perceived need to hide the pregnancy and the subsequent termination, likely forced her family to question the emotional, psychological, and spiritual safety of female family members after falling into sin.

In the context of society, the famous 1973 Roe vs. Wade case, in which the United States Supreme Court ruled in favor of a woman's right to an abortion, clearly demonstrates the legal and social implications of what is often perceived as a "personal decision." In fact, writer Alex McBride says that the case remains "one of the most intensely debated" rulings to date. He says, "In no other case has the Court entertained so many disputes around ethics, religion, and biology, and then so definitively ruled on them all" ("Landmark Cases: Roe vs. Wade [1973]").

Should a Woman Have To Choose?

After leaving Layla's apartment that day, I was unable to view abortion as something wholly disconnected from me. Her view that the option itself is oppressive to young women gave me pause, as it continues to do today. I have no idea if the abortion option is truly a form of oppression, nor do I know whether or not it is ever justifiable in Islam. But I do believe that the judgmental contexts in which so many Muslim women live force too many pregnant women to feel as if the decision has already been made for them—regardless of whether or not they have repented for any prior mistakes or sins in front of Allah.

This essay was first published via onislam.net

20
"He Raped Me, But My Honor Remains"
Coping With Life After Rape

"Honor cannot be stolen. It can only be surrendered. Surely, in the act of rape, it is the perpetrator, not the victim, who surrenders honor."
—Leeza Mangaldas, "Misogyny in India: we are all guilty" (edition.cnn.com)

~

I walked into my friend's house and greeted all the guests with salaams and a handshake. When I reached the young Arab woman cradling a baby in her arms, I could not keep from glancing repeatedly in her direction even after I had settled down on the carpet surrounded by other women. For some reason the Arab woman didn't seem to belong, and I was searching in her countenance for the answers to my unspoken questions. It wasn't the predominately African-American group of women that made the woman seem out of place. In all parts of the city, even in the lower socioeconomic area where we were right then, there were multitudes of ethnicities, colors, and nationalities, Arabs amongst them. But she seemed to be feeling out of place herself…

"She recently came to America," my friend told me later. "Her family disowned her, so a brother from our community married her and brought her here."

I creased my forehead in confusion. "Disowned her? Why?"

"She was raped," my friend said, her expression conveying that she herself was puzzled by her words. "So they didn't want anything to do with her anymore."

Rape at a Glance

Rape is the act of forcibly having sex with someone without their consent, and although anyone can be a victim of rape, women are disproportionately the victims, and the aggressors men.

Recently, the issue of rape made international headlines when the India gang rape case, in which the victim ultimately died from the injuries sustained after five men sexually assaulted her on a private bus, sparked new questions regarding what motivates sexual aggressors and what laws should be in place to better protect women and prosecute criminals.

However, while the world debates psychology, motives and legalities, there are thousands of victims of rape who must face life after rape—often without social, psychological, or legal support.

Wounds of Rape—Physical and Psychological

Rape is often thought of as primarily sexual in nature. However, rape is more an act of aggression than it is an act of "intimacy." More than anything, rape is a violent crime—intended by the aggressor to exert power over the victim—and can cause more long-term damage to the body than an act of physical assault. Some of the physical after effects of rape include the following:

- painful intercourse (with significant other)
- urinary infections
- uterine fibroids – non-cancerous tumors in muscle wall
- pregnancy
- sexually transmitted diseases (STDs) – HIV, genital warts, syphilis, gonorrhea, chlamydia, and others

Though the physical after effects of rape are quite damaging, some of the most traumatic after effects are psychological. "Healthy Place" writer Samantha Gluck says:

"One of the most common psychological consequences of rape is self-blame. Victims use self-blame as an avoidance-based coping tool. Self-blame slows or, in many cases, stops the healing process."

She goes on to list the following emotional and psychological effects of rape:

- post-traumatic stress disorder (PTSD) – feelings of severe anxiety and stress
- depression
- flashbacks – memories of rape as if it is taking place again
- borderline personality disorder
- sleep disorders
- eating disorders
- dissociative identity disorder
- guilt
- distrust of others – uneasy in everyday social situations
- anger

- feelings of personal powerlessness – victims feel the rapist robbed them of control over their bodies

Victims Reclaiming Their Lives

Although rape is undoubtedly one of the most traumatic experiences for many women, experiencing rape does not mean that life stops for victims. Many rape victims are able to live normal lives after the experience, and many go on to have healthy intimate relationships later in life.

Or in the words of Dr. Laura Berman: "Rape is one of the worst violations a person can suffer, and the scars can be everlasting — but you can reclaim your life."

When we hear about the more than 15 million women who have been victims of rape, the numbers can be disheartening. But amongst these millions of women are survivors who refused to allow a single incident, no matter how traumatic, to define their entire existence. In other words, they reclaimed their lives.

And amongst these remarkable survivors are Muslim women.

Amatullah's Story

I met Amatullah as anyone would a good friend, during a social gathering of Muslim women, and I liked her right away. We shared common goals in life; we loved reading and writing; and we were excited to attend as many faith-boosting seminars that the masjid could offer. Her husband and my husband also got to know each other, so we spent lots of time together whenever we could. In a sentence, she was one of the most balanced, down-to-earth sisters I'd met.

So I was surprised when she mentioned to me that when she was fifteen years old, she had been raped.

At the time, I held a stereotypical view of rape victims. I imagined that they were so emotionally and psychologically traumatized that "normal social behavior" was unlikely and a happy marriage almost impossible. But Amatullah proved me wrong.

And what was most therapeutic for Amatullah was her faith.

"I turned to Allah," she said. "But it was a really confusing experience for me because I just couldn't understand why it was happening to me."

She told me that the rape occurred one night when her parents were out and she was babysitting her younger brothers and sisters. The aggressor, who she says appeared to be in his late teens, entered her home and dragged her away from her younger siblings then raped her.

As she fought the rapist—but to no avail—she says that all she kept saying to herself was *"But I'm Muslim. But I'm Muslim…"*

"I grew up Muslim and I followed all the rules," she said. "I never dated or had relations with boys, so in my mind this wasn't supposed to happen to me. I was saving myself for marriage like Allah told me to, and I never imagined that this would be my first experience [with sex]."

"But I'm Muslim"

How well a victim fares after an incident of rape depends largely on the culture in which she lives—both in her home environment and in the society at large.

"I didn't tell anyone about it," Amatullah says. "It wasn't that I didn't think I'd get help. It was just that I couldn't believe it happened. So when he finished with me and left, I just put back on my clothes and went to check on my brothers and sisters."

She says, "Till today, I have no idea who that guy was, and I never tried to find out."

But for many victims of rape, the decision to not tell anyone is a very conscious one; and sadly, this tendency is rather common amongst Muslim women.

Unfortunately, in many predominately Muslim societies that have deviated from Islam and embraced tribal customs, the decision to not reveal an incident of rape is motivated by a construed notion of "honor"—the idea that the moral and social nobility of a woman or her family rests in a female's private parts, regardless of whether or not she is guilty of moral transgression. In some of the more barbaric societies that exist today, a woman could be murdered if her name is connected to even the rumor of "dishonor," hence the term "honor killing."

Thus, for many Muslim women, the decision to not report an incident of rape is not a question of morality; it is a question of survival.

"Your Honor Is Most Important"

I was teaching a class of female high school seniors (most of whom came from predominately Muslim countries) when some of my students shared with me the advice their parents had given them as graduation approached.

"My mother told me to be careful," one of my students shared. This student had received a full scholarship to study abroad and would be living far from her family, and her mother wanted her to be very cognizant of any contact with males. "She told me, 'Remember, your honor is most important.'" My student contorted her face. "I told her, 'No it's not.'"

I nodded, proud that my student had come to this realization despite her home culture. "That's true," I said. "Your honor is not most important. Your soul is."

And it is through focusing on our souls—by turning to Allah for help and direction no matter what our backgrounds or experiences—that keeps our lives healthy, rejuvenating and "honorable," no matter what our bodies may suffer during life's sojourn.

This essay was first published via onislam.net

21
Her Body Says No To Sex
Understanding Vaginismus

~

A few months ago, a group of Muslim girls relaxed in my friend's living room watching television with my friend's daughter. I was upstairs chatting with my friend about some projects we were working on for the youth. Later one of the girls came to me, clearly upset.

"Why do Muslims do that?" she said.

"What happened?" I asked her.

"When we were flipping through the channels, we saw a man and woman kissing," she explained, "and all the girls screamed, 'Ewwww! That's disgusting!'" She shook her head then continued, "And I told them, 'No it's not disgusting. They just shouldn't be doing it on TV, and they should be married.'"

She then looked at me, a question in her eyes before she asked, "Why do Muslims act like that? Like it's nasty to kiss and have sex? I don't want to think like that. I want to enjoy those things when I get married."

Sex and Shame

It is possible that the teenage girls' reaction of disgust to the man and woman on television had more to do with seeing intimacy displayed so shamelessly than with disgust regarding the intimate act itself. Nevertheless, it is undeniable that in many cultures, sex and intimacy are viewed as shameful acts even when they are not displayed on television—and even when the intimacy takes place between a husband and wife.

As I discussed in the blog "Let's Talk About Sex" as part of a series on Muslims and sex, viewing intimacy as a shameful act, particularly as it relates to women's sexuality, is unfortunately tied to the concept of *hayaa'* (Islamic modesty) in many predominately Muslim cultures; and consequently, both husbands and wives suffer from this false sense of modesty. In the blog, I write:

Often, both men and women remain sexually unsatisfied because while a woman's ignorance of her body and sexuality might be sexually arousing to some men on wedding night, this glorified ignorance gets old and tiresome over time, especially for those who wish to stay within the limits set by Allah and derive sexual satisfaction from only their spouse.

Tragically, the women themselves suffer psychologically, as many feel ashamed of their sexual desires and view it as "inappropriate" to speak about what arouses them or to initiate any sexual contact.

Though this problem is not discussed much in Muslim circles, the psychological ramifications of viewing female sexuality as a form of immodesty, even in the bounds of marriage, can be quite tragic for married couples. And this tragedy often goes beyond sexual frustration during sexual intercourse itself. It sometimes results in a woman's body rejecting penetration altogether, thus preventing sex from taking place at all, hence the condition *vaginismus*.

Vaginismus, the Vagina's Panic Attack

"Vaginismus is a panic attack in the vagina," says Drs. Ditza Katz and Ross Lynn Tabisel in their book *Private Pain: Understanding Vaginismus & Dyspareunia* (2013, p. 3).

In other words, vaginismus occurs when the vagina involuntary constricts to prevent any penetration, whether during a routine vaginal exam, while inserting a tampon, or upon male genital penetration preceding sexual intercourse. Though a physical or medical condition can cause this condition, vaginismus often occurs while no physical or medical condition is present. There are many non-medical reasons for vaginismus, and one of them is the cultural and psychological association of sexuality and/or the vagina (or penis) with something shameful, immodest, or "dirty."

Her Body Says No to Sex

I first heard the term *vaginismus* when a young Muslim woman contacted me after reading my blog "Let's Talk About Sex." She thanked me for writing about the taboo issue of sex in the Muslim community, and she shared with me that, due to how her own culture had taught her to think about her body and sex, she suffered from the condition vaginismus.

At the time that the young woman reached out to me, she and her husband had been married for more than a year and a half, and they still had not consummated the marriage. After multiple failed attempts at penetration, she sought professional help and underwent intensive therapy to overcome this condition. Fortunately, she has since contacted me to tell me the current result of the therapy: After more than one and a half years of marriage, she and her husband successfully had sex for the first time.

Helping Others

In an effort to help other females suffering from this condition, the young woman decided to share her story with the world. So in "She Couldn't Have Sex," we interview 23-year-old Tasniya about her struggle with vaginismus.

This essay was first published via ummzakiyyah.com

22
She Couldn't Have Sex
Interview with Tasniya: Part 1

~

In this interview, Tasniya, a young Muslim woman discusses how vaginismus prevented her and her husband from having sex for more than one and a half years.

Umm Zakiyyah (UZ): *Please tell us a little bit about yourself: your name, age, ethnic background, marital status, and where you spent your childhood and young adulthood.*

Tasniya Sultana (TS): My name is Tasniya Sultana and I am 23 years old. I was born in Bangladesh. When I was around 3 years old, I went to Australia and I spent my childhood there. At the age of 10, I came to USA which is where I live. I got married straight after college in 2012 and now I am living with my husband.

UZ: *Before we talk about what led to the condition vaginismus, can you please tell us what vaginismus is, what the symptoms are, how it develops and why, and who is most susceptible to this condition?*

TS: [According to Women's Therapy Center], the basic definition of vaginismus is [the following]:

> *"...the instantaneous, involuntary tightening of the pelvic floor muscles in anticipation of vaginal penetration. This reaction will occur if penetration is perceived as upsetting, painful (even before attempting it!) frightening, or dangerous, making the body scream out loud, 'NO ENTRY!' Occasionally, vaginismus will be caused by a physical problem such as a birth defect, or surgery. Either way, it is a vagina in panic..."*

[In the book, *Private Pain: Understanding Vaginismus & Dyspareunia*, the authors tell us]:

> *"Vaginismus affects adolescent girls and women of all ages, all cultures, all religions, all socioeconomic and education levels, singles, married, and lesbian couples alike. A common myth is that vaginismus is caused by a physical problem like an infection in the vagina or an allergic reaction but that is not the case. Usually, males explore their genitals from a very early age since their genitals are visible and they can see*

them quite clearly. Therefore, men usually understand their body and know what they like and what they don't. However, females' genitals are internal, invisible, and not usually explored. Therefore, there is this mystery associated with the vagina because many females never explore or even look at it before they are sexually active. For this reason, the 'mysterious and unknown vagina' can be very scary to many females. In addition, a person's upbringing and emotional health will also play a part in determining whether she will develop vaginismus or whether she will be able to explore her body and emotions. Any traumatic experience, especially to the genital area (whether it's physical, verbal, emotional, psychological) can have an adverse effect on the body and the mind and can bring about vaginismus as well" (Katz and Tabisel, 94-95).

[About women's sexuality, the authors say further]:

"We also need to understand that in a sexual relationship, often the women carries the emotional burden of being 'done to' while the man is the 'doer.' Therefore, this carries an enormous weight on the female because they usually have a lack of control and are "choice-less" even if the man is understanding, non-forceful, and the act is consensual. This same emotional feeling also transfers when a woman has to go through a pelvic exam, where the gynecologist is given permission to enter the woman's body yet the women is reluctant to accept this penetration due to a lack of control" (Katz and Tabisel, 95-96).

As a summary, some of the causes of vaginismus according to Katz and Tabisel [are]:

- *Fear of the body and its function, fear of the "unknown."*
- *Being worried about the fragility of the vagina*
- *Fear of pain*
- *Past illness/surgery/medical procedures*
- *Religious inhibitions and taboos*
- *Cultural variations*
- *Parental or peer misrepresentation of sex and sexuality*
- *The inability to say No to an unwanted sexual situation. [This] causes the feeling of being forced, of being option-less, of the need for self-protection, and thus vaginismus*
- *Childhood sexual abuse*
- *Parental indulgence and over-protectiveness*
- *Failed penetration experiences*
- *Fear of penetration and infection*
- *Loss of control*
- *Physical and social causes*

For more detailed information about each of the causes, I highly recommend to buy the book *Private Pain*.

UZ: *How can sufferers of this condition get help?*

TS: Sufferers of vaginismus can get help by visiting www.womentc.com. It is called the Women's Therapy Center and this is the place where I went to get cured and I got cured 100%. *Alhamdulillah* [All praise is due to God], the doctors are amazing and really know what they are doing. I highly encourage anyone who is suffering to reach out to this clinic because it has changed my life.

UZ: *Thank you for taking time to educate us on this condition. What inspired you to do this interview?*

TS: When I got married and I wasn't able to consummate my marriage, I was very confused. I went to several counselors, Imams, and gynecologists but no one really understood me. I felt isolated and depressed because I thought I was the 'only one' going through this. For example, my gynecologist gave me an exercise to do: she told me to buy the smallest tampon in the store, put lube on it, and try to insert it into my vagina. It was a nightmare for me! I just couldn't do it and I felt like a failure every single time. Therefore, at one point, I seriously considered leaving my husband because I felt as though I was being unfair to him and he deserved better. Feelings of shame and guilt overwhelmed to the point where I was really having difficulties living a normal life. *Insha'Allah* [God-willing], my husband and I want to start a family some day and I thought that I could never do such a thing because I couldn't even have intercourse!

Alhamdulillah, after making *du'aa* [prayerful supplication] to Allah (SWT) and doing some research, I came across the clinic in NY [New York]. I realized my condition actually has a name and I'm not some sort of weirdo because there are others out there just like me! Then, I realized that if I am a Muslim woman who was suffering silently, I am sure there are other Muslim women who are also suffering silently. This is a taboo topic to talk about and no one likes to admit that they can't have intercourse (especially after marriage). That is when I decided that I have to spread awareness about this so I can help the ummah. I want our ummah to know that there is a cure and vaginismus can be a thing of the past *insha'Allah*!

UZ: *What are some of your memories as a child and young adult that you feel are significant in shaping how you felt about your body, specifically as a female?*

TS: I always felt uncomfortable in my body. I have low self esteem and body image issues. I was always under the impression that things like the period or menses are a dirty thing. I would always be ashamed of my pad leaking, which I believe contributed me to ultimately be ashamed and disgusted by my vagina. Because I didn't realize that menses are a normal part of the life, it became something that was unnatural to me.

I also associated pain, shame, and disgust with things like intercourse. I don't think I was ever taught that intercourse is a pleasurable thing for the husband and wife. No one ever told me that intercourse is pleasurable in the eyes of Allah (SWT) when it is done in the confines of marriage. Therefore, mentally I conjured up this negative image of intercourse and associated pain and disgust with it, which ultimately led me to having vaginismus.

UZ: *When you reached puberty, did you know what was happening? If so, what did you know about this physical change? If not, why not?*

TS: When I reached puberty, I had no idea what was going on with my body. The first time I had my period was a traumatic experience. I thought I had cancer and I was afraid to tell my parents because I didn't know what they would think. Finally my mom saw me crying and I told her what had happened. She gave me a pad but I never really understood what was going on and why I was having my period all of a sudden. Therefore, this lack of understanding of what truly happened in my body could have resulted in having vaginismus.

UZ: *As a teen and young adult, how did you feel about your natural feelings toward the opposite sex? Did you talk to anyone about these feelings? If not, why not? If so, who, and how was the topic addressed?*

TS: I always felt ashamed of having feelings toward the opposite sex. In my mind, I thought I was sinning and God would punish me for having these feelings. I would try to contain them but I couldn't. I would talk to my friends about these topics but that's about it. We were all going through the same thing and we really didn't understand what was going on. I would enjoy talking about boys with them but afterwards I'd feel guilty because I thought I would go to Hell for even talking about such things.

UZ: *Do you recall feeling confused or frustrated as a child or young adult regarding any "taboo" subjects? Please explain.*

TS: I always felt upset when I couldn't openly ask or speak about certain topics with my family members. I remember an aunty of the family once telling my mom how 'advanced' children have become these days because they know so much about topics like intercourse and sex. She remarked how back in the day children were so innocent and because they didn't know what intercourse or sex was until they got married. It almost seemed that because children are learning about these topics at an early age, they are somehow "messed up". So it would often frustrate me because I felt like those aunties were talking about me. I learned a lot about sex from my classmates and health classes in school. However, I didn't think I was a "messed up" child for knowing these things. It almost seemed that being ignorant about the world was a sign of purity and being knowledgeable was a sign of impurity. It just didn't feel right and I felt very conflicted.

UZ: *When did you first discover you had vaginismus? How did you know there was a problem? What happened?*

TS: Before marriage, I had a gut feeling that something would go wrong. Every time I would think of having intercourse, I felt nervous or afraid. However, I thought all girls felt that way because it is something new for them. I first discovered I had vaginismus after I got married. I couldn't consummate my marriage so I knew something was wrong. We would try for hours and hours to have intercourse but I just couldn't. I would start panicking and crying in bed. I was so afraid to open my legs up even when my husband would try to. If he tried to touch my vagina or anywhere near that area, I would move his hands away and push him.

When he tried to enter me, it literally felt like he was hitting a brick wall. I started to think something was wrong with me anatomically and maybe I didn't have a hole or something. It was frustrating and I knew something was wrong. I just didn't know exactly what it was and the traditional doctors or gynecologists did not know either.

Another experience that confirmed that something was wrong with me was when I went to have my first gynecological exam. It was a nightmare. I was freaking out and my heart was racing. When the gynecologist came to do my pap smear, I was so terrified. I was not about to let her put that instrument inside me. It looked so big and scary! She tried to put her small finger inside me and the pain was excruciating. I started crying and I told her I did not want to go through with the exam. So my husband and I left. I was so embarrassed. I felt like I failed him. I failed us. Again, I had no idea what was wrong with me but there was something wrong indeed.

UZ: *What do you believe was most significant in causing this condition for you?*

TS: I believe the lack of understanding and knowing my body was one of the primary causes for this condition. In addition, having self esteem and body image issues was also a major contributing factor.

To learn more about vaginismus and other female sexual health issues, visit the website for Women's Therapy Center at womentc.com or read Private Pain: Understanding Vaginismus & Dyspareunia *by Ditza Katz, PT, Ph.D. and Ross Lynn Tabisel, LCSW, Ph.D.*

This essay was first published via ummzakiyyah.com

23
She Couldn't Have Sex
Interview with Tasniya: Part 2

~

In Part 2, Tasniya discusses what women suffering from this condition (vaginismus) should do and how parents, husbands, and Muslim communities can help. She also shares common mistakes made by friends, family, and Muslims that only worsen the condition for sufferers.

UZ: *If a woman believes she's suffering from this condition, what advice would you give her?*

TS: If you believe you are suffering from this condition, please know that you are not alone. Please know that Allah (SWT) has not abandoned you and He is listening to every prayer and every tear of yours. Keep making *du'aa* to Him and He will bring ease in you and your family's hearts. Also know that there is a name for this condition (vaginismus) and there is a cure. *Alhamdulillah*, I got cured by going to the Women's Therapy Center (www.womentc.com) and so have others. The hardest thing is to take that first step and seek help. But the doctors there are so amazing and so understanding. *Alhamdulillah*, they have changed my life and they can help you too *insha'Allah*. Trust in Allah (SWT) and reach out to them! They can help. In the mean time, there is a book called *Private Pain* by Ditza Katz and Ross Tabisel. They are the doctors who helped me and they wrote this book. You can get it on Amazon and read more information and stories about sufferers who went through this!

UZ: *What can parents do to prevent this from happening to their daughters?*

TS: I think parents need to educate their children about their bodies in a healthy manner. They should also be open about topics such as menses, intercourse, wet dreams, etc. I believe that one of the main reasons I had vaginismus is because of my lack of understanding my body. I never knew what my vagina looked like until I went to the clinic. When the doctors asked me look in the mirror and see what my vagina looks like, I literally had a panic attack. However, I needed to go through that. After that, I came home and looked at my vagina for a couple of minutes a day just to show myself that it really isn't a big deal and this is a part of my body just like my eyes, nose, and mouth are.

Therefore, when I have children *insha'Allah*, I am going to have these conversations about the genitalia, and 'taboo' topics that are not discussed in the Muslim family. I believe that education truly empowers a person— even when it comes to their body. Once I understood my body and I was able to get over the fear and negative feelings associated with the vagina, I felt much more liberated and slowly I got better *alhamdulillah*.

UZ: *How can husbands help their wives overcome this condition?*

TS: The biggest thing a husband can do is be patient with his wife. Do NOT force her to have intercourse because that will just make things worse. *Alhamdulillah*, my husband was really patient with me and never complained or regretted that he does not have a 'normal' marriage. That kept me strong and helped me fight through vaginismus. So be patient, ask Allah (SWT) to help you through this, and understand that this is NOT your wife's fault and she is NOT doing it on purpose. Wives will already feel guilty and ashamed for not being able to have intercourse and the worst thing a husband can do is to make them feel more guilty on top of that. So please be patient, if not for her, then for the sake of Allah (SWT).

UZ: *What can Muslim communities and masjids do to help sufferers overcome this condition, given that they may never know who is suffering specifically?*

TS: Again, I believe the number one thing that Muslim communities and masjids must do is to educate themselves and others. Before I knew about vaginismus, I went to an Imam and told him about my condition. I asked him if other women had the same issues. He said they did and that because intercourse is new for me, I am having a hard time with it. [He also said] *Insha'Allah* if we try it a couple of more times, I will be able to get over it. *MaashaAllah*, he was a very nice Imam and may Allah bless and preserve him for being caring towards me. However, I did not have intercourse after trying couple of times. As a matter of fact, I couldn't have intercourse for more than a year and a half.

Therefore, Muslim communities first need to educate themselves and acknowledge the fact that there is something called vaginismus and it affects many women regardless of age, race, or religion. And Imams especially need to know about vaginismus and know about the Women's

Therapy Center in NY [New York] so that they can point couples to the right direction *insha'Allah*.

I also believe that our *khutbah* topics need to be focused more on taboo topics such as vaginismus, domestic violence, or alcohol and drug abuse, so that we can create more awareness. *Jummah* [the Friday prayer] is the few time that many Muslims gather at one place so we need to seriously make use of that time by spreading awareness and giving resources that can guide the ummah *insha'Allah*.

UZ: *What are some mistakes that friends, family, and Muslims do to worsen the condition for sufferers, in your experience?*

TS: People really need to be sensitive about topics like pregnancy and children. After I got married, one of the first things that people in my community asked me was about having children. I know they mean no harm but for someone who was suffering from vaginismus, it was a blow for me. Every time I used to go to the masjid, the sisters would ask me about children and whether I am trying to have children. I would come home in tears every single time because a part of me felt like I could not have children due to vaginismus. I felt more isolated, depressed, and out of place. So I would highly recommend if people would be more mindful when they ask such questions. Honestly, it is the couple's business whether they will have children or not and when they will have children. I wish people would stop nagging married couples because we never know what someone is truly going through.

I also realized that people got surprised when I finally opened up about my condition. Instead of being empathetic and understanding, I had people ask me things like "Are you sure this is real?" Again, when someone asks things like this, it reinforces in the sufferers mind that they are just an odd ball because they have something that others don't. Do you ever ask a cancer patient if cancer is real? I bet not.

UZ: *Other than professional help, in your experience, what are some things that are most helpful in helping your recovery?*

TS: The main thing that was helpful in my recovery was making *du'aa* to Allah (SWT). Whenever I felt like the world did not understand me or misunderstood me, I could find solace in Him. Allah truly guided and helped us through this. He gave patience in my husband's heart and gave me strength to endure the pain. *Alhamdulillah*, I am truly grateful that Allah SWT gave me vaginismus because I learned so much from it.

UZ: *Do you believe full recovery is possible? If so, how? If not, why not?*

TS: Absolutely! *Alhamdulillah*, I am fully recovered! Anyone who goes through the treatment are also fully recovered! I can have intercourse without any problem, I can use a tampon of any size, I can use spacers, and I can have a gynecology exam without freaking out! *Allahu Akbar* [God is the Greatest]!

UZ: *What do you hope readers will learn from your experience?*

TS: I hope readers will understand that there is something called vaginismus and it is real. If you or a family member or friend is going through this, know that there is help. Please visit www.womentc.com to learn more about vaginismus and the Women's Therapy Center. I hope that readers understand that it is not the sufferer's fault for having this and the best thing they can do is to be empathetic, non-judgmental, and patient with the sufferer.

To learn more about vaginismus and other female sexual health issues, visit the website for Women's Therapy Center at womentc.com or read Private Pain: Understanding Vaginismus & Dyspareunia *by Ditza Katz, PT, Ph.D. and Ross Lynn Tabisel, LCSW, Ph.D.*

This essay was first published via ummzakiyyah.com

24
Gay and Muslim?

~

A Cry for Help

I have a question and I really don't know where to turn. This is something I can't even talk to my parents or friends about, so I hope you can help me. I am a 19-year-old Muslim girl and I'm sexually attracted to other girls. Please don't judge me. I know it's not right to act on my feelings and so far I haven't, alhamdulillah. But I come from a good Muslim family, and now I live away from home for college and it's getting more & more difficult to stay away from sin. I'm part of the MSA (Muslim Student Association) & I tried to bring up this topic once (without telling them it was about me); and the Muslims got all upset & some people started making jokes about "It's Adam and Eve, not Adam and Steve." And I was just asking what someone with these feelings should do to stay away from sin. I didn't say homosexual acts are okay! Now I'm getting really depressed and feel so alone. I'm even starting to question my faith. I mean, why can't Muslims with gay & lesbian feelings get advice or help when Muslims have no problem giving advice to Muslims who don't wear hijab, who drink, who commit zina, and even Muslims who don't pray! Do you know of any online resources or support groups for Muslims I can join anonymously? I don't want to lose my faith. Please help me.
—Don't want to be Gay Muslim

This is an example of the type of questions I regularly receive from Muslim youth wanting advice.

How Can We Help?

Undoubtedly, any Muslim who reaches out for help in practicing his or her faith deserves not only help and guidance, but also patience, compassion, and empathy. No believer should be shamed or blamed for simply wanting advice in fighting sin, whether that sin is major or minor, normal or abnormal. None of us is without sin. Prophet Muhammad, *sallallahu 'alayhi wa sallam*, taught us that all of the children of Adam sin, and the best of those who sin are those who constantly repent.

Therefore, as we strive for Paradise, we should help each other in our efforts of repentance, even if the sin is shocking or repulsive, as homosexuality is to many people.

Homophobia: Remaking Religion in a New Image

Ironically, one of the greatest barriers to helping Muslims like the nineteen-year-old Muslim girl above is the alleged fight against homophobia. Literally, *homophobia* means an irrational fear of or paranoia regarding homosexuality or homosexuals. However, socially and politically, homophobia has come to mean anything that offends gays and lesbians, specifically those gays and lesbians who either reject God and religion altogether or those who wish to remake God and religion in their image.

Unfortunately, the latter group now includes professed Muslims. Some of these Muslims identify with a gay or lesbian orientation while others are merely silent (or vocal) supporters of "the cause"—whose primary goal is to dismantle the moral teachings of the Qur'an under the guise of "new interpretations."

Gay Struggle vs. Gay Agenda

In the Qur'an, Allah discusses the stipulations of *nikaah* (Islamic marriage):

"And give to the women [whom you marry] their dowry [*mahr*] as a free marital gift..."
—Al-Nisaa (4:4)

However, one lesbian blogger who professes to be Muslim claims that Allah's instructions are outdated. *"I think the concept of nikkah is largely outdated,"* the lesbian blogger told me in an email.

She went on to say that Islamic marriage is, for all intents and purposes, a reprehensible financial transaction that involves selling and buying a woman's sexual organs, a concept that is inferior to her homosexual "marriage":

In the fiqhi discussions, the nikkah contract at its most basic is one whereby the husband purchases with the mahr access to the wife's sexual organs usually from one of her male relatives. This is why this is little discussion or understanding of marital rape or the wife's right of consent before engaging in sex with her husband. This concept of purchasing or

105

a contract stipulating access to a spouse sexually is anathema to the relationship I have with my wife. Our marriage is based on more egalitarian principles of mutual love, support and commitment.

Interestingly, this explanation utilizes the same approach used by Islamophobes, wherein they describe praiseworthy Islamic concepts in reprehensible terms to make their "alternative" appear not only logical and justifiable, but also more desirable than anything offered by Allah in Islam.

Clearly, this view is not indicative of a Muslim's "gay struggle," wherein one struggles with gay feelings but merely needs support and empathy from believers in striving against temptation to sin. Rather, this view is indicative of a "gay agenda" designed to dismantle Islamic teachings altogether.

As we seek to be supportive and empathetic with Muslims struggling with homosexual desires, it is important that we don't mistake a gay agenda for a gay struggle. The former is a path to *kufr* (disbelief) while the latter is a path to *tawbah* (repentance).

Is a Gay Orientation "Natural"?

In her email, the lesbian blogger argued, "God created us perfectly, irrespective of orientation." She also said that "a person's sexual orientation is not a mistake, sinful, or something to feel ashamed about nor hidden or suppressed."

In other words, Islam's requirement to avoid acting on our underlying sinful desires (homosexual or otherwise) and the perpetual existence of our underlying sinful desires are somehow mutually exclusive to each other… Or they are evidence that no Islamic law exists to prevent us from acting on our sinful desires *as long as we can convince ourselves that our sinful desires stem from a static "orientation" that is part of our "perfect nature."*

Put simply, if we can blame Allah for our ongoing struggles and desires in this world, we are allegedly absolved of any responsibility for following His laws in the process.

This is an interesting argument given that not a single one of us *controls* the tests we are handed, only how we respond.

Sexual Orientation Argument Debunked

If we use the blogger's definition of orientation (an underlying consistent sexual desire that the person himself/herself did not choose), then we have to recognize that there are people who have an underlying "orientation" toward animals, inanimate objects, and even children—orientations that they too did not choose. Thus, if we remove acts of homosexuality from the category of sin based on the consistency of the underlying sexual desire beyond one's control, then we must accept that a host of sexual desires can be acted on without falling into sin.

Though the modern Western world typically uses the "consenting adults" argument to dismiss the validity of acting on sexual desires toward children, **the "consenting adults" argument is inherently flawed when approving homosexual acts.**

In other words, if you believe homosexual acts are <u>not</u> sinful but you apply the condition of "consenting adults," then you are agreeing to the same principle that rules homosexual acts as sinful in the first place—that, ultimately, morality trumps desire. The only question is: What is *your* definition of "morality"?

Muslims, like Jews and Christians, recognize only one ultimate authority in defining morality: God. Thus, any underlying "nature" is irrelevant in discussions of sexual morality. Although many Muslims (as well as Jews and Christians), argue that homosexuality is "unnatural," this is really a moot point as far as the religious concepts of sin and obedience are concerned.

Islam, as a general rule, is most concerned with sinful acts, not with the underlying desire itself, irrespective of whether or not the desire is rooted in nature (i.e. a man and a woman sexually desiring each other) or a perversion of nature (i.e. a person desiring sexual relations with an animal).

However, viewing certain desires as unnatural (as some desires certainly are) is helpful for those seeking to understand and subsequently root out their perverted desires. But, in the context of religious morality, the categorization of the sexual desire as natural or unnatural is irrelevant when discussing sinful behaviors.

In other words, in Islam, we are not held accountable for *desiring* something sinful. We are held accountable only for *acting on* something sinful.

When We Betray Those We Can Help

When offering advice to others about a sinful lifestyle, there are only two possibilities: We frame our advice according to how the sin is viewed in Allah's Book and the Sunnah; or we frame our advice according to some other point of view. When we choose the latter approach, we are betraying those whom Allah has entrusted us to help.

Whenever we are given both *emaan* (Islamic faith) and a severe trial, it as if we are being given an answer key along with a test. And if we are able to share with others the lessons we learn during our tests in life, we are offering a hand to others with struggles like ours. In fact, as believers we have a *responsibility* to help others during our brief sojourn on this earth, especially if Allah has equipped us with both the life experience and the Islamic knowledge necessary to help others remain on the right path.

I just wish there were more experienced, knowledgeable people to help Muslims like the nineteen-year-old Muslim girl struggling with lesbian desires, help that strikes a balance between not judging her for her struggle and not inviting her to effectively indulge in the very sin she is crying out for help in fighting.

…Or inviting her to leave the very faith she wants to hold onto by encouraging her to replace her gay struggle (a path to *tawbah*) with a gay agenda (a path to *kufr*).

This essay was first published via muslimmatters.org

25
We Are All Being Tested

"Do you believe that <u>your</u> struggle is more severe than the personal trials of every other Muslim? Why then do you say yours is "unfair"? Is it unfair because you are facing it, or is it unfair because you believe no other trial is at least as severe?"
— from the journal of Umm Zakiyyah

~

During the most difficult and confusing times of our lives, our faith is often shaken. We begin to question who we are and what we believe. Sometimes when there is no one around to hear us but the walls of our room and God above the heavens, we cry out, "Why me? Why is this happening to me?"

Our despair can be due to the death of a loved one, to a terminal illness diagnosis, or even the loss of a coveted career or educational opportunity. But regardless of the details of our individual trials, beneath each episode is the excruciating feeling of helplessness because we have lost—or we are at risk of losing—something that is dear to us or something that we believe is essential to our sense of self or the meaning of our lives.

No one is exempt from life's trials, not even prophets and righteous people.

Allah says,

"Or do you think that you will enter Paradise while such [trial] has not yet come to you as came to those who passed on before you? They were touched by poverty and hardship and were shaken until [even their] messenger and those who believed with him said, 'When [will come] the help of Allah?' Unquestionably, the help of Allah is [always] near."
—Al-Baqarah (2:214)

Can You Help Me?

Being in a position where I'm regularly contacted by people seeking advice during some of the most difficult and trying times of their lives is very humbling. Emails, phone calls, and whispered stories in which

109

someone seeks help and guidance are parts of my daily life, as it is for many public figures, community leaders, and respected members in the Muslim community.

Though the details of each story are unique, many of those seeking advice have very similar (and sometimes identical) struggles. But not every narrative is shared for the purpose of receiving spiritual direction. Some people need only a shoulder to cry on or someone to listen with empathy and without judgment to their pain and confusion. For most of us, both are essential to getting through a difficult trial. Thus, it is a combination of both religious honesty and nonjudgmental compassion that we all need when we reach out to someone and say, "Can you help me?"

When We Don't Care What's Right

In facing the inevitable trials of life, there are times when we don't care what is right or wrong and we merely want what we want even if it means displeasing Allah. In these circumstances, our reaching out and seeking advice is usually for the purpose of eliciting from someone affirmation that, in response to our trial, we don't actually *have to* do what we know full well Allah has required us to do.

What makes this spiritual trauma both crippling and self-destructive is that we are not always conscious of our illicit intentions. It often takes an outsider looking in to point out the sometimes obvious inconsistencies in our words and actions, inconsistencies that go far beyond the natural, inevitable inconsistency that we are all riddled with as humans. Destructive spiritual trauma occurs when our trials exacerbate the darkness of our souls, when we are effectively throwing ourselves headlong into sin and, more tragically, disbelief.

The Prophet (peace be upon him) said, "The believer is the mirror of the believer." Thus, during these times, our entire perception of reality hinges on someone holding up a mirror in front of us and showing us our reflections, no matter how repulsive our image might be.

Spiritual Destruction

When our trial involves open disobedience to Allah, it is excruciatingly difficult to face ourselves, so we often lash out at others and blame them for holding up a mirror in front of us. We often become meticulously critical of and ultra sensitive to everything that is said to us or to even how people behave around us. In this way, we project our guilty conscience on others and interpret nearly every word of advice as a personal attack.

Sometimes we become, quite frankly, pretty nasty people to be around. Loved ones may even tiptoe around us, afraid that even the innocent "How are you?" will be interpreted negatively.

Sometimes we even *provoke* discord so that we can accuse someone of being mean to us, especially those who are reminding us of Allah and pleading with us to repent and change our ways. We might rush to social media so that we can play victim behind our Facebook or Twitter accounts, cushioned by the multitude of "likes" and "followers" who will nearly always support our pity parties…because we craftily frame our posts such that we evoke the most sympathy and the least scrutiny, sometimes even hiding behind someone else's words or blog that we share on our page.

Some of us make the spiritually tragic choice to use social media to not only publicize our sin, but also to openly promote it. This promotion is often carried out under the guise of some greater cause or "spreading awareness" about an issue that we claim is close to our hearts (an issue that conveniently allows us to continue our sin guilt-free while painting others as harassers and aggressors if they, publicly or privately, tell us that we are wrong).

If we are promoting our un-Islamic lifestyle of drinking alcohol or interacting inappropriately with the opposite sex, our "greater cause" will likely be "Don't judge." If we are promoting our non-hijabi status, we will likely—in addition to championing the "Don't judge" cause—criticize and shame movements that praise or support successful hijabis who are athletes, journalists, or public figures. "So are the only *real* Muslim women those who wear hijab?" we might cry out indignantly, even as the pro-hijab movements claimed nothing of this sort.

Thus, when our response to our test is so spiritually destructive that we have moved from feeling shame for our sin to openly bragging about it or even promoting it, it's not good enough to merely have multitudes of people being kind and empathetic due to our struggles in the faith. We feel the need to go a step further and tear down those who are being positively recognized for their strengths in the areas that we have refused to work on spiritually.

Whose Trial Is More Difficult? Mine or Yours?

In my short story, "The Invitation," we learn the trials of two best friends, Faith and Paula. Faith is struggling with her attachment to her high school boyfriend, John, as she comes to terms with her spiritual obligations after becoming Muslim. And Paula is struggling with her faith and sexuality after she decides to come out as gay—and convert to Islam.

Whose trial is more difficult? Faith's or Paula's? Oftentimes, when pondering the answer to this, we use our opinions, experiences, and selfish perceptions to come to a conclusion. However, we have no way of knowing whose test is more difficult because, ultimately, the most excruciatingly difficult tests are faced by those with the most *emaan* (faith) in their hearts.

Prophet Muhammad (peace be upon him) was once asked, "O Messenger of Allah, who are the people who are most severely tried?" He replied, "The people who are tested the most severely are the Prophets, then the righteous, then the next best and the next best, and a man will be tested in accordance with his level of faith; the stronger his faith, the more severe will be his test" (Ahmad, *sahih*).

Thus, the level of difficulty a person faces through his or her tests is a matter of the unseen, as we have no way of knowing the level of righteousness in a person's heart.

This Is So Unfair!

It's difficult *not* to look at someone else's life and think that they have it easier than we do. After all, we experience firsthand only our *own* trials, not anyone else's. As such, we have intimate knowledge of the painful nuances and visceral realities of whatever trial we're facing. We have no way of having that same level of knowledge regarding someone else's life, no matter how close they are to us, in our hearts or circumstance.

"This is so unfair. This is so f—ing unfair."

These are Faith's angry words from "The Invitation" in response to her difficult trial—and they mirror how so many of us feel about the tests Allah gives us, even if we don't speak these words aloud.

None of us is immune to the degeneration of the human spirit. We can all fall victim to the darkness of sin that mars our souls. And we can all fall victim to imagining that Allah is being unjust or "unfair" by giving us a trial that no one else has to face.

But ultimately, we are *all* being tested…and we can all pass our tests, with the help of Allah.

And, unquestionably, the help of Allah is always near.

This essay was first published via muslimmatters.org

26
Being Gay Is Definitely Harder?
A Reader Responds to "We Are All Being Tested"

~

After MuslimMatters.org published the blog "We Are All Being Tested" (which briefly references the fictional characters Faith and Paula from my short story "The Invitation"), a reader posted the following comment in reference to Paula's struggle with homosexual desires in comparison to Faith's heterosexual struggle with her boyfriend [and I'm sharing it here because it highlights a very important topic]:

> Being gay is definitely harder. Faith can eventually overcome her boyfriend and find another muslim to love and marry. Paula can never get married because she is gay. Paula also probably feels constant shame and guilt like all of us gays who do not act on our desire. To be gay is such a hard test, one of the most severe. The people who acted on it were punished the worst, as mentioned in the Quran in Surah Lut. Muslims who are gay either leave Islam or commit suicide. This speaks volumes about the severity of this test.. On top of being hard, it's just so confusing. Why am I gay if Allah hates it? Did Allah make me gay? I didn't choose to be gay. How do I become un-gay? It's virtually impossible. How do I even imagine the joys and spouses of Jannah if I don't even swing that way? Am I supposed to live my life all alone? People will start to suspect my homosexuality if they see I chose not to get married....
> May Allah SWT give all the gays who don't act on their desires the highest level of Jannah.

My Response:

Thank you for your comment. *Ameen.* May Allah give all believers who strive against their desires and hold on to their faith *Jannah* without account.

I agree with you 100% that the test of being gay is definitely harder than not being gay, if we are looking at the lens of life through sexuality alone. However, life is much more nuanced than this. If we pick any trial and look at life through that lens alone, then whoever has the obviously more difficult challenge will have the harder test. Sexuality is not a small matter, but neither is hearing, seeing, communicating, having good health, not living in poverty, living in a war-free region, not being physically tortured everyday, not being imprisoned, and the list goes on.

The point of my post was to point out that the trials of life touch everyone, and the extent that those trials try that person to the very core is a matter of the *ghayb* (unseen) about which only Allah knows. Yes, being gay is technically a harder trial than not being gay. However, this doesn't mean that every gay person has a more difficult life than every non-gay person.

The Prophet, *sallallaahu'alayhi wa sallam*, taught us that those with the most difficult trials are the prophets and messengers, then those with the most *emaan* accordingly. Thus, can anyone argue that a gay person today has a harder life than Allah's prophets, or the Companions, and the most faithful of the believers?

I definitely believe the suicide rate amongst gays and their rate of leaving Islam points to a very trying test. However, the truth is, it is the minority of all of humankind who will die as believers. So the trial of holding on to one's faith, like the trials of life itself, is not merely about sexuality. In fact, some trials are so severe that some people lose their appetite for physical pleasures altogether.

The goal of anyone who is striving with any personal trial should not be to question Allah, but to focus on the Hereafter, as Allah decrees trials in ways we do not understand. [From the Qur'an] in *Surah Al-Baqarah* (2:102), Allah tells us about the Angels Harut and Marut who taught the people *sihr* (magic): "But neither of these two [angels] taught anyone [such things] till they had said [to them]: 'We are only for trial, so disbelieve not [by learning magic from us]…'"

Why send these angels with something that would only cause people to disbelieve? we might ask. Yet Allah says, "He (Allah) cannot be questioned as to what He does, while they (humans) will be questioned" (21:23).

Thus, for any of us to go astray or commit suicide due to frustration with the tests Allah has given us is something we'll be questioned about, and if this is combined with disbelief, we will not be pardoned or forgiven for it. In light of the severity of life itself, it is of little benefit to argue whose test is harder, as we already know that *emaan* comes with the greatest trials, regardless of any other trial that comes along with it.

May Allah make our affairs easy for us, and may He give us tawfeeq upon His religion. And may He protect us from the whispers of Shaytaan, the evil of ourselves, and all forms of misguidance and kufr. And may He forgive our sins, have mercy on us, and take our souls in the best way and grant us the highest success in this world and in the Hereafter, though we could never deserve this great blessing.

This discussion was first published via muslimmatters.org

Also by Umm Zakiyyah

If I Should Speak
A Voice
Footsteps
Realities of Submission
Hearts We Lost
The Friendship Promise
Muslim Girl
His Other Wife
UZ Short Story Collection
Pain. From the Journal of Umm Zakiyyah

Order information available at ummzakiyyah.com/store

Read more from Umm Zakiyyah at uzauthor.com

About the Author

Daughter of American converts to Islam, Umm Zakiyyah (also known by her birth name Ruby Moore), writes about the interfaith struggles of Muslims and Christians, and the intercultural, spiritual, and moral struggles of Muslims in America. Her work has earned praise from writers, professors, and filmmakers and has been translated into multiple languages.

To find out more about the author, visit ummzakiyyah.com or uzauthor.com, subscribe to her YouTube channel: uzreflections, follow her on Twitter and Instagram: uzauthor, or join her Facebook page at facebook.com/ummzakiyyahpage.

Lightning Source UK Ltd.
Milton Keynes UK
UKHW040745041222
413249UK00005B/656